JOURNAL FOR THE STUDY OF THE NEW TESTAMENT SUPPLEMENT SERIES

15

Executive Editor, Supplement Series
David Hill

Publishing Editor
David E Orton

JSOT Press
Sheffield

HOSTILITY to WEALTH
in the
SYNOPTIC GOSPELS

Thomas E. Schmidt

Journal for the Study of the New Testament
Supplement Series 15

for Catherine

Published by JSOT Press
JSOT Press is an imprint of
Sheffield Academic Press Ltd
The University of Sheffield
343 Fulwood Road
Sheffield S10 3BP
England

Typeset by Sheffield Academic Press
and
printed in Great Britain
by Billing & Sons Ltd
Worcester

British Library Cataloguing in Publication Data

Schmidt, Thomas E.
    Hostility to wealth in the Synoptic
    gospels.— (Journal for the study of the
    New Testament. Supplement series, ISSN
    0143-5108; 15).
    1. Bible. N.T. Gospels—Criticism,
    interpretation, etc.   2. Wealth—Biblical
    teaching
    I. Title   II. Series
    226.08′33941   BS2555.2

    ISBN 1-85075-092-0
    ISBN 1-85075-091-2 Pbk

CONTENTS

PART III:
HOSTILITY TO WEALTH IN THE SYNOPTIC GOSPELS 101

PREFACE

This work grew from my curiosity about the nature and sources of some disturbing sayings attributed to Jesus. That curiosity led me to the University of Cambridge, the able tutelage of Dr Ernst Bammel, and the superior facilities and fellowship of Tyndale House. The work was accepted for the degree of Ph.D. in 1985 and appears here with minor revisions.

Dr Bammel's direction, his example of competent scholarship, and his personal interest and support were of inestimable value in the production and revision of the manuscript. Useful comments and criticisms were offered by Bruce Chilton, David Hill, and E.A. Judge. Special thanks are due to William Horbury for his sensitivity and faithfulness in conveying constructive suggestions at many points. Errors of omission and transgression that remain are entirely my own, and I gratefully acknowledge future critics who will correct and clarify where necessary.

It is a privilege to study, and it is a joy to study amongst friends. Memories of research and writing will always be intermingled with thoughts of the Longs, David Olford, the Diamonds, the Savages, and the Duncans. Support on this side of the Atlantic came from our dear parents and, more recently, from colleagues and students at Westmont College. My wife Catherine left family and friends, houses and lands to become a servant in this cause. May she receive a hundredfold in this life, beginning with the small token of dedication of this book to her.

ABBREVIATIONS
(Standard reference works and texts)

AEL	*Ancient Egyptian Literature*. 3 vols. Ed. and ET M. Lichteim (Los Angeles, 1973-80).
ANET	*Ancient Near Eastern Texts*. Ed. and ET J.B. Pritchard (Princeton, 1950).
APOT	*The Apocrypha and Pseudepigrapha of the Old Testament*. 2 vols. Ed. and ET R.H. Charles *et al.* (Oxford, 1913).
BAG	*A Greek-English Lexicon of the New Testament and Other Early Christian Literature*. W. Bauer. ET W.F. Arndt and F.W. Gingrich (Chicago, 1957).
BD	*A Greek Grammar of the New Testament and Other Early Christian Literature*. F. Blass and A. Debrunner. ET R.W. Funk (Chicago, 1960).
BDB	*A Hebrew and English Lexicon of the Old Testament*. F. Brown, S.R. Driver, and C.A. Briggs (Oxford, 1907)
BPP	*Babylonian Penitential Psalms*. Ed. and ET S. Langdon (Paris, 1927).
BWL	*Babylonian Wisdom Literature*. Ed. and ET W.G. Lambert (Oxford, 1960).
LAE	*The Literature of Ancient Egypt*. Ed. and ET W.K. Simpson (New Haven, Conneticut, 1972).
Liddell–Scott	*A Greek-English Lexicon*. H.G. Liddell and R. Scott. 9th edn (Oxford, 1940).
NERT	*Near Eastern Religious Texts Relating to the Old Testament*. Ed. W. Beyerlin, ET J. Bowden (London, 1978).
OTP	*The Old Testament Pseudepigrapha*. 2 vols. Ed. J.H. Charlesworth, ET J.H. Charlesworth *et al.* (Garden City, New York, 1983, 1985).

Payne Smith   *A Compendius Syriac Dictionary*. J. Payne Smith (Oxford, 1903).

SB   *Kommentar zum Neuen Testament aus Talmud und Midrasch*. H.L. Strack and H. Billerbeck. 4 vols. (München, 1926-34).

TDNT   *Theological Dictionary of the New Testament*. Ed. G. Kittel and G. Friedrich, ET G. Bromiley. 10 vols. (Grand Rapids, 1964-76).

INTRODUCTION

The prevailing sentiment in biblical scholarship, as in life, appears to be that the poor require much attention, whereas the rich can take care of themselves. Thus those who are hungry for material about charity and the poor are filled with good things, but those who seek information about the rich are sent empty away.

This state of affairs is due in large measure to the ancient texts themselves, which only rarely treat poor and rich as antonymic categories. While poor and rich are natural social opposites, their opposition in terms of ethical and religious prescription creates some problems. If one must act benevolently toward the poor, how must one act toward the rich? If the poor must hope in God because of their poverty, in whom must the rich trust, and why? Such questions justify a distinct tradition with regard to wealth; and therefore, a distinct treatment of that tradition on the part of biblical scholars.

To date, no treatment of the development of the tradition and its relation to the teaching of Jesus has appeared.[1] New Testament scholars in the last decade have centered their efforts not on this ideological background of the Synoptic material, but on reconstruction of the social situation in which the material appears. This situation, it is argued, is reflected by some Synoptic texts, and it is best understood in sociological terms. Where internal evidence is lacking, sociological data from the New Testament period are supplied to describe the immediate historical context; and where gaps still appear, a model is posited for which additional material can be supplied from contemporary phenomena whose particulars provide analogies to the New Testament period. This approach, which has gained almost unquestioning acceptance, requires a thorough review, both in terms of the historical evidence used to support it and in terms of the method itself. Although numerous works reflect the prevalence of this method,[2] we will focus our attention on the writings of G. Theissen, D.L. Mealand, and J.G. Gager, which apply the method directly and most fully to Synoptic texts.[3] The critique will offer reasons to regard with skepticism many of the findings and much of the approach of these authors.

Into the vacuum created by this skepticism will be placed not a different set of findings based on the same approach, but a different approach which intends to describe the development of the tradition in logical and chronological sequence from its origin to the New Testament period. This approach will serve a dual purpose as further refutation of the prevalent view and as evidence of the religious-ethical import and broad historical background of the tradition.

It must be emphasized that the two approaches are not necessarily mutually exclusive. Both intend to offer a more thorough understanding of the Synoptic teaching, and both can be employed as means to that end. But one has not been systematically criticized, and the other has not been systematically advanced. The former approach, as a relatively new tool, requires refinement in order to be more useful. The latter approach, as a more familiar tool, requires use to insure a thoroughly wrought undertaking.

With respect to the Synoptic material itself, the possibility of disparity within and between the Gospels is an important constituent of any treatment. This possibility has all too often been overlooked by writers who devote their energies exclusively to one book or source, and assumed as a certainty by writers who characterize a book or source to advance a particular form-critical or sociological reconstruction. These factors call for a new passage-by-passage examination which stresses both redaction and preservation of tradition. In this context the arguments of previous important works will be reviewed, and several new arguments will be advanced. But more importantly, the tradition itself will be put forward as the culmination of a logical development in semitic religious-ethical thought.

The three sections of the study answer to the three needs outlined above for a methodological critique, a description of the development of the tradition, and a new exegetical treatment of the Synoptic material. Together, the three sections provide evidence for the thesis that *hostility to wealth exists independently of socio-economic circumstances as a fundamental religious-ethical tenet consistently expressed in the synoptic Gospels*.

The statement contains several terms whose amplification at this point will facilitate understanding as the argument develops.

Hostility. This word was chosen to denote a range of meaning in the relevant literature, from an attitude of cynicism to one of condemnation, and from an action of inner detachment to one of outward separation. The general orientation is negative, and the precise manifestation of hostility prescribed in a given instance must be understood in terms of its context. The abbreviation HW will be employed to indicate this negative orientation; conversely, the abbreviation VW (valuation of wealth) will indicate the opposite, positive orientation.

Wealth. As a social category, wealth is simply that which the wealthy possess. As exasperatingly vague as this may appear, it is as precise as we can be whilst remaining fair to the texts in question, which only rarely give an indication of quantity. As a religious or ethical category, wealth is more apt to be considered in the abstract and defined in terms of that which precludes dependence on God or that which exceeds basic requirements for survival. Although such distinctions are not as precise as we might wish, they do indicate that wealth is a category broad enough to include any or all possessions. For the purpose of our discussion, then, wealth must not be defined in terms of some arbitrary percentage, but must include all possessions. Again, the context of a given passage will help to determine more precisely the group or amount in question.

Exists. HW is present in the text; i.e., the author intends to convey it to his readers, and/or it is likely to be perceived in the text by his readers.

Independently. The presence is not determined by; i.e., it has a function and history apart from.

Socio-economic circumstances. These are the particulars of class, status, and wealth of an individual or group; specifically, of an evangelist or his community. The phrase will normally be abbreviated SEC.

Fundamental religious-ethical tenet. This phrase signifies the integral relation between discipleship and orientation toward possessions. The phrase *'fundamental . . . tenet'* implies that this orientation is essential to, or expressive of, the life of discipleship. The word *'religious'* stresses that the orientation is primarily expressive of the relation between the individual and God; and the word *'ethical'* stresses that the orientation is manifested both in thought and in conduct. It is helpful in this regard to distinguish that which man must do in relation to God from that which God does or will do in relation to man. The latter is more apt than the former to find expression in terms of soteriology, to occur in prophetic/apocalyptic (as opposed to wisdom) material, and to reflect a social or political stance. We will observe that references to specific oppressors and to the poor are more likely to fall into the latter category.

Consistently expressed in. In general terms, the effect of the tradition on a reader of any of the synoptic Gospels would be substantially the same: he would perceive the same intention of the author with regard to his conduct and with regard to the reasons for that conduct. In specific terms, the tradition finds recurrent expression and recurrent constituent elements within each and between the three synoptic Gospels; moreover, there are no prescriptions or descriptions that constitute a rescission or mitigation of the tradition.

Each chapter will conclude with a series of summary statements and a brief explanation of their relation to the general thesis. Following the last chapter, these summaries will be restated in a general conclusion, and some observations of a more general nature will be made regarding the relation of the thesis to the Synoptic situation and to the rest of the New Testament.

PART I

HOSTILITY TO WEALTH AND SOCIOLOGICAL METHOD

Chapter 1

SOCIO-ECONOMIC CIRCUMSTANCES
IN FIRST-CENTURY PALESTINE

The dominant theory of early Christian social constituency states that representatives of the increasingly oppressed lower classes, who were the primary constituency of the first communities, created, altered, and/or preserved the extant material in order to express their own attitudes toward wealth. Implicit in this statement is the view that the primary determining factor was the economic condition of these people.[1] It is not the purpose of this study to label or to refute the philosophy of history that may lie behind the works under consideration, but only to bring to light some weaknesses of findings and method that warrant a greater attention to the idealogical background of the Synoptic material. A more serious charge than that the works of Theissen *et al.* assume or effect a Marxian view of history is that their methods and conclusions are gaining wide acceptance before their groundwork has been established by thorough historical research and exegesis. Some essential questions are these: Have these authors read the historical evidence correctly? Have they employed a defensible method? Have they paid adequate attention to literary background? Have they engaged in a thorough study of Synoptic texts? Part I will address the first two questions (Parts II and III will address the other two questions) and will point to flaws in the theory that Synoptic economic ethics can be explained largely by reference to socio-economic circumstances.

This theory regards the authenticity of Synoptic material as next to inconsequential since Jesus is, at most, voicing the group ethic. The 'teaching of Jesus', then, follows the group logically and perhaps to a large extent chronologically. It is not the aim of this study to suggest that, on the contrary, we possess the *ipsissima verba* of Jesus with regard to wealth. Later sections will allow for at least the *ipsissima vox* by maintaining a common background for the teaching

Objetivo

and the consistency of its expression. At this stage, the objective is simply to observe flaws in the popular theory that warrant consideration of other approaches to the explanation of the extant material. But the question of authenticity points to a crucial assumption of the theory that needs to be unmasked at the outset.

The normal sequence of background description followed by consideration of biblical texts tends to disguise as an inductive approach what can only be supported by a process of deduction. We are told 'how bad the situation was' and 'how much worse the situation became'. Then the text is introduced to show 'what the situation produced'. But this sequence demands closer scrutiny. Excepting the most radical viewpoint possible, that Jesus had nothing at all to say on the subject, we must posit some small, perhaps unrecoverable, body of teaching ascribed to him at a very early point and give to that body of teaching the functional appelation 'dominical'. If indeed Jesus voiced the group ethic; or in other words, if there is some identity between its attitude and the attitude of Jesus on the subject of wealth, the choice between creation and preservation on the part of the community becomes a question of some indeterminable percentage. Any material added from the time of Jesus to the time of Gospel production, insofar as it is consistent with dominical material, is only expressive of the attitude of early believers as an extension of the attitude of Jesus. Alteration, then, is the crucial factor. Diversity within and between the Gospels is the starting point for enquiry, *not* the group ethic and *not* the SEC of first-century Palestine. This is the only satisfactory explanation of the record of selective presentation and misapplication of data on the part of many modern scholars. The method rests on a further and more dangerous idea that should be termed an assumption: that is, that diversity within or between the Gospels must reflect progressive accommodation to changing economic conditions in the church between AD 30 and 70. Nowhere is this more clearly stated than in the introductory chapter of David Mealand's book, *Poverty and Expectation in the Gospels*: Mealand distinguishes between material reflecting 'the precarious economic circumstances of Christians in newly found communities', 'the economic crises of AD 48-70', and the situations of Matthew and Luke, who were 'presumably in circumstances different from those of Palestinian Christians between AD 30 and AD 70'. Thus, upon the dubious distinction between *precarious circumstances* and *crises*, and upon the

imprecision of a phrase like *presumably different circumstances*, rides
the thesis of one book that promises to demonstrate 'some correlation
between the economic circumstances . . . and the different strata of
teaching on poverty and wealth in the gospels'.[2] It is the aim of this
chapter to call into question the validity of these distinctions by
examining the evidence for the situation that lies behind them.

Tesis

The theory that socio-economic circumstances played a primary
role in the production of the extant material can be divided into two
major tenets, one relating to the economic conditions of the time and
the other relating to the constituency of early Christian communities.
We will consider these in turn, focusing on the historical data used to
support particular aspects of each.

Economic Conditions

The picture that we are often given of first-century Palestinian
economic conditions is a bleak one. We are told that there was
widespread oppression of the overpopulated mass of the lower
classes. High taxation, natural disasters, and societal polarization
aggravated the situation. Not only was there 'immense and continual
unrest',[3] but the period saw an 'increase in socio-economic pressure',[4]
culminating in the revolt of AD 66.

Descripción

Any consideration of the general conditions of the time must begin
with a statement of the perimeters of discussion. If indeed the
situation went from bad to worse, we must look carefully not only at
the facts that document the situation, but also at the standard used
for comparison and the time lapse between standard and situation.
The fact that scholarly opinion usually puts the production of the
Synoptics in the two decades following the revolt[5] should not, of
course, make that period a latest possible date for the oral and
written traditions from which the writers worked. The evangelists
received a substantial ethical tradition that must have been in
process of formation well before the war.[6] No matter how short a
gestation period one requires for the formation, articulation, and
ascription to Jesus of a group attitude, it is hard to imagine that
process *beginning* for the relevant texts as late as the 60s. Surely the
burden of proof would lie with anyone who considers events within
five years either way of the war as determinative with regard to
Synoptic ethics. Although no one has assumed such a burden, the
point applies equally well to the common tendency to include that

particular period in general descriptions of 'the times'. It is hardly more acceptable to deduce from the war events and attitudes that 'led up to it' from as many as three generations earlier. Revolt does not require so long a gestation period. Furthermore, as some modern revolutions have shown, a general desire for a better life may become associated with a particular group or cause only after the appearance of a persuasive and initially successful leader. Such may well have been the case here; in any case, the more immediate causes of the conflict must be given the weight of consideration in the absence of clear evidence that *gradual* religious, economic, and political upheavals caused the war.[7] With regard to the economic conditions of first-century Palestine, we are led by these considerations to focus upon the situation in the decades AD 10-60. Moreover, we should regard earlier evidence within the period as more important, since this allows a longer 'gestation period' for the development of the tradition.

Determination of a beginning point of inquiry is less certain, because stories and sayings adopted by Jesus and/or the early community reflect a long ethical tradition, even the more recent aspects of which do not necessitate identity of background or cause. In other words, we must exercise a similar caution with regard to the use of apocalyptic or wisdom literature in ethics to that which we exercise with regard to the use of the OT by NT writers. If, however, we adopt AD 10 as the beginning of 'the situation', we allow a reasonable time for the impact of recent events upon popular attitudes at the time of Jesus' ministry. The further back we go from such a date to describe the times or even to find a standard of comparison, the more we run the risk of imposing our greater historical perspective upon a limited period. We should not expect these people to have formed their values on the basis of a comparison of their own economic lot to that of preceding generations. Surely the day's own trouble was sufficient for the day, and that day should be the focal point of discussion.

General statements of economic conditions
The generally negative picture that is given of the period AD 10-60 is anything but certain. On the contrary, the level of prosperity enjoyed at the time might serve as a favorable standard of comparison for any period between 100 BC and AD 100.

Josephus's sources inform him that Herod 'had sunk the nation to poverty'.[8] Writing fifteen years later, he gives an embellished account:

> He had indeed reduced the entire nation to helpless poverty after taking it over in as flourishing a condition as few ever know, and he was wont to kill members of the nobility upon absurd pretexts and then take their property for himself (*JA* 17.307).

We have reason to doubt the 'flourishing' condition of Herod's new kingdom following a series of internally financed wars of expansion and resistance by his Hasmonean predecessors.[9] In addition, we should note the qualifying limitation of impoverishment to members of the nobility, whose concerns were naturally better known and more keenly felt by Josephus than those of the general population.[10] But even if we accept his account as accurate, we must regard its relevance as temporally limited. Josephus reports that Jewish leaders had complaints about Herod's successor Archelaus (*JA* 17.228-39), but these were clearly not in the economic sphere: Archelaus eagerly assented to demands for reductions in yearly payment and the removal of sales taxes (*JA* 17.205). Significantly, we hear no more complaint from Josephus about the economic conditions from this time (4 BC) until the period just before the revolt. Such silence forces Grant, for example, to resort to a reference to the '*secret and growing* discontent of those upon whom the burden of taxation fell most heavily' [italics mine].[11]

A more relevant text is found in Tacitus's *Annals* 2.42, where we are informed that in AD 17, a delegation from Syria and Judaea requested a reduction of the required tribute because they were 'exhausted by their burdens (*fessae oneribus*)'. Since Tacitus's only claim of independent knowledge of the situation is that 'under Tiberius all was peaceful',[12] we must presume that the phrase in question is a summary of the applicants' appeal. We should hardly expect a less urgently worded entreaty, but we have neither specific information about the situation in AD 17 nor the Roman response to the request to assist our evaluation of its cause and effect.[13]

The general information that we possess about the period suggests to some scholars a time of relative prosperity. Smallwood concurs with the verdict of Tacitus: despite particular incidents during the tenure of Pilate, 'the early governors were moderate enough in their behaviour to be acceptable to their subjects'.[14] Both Rostovtzeff and Bammel apply this judgment specifically to the economic sphere by positing prosperity as the corollary of peace and security.[15] Freyne, commenting specifically on the Galilean situation, observes that there was neither social unrest nor an increase in taxes through the period, and that

> the only mention of poverty as a contributory factor in the events leading up to the revolt was significantly enough in the urban center of Tiberius, where the destitute class are singled out as one definite element in the troubles there (Life 66).[16]

Freyne concludes that 'the country-people of the province were in a more stable position economically than those of other areas of the country'.[17] This conclusion is significant both because it depends largely upon first-hand evidence from Josephus and because such Galilean country-people formed an essential part of the leadership of the early Christian movement.

Taxation

In order to assess more carefully the theory of economic crisis and decline, we must consider specific factors cited in its support. One of the most important of these factors is the burden of taxation. Grant gives the estimate that

> the total taxation of the Jewish people in the time of Jesus, civil and religious combined, must have approximated the intolerable proportion of between 30 and 40 per cent.[18]

Grant offers as a corollary to this the contention that the burden was 'beyond the powers of utmost thrift to sustain'.[19] His verdict, however, involves two unnecessary assumptions: that this tax burden was introduced at this time, and that the total of possible taxes was actually paid by significant numbers of people. We have already seen evidence contrary to the former assumption in the generally peaceful conditions of the time and in the lack of evidence for increases in the tax burden. More specifically, we know that tribute had been paid to Rome since 63 BC in the form of a tax on the produce of the land,[20] which in itself was a drastic diminution (from 33% to 12½%) of a similar type of tax administered by the Seleucids.[21] Provincial status added only the *tributum capitis*, or head tax, which was assessed per annum at the nominal rate of one denarius.[22]

With regard to the second assumption, that the civil and religious tax burden was consistently assessed and paid, we have additional evidence to the contrary. The tax on produce of the land, the *tributum soli*, was paid only by the well-to-do,[23] and in some places those who paid the land tax were exempt from the head tax.[24] Urban dwellers were by definition exempt from the former. With regard to religious dues, the most universally applicable, the annual half-shekel Temple tax, required the wage of about one day from a labourer. Others (Grant lists twelve)[25] were directed almost exclusively at the agricultural sector and were dependent on the piety of the individual. Tithes were payable in produce—a system that exempted durban dwellers and thereby fostered resentment.[26] The majority of the people simply did not tithe.[27] We know that some wealthy priests cruelly exacted tithes from poorer priests in Jerusalem (*JA* 20.181, 206), but we have no reason to regard these as anything but sensational incidents of the period AD 60-64.

The sources do not describe any tax increases during the period AD 10-60; nor, for that matter, between this and the previous fifty-year period. Indeed, Josephus reports five tax *remissions* from the time of Herod to the increase under Albinus in AD 62-64.[28] Still, Grant declares that

> it is possible that the actual amount of money demanded increased as time went on and the Roman revel of prosperity became a drunken debauch of profligacy and extravagance.[29]

But graphic prose cannot disguise the weakness of an argument that rests on the phrase 'it is possible'. A more sensible judgment is taken from Stern, who points out that

> we have no information on the total sum collected in taxes in Judaea, or whether the Roman government of the province enjoyed a surplus of revenue over expenditure.[30]

Theissen finds his only evidence for a worsening tax burden in *JA* 18. 23-28, where the residents of Batanaea are said to go from tax-free status to taxes which 'ground them down' under the Agrippas (AD 37-100) and 'crushed them' under succeeding Roman rule.[31] Aside from the geographical distance of the area and the chronological distance from the period in focus, the loss of tax-free status by a new colony can scarcely be considered typical of the general situation. We must conclude that the evidence concerning taxation for the years AD 10-60 does not warrant the position that a general or growing crisis occurred.

Population

We have less specific data on the subject of population. Byatt offers reasons to trust the total of two and a quarter million based on the figures of Josephus, but he acknowledges uncertainty.[32] But even granting these figures as accurate, we do not know what would have constituted *over*-population. Byatt considers the economy at least of densely settled Galilee as able to sustain its proportion of the population.[33] Grant works from the axiom that in the Christian era 'Jewish territory is always over-populated'[34] to the assertion that during his particular period the Jews 'expanded to the very limits of the food supply, and beyond'.[35] Theissen offers the vague claim that 'we must reckon with the possibility of a degree of over-population in Palestine'.[36] But where is the evidence to substantiate any of these opinions? The essential data for a calculation of need versus output is simply not available.[37] Estimates of population vary considerably.[38] Precise knowledge about land, climate, crops, and methods of cultivation is lacking.[39] We have already observed a lack of information as to the percentage of output removed by taxation. Equally elusive are details of contributions from the Diaspora and of indigenous skill in managing limited resources:[40] certainly an alternative to Grant's axiom is that Jewish industriousness has usually been more than a match for Jewish over-population. But data, and not axioms, are requisite for a determination of the ability of a particular economy to sustain a particular number of people. In this case, we have insufficient data; therefore it seems better not to hazard an opinion than, like Theissen, to encumber an opinion with qualifications that render it virtually meaningless.

It is possible that emigration during the period signifies more than a safety-valve for a crowded country. The hint of large-scale movement to Alexandria in *P. Lond.* (lines 96-98) coupled with Sperber's findings that Palestinian wages, and prices of grain and clothing, were twice those of Egypt,[41] suggest that the Palestinian emigré had reasons to move other than the desire for living room.

Natural disasters

The impact of natural disasters on an already strained economy is said by Theissen to have had 'momentous consequenes' in the first century AD,[42] and by Mealand specifically to have produced 'bitter outcries in the gospels against the rich who feast while the poor starve (Luke 6.20-26; 16.19-31)'.[43] We must consider carefully the evidence for these claims.

Jeremias documents nine catastrophes between 65 BC and AD 69.[44] ~~Jeremias~~
There was a drought in 65 BC (*JA* 12.378) followed by a hurricane in
64 BC (*JA* 14.22); both of these are beyond our scope of interest.
During the reign of Herod I, four disasters occurred in a thirteen-
year period: a famine in 37 BC (*BJ* 1.347; *JA* 14.471; 15.7), an
earthquake in 31 BC (*BJ* 1.370; *JA* 15.121), an epidemic in 29 BC (*JA*
15.243), and a famine in 25-24 BC (*JA* 15.299, 310). Josephus does
not speak of a negative long-term impact of these closely successive
disasters, and he reports the rest of Herod's reign as free from them.
The next mention of a natural disaster is the famine around the year
AD 48 (*JA* 20.51, 101)—a gap of nearly seventy-five years. Following
this disaster—and we must remember that we are now within the
scope of Josephus's own memory—another gap occurs until the time
of the first revolt. Rabbinic sources indicate a drought just before the
war (*b. Taan.* 19b-20a *Bar.*; *y. Taan.* iii. 13, 67a.40), and Josephus
reports a mid-war drought (*BJ* 5.410; *JA* 18.8). These last two
disasters are probably too late to figure seriously in the formation of
Synoptic ethical tradition. They fit best with the prophecy of Mk
13.8 that earthquakes and famines would be a sign of 'the beginnings
of the birth-pangs', since the context (Mark 13.2, 8) clearly describes
the war.[45] Thus Theissen is mistaken in applying the passage to the
entire period as 'signs of the present'.[46]

We are left with one disaster: the Jerusalem famine. Jeremias, who
gives the fullest acount of the situation, gives this sequence:

> Summer 47, the harvest failed, the sabbatical year 47-48 aggravated
> the famine, and prolonged it until the next harvest of spring 49.[47]

Jeremias and Mealand cite *JA* 3.320 as evidence that the price of
bread rose to thirteen times the normal price during 'a famine', but
there is reason to doubt that the figure is correct or pertinent.[48] We
do not know that 'many were perishing' when Queen Helena and her
son Izates 'distributed among the needy' and thus 'delivered many
from the extremely severe pressure of the famine' (*JA* 20.51-53).[49]
Relief was offered to the Christian population by believers in Antioch
(Acts 11.28-30).[50] Since Josephus mentions the famine only as an
occasion for praise of Queen Helena and her son, perhaps as an
implied comparison to emperors who distributed to the needy,[51] we
must be wary of reading too much into the situation. Josephus
describes no long-term effects, nor does he mention the famine again
as contributory in any way to unrest at that time or in the subsequent
period. By definition, any famine's effects 'must have been terrible,

especially on the poorer citizens'.[52] But to deduce from this a pluralization of disasters, long-lasting social consequences, and the production of key elements in the Synoptic ethical tradition, is to build a card-house of conjecture.

Polarity between classes

'A progressive concentration of possessions'[53] is the phrase used to describe increasing polarization between rich and poor during the period. Kreissig gives the fullest account of social stratification and the struggle between classes,[54] but his view of an extensive and growing problem has serious flaws. His theory of price undercutting by large landowners rests on a mistaken assumption of consistent commercialization.[55] Even more serious is his lack of comparison to earlier periods.[56] And within the period of concern, Kreissig fails to supply evidence for a dangerously large (e.g. rapidly growing) proportion of destitute people. He cites Josephus's account of Herod's oppression and some rabbinic allusions to poverty that cannot be dated with certainty to this period.[57] Finally, he cites as Synoptic evidence the phrase in Matt 9.36 that the people were 'harassed and helpless (ἐσκυλμένοι καὶ ἐρριμένοι)'.[58] As potentially the strongest internal narrative evidence for widespread poverty in the Synoptics, this passage demands careful consideration. The phrase 'they were ... like sheep without a shepherd', taken from Matt 6.34, might be construed as an allusion to Ezek 34, which describes Israel as, among other things, a victim of economic injustice.[59] But the majority of commentators rightly regard the entire sentence as an allusion to passages such as Num 27.17, 1 Kgs 22.17, and 2 Chr 18.16, where Israel is seen as lacking spiritual leadership.[60] Only this interpretation makes 9.35-38 appropriate as a backdrop to the mission charge (10.1-15), in which the Twelve are sent to heal and to preach. Moreover, it would seem strange to find the only reference to widespread poverty in the work of a writer whose church's economic circumstances were allegedly 'less harsh than those of earlier communities',[61] and who adds the phrase to a sentence borrowed from Mark. We are led to conclude that Matt 9.36 should not be used as descriptive of economic conditions in the first century.

Internal non-narrative evidence might include Matt 18.23-25; 20.1-16; Mark 12.1-12; Luke 16.1-7. But these passages, albeit possible indications of a social situation, do not require that we consider them typical, much less prevalent. Furthermore, as descriptions of Jesus' audience, they could be countered by Matt 24.38, 48-49, and especially Luke 17.27-28; 21.34.

All this is not to deny that a part of the population lived on or over the edge of poverty during the period in question. It is safe to assume that these and others wanted to improve their economic conditions. Presumably some were among those who turned to brigandage as the weakness and corruption of the country's leadership became apparent in the 50s and 60s.[62] But neither an approximate proportion of destitute people, a degree of hardship experienced by them, nor an adverse comparison to previous periods has been demonstrated. The economic system of the time may in fact have worked to increase the wealth of the rich and the numbers of landless poor; but again, the lack of quantification should forestall the assumption of a negative result. Some degree of agricultural centralization may have increased efficiency of production and marketing, thereby raising the level of general prosperity. Grain and oil exports (Acts 12.20; *Vita* 119; *BJ* 2.592), which Theissen complains of as monopolies,[63] may in fact indicate a surplus of these important products. However beneficial or detrimental the economic system was to the general population, then, we must regard with skepticism the ambiguous claim that a problem was 'large' or 'growing'. Indeed, the modern notion of the poor as a permanent class that varies in size and resentment according to conditions[64] has no correspondent in the first century. Malina surveys NT descriptions of the poor and explains that, in the mindset of NT authors,

> A poor person seems to be one who cannot maintain his inherited status due to circumstances that befall him and his family, like debt, being in a foreign land, sickness, death (widow), or some personal physical accident. Consequently, the poor would not be a permanent social class, but a sort of revolving class of people who unfortunately cannot maintain their inherited status. Thus day laborers, landless peasants, and beggars born into such situations are not poor persons in first-century society, and poor would not be an economic designation.[65]

Malina's explanation is an important correction of the tendency to read modern economic class distinctions into ancient texts.[66]

Early Christian Social Constituency

The second major tenet of the theory in question relates to the constituency of early Christian communities. The texts that evince hostility to wealth, declares Gager, 'reveal . . . the economic status of believers'; that is, 'early believers came primarily from disadvantaged groups'.[67] Obviously, any movement of the period that represented a cross-section of society would include many economically deprived people, but more precise definitions of 'disadvantaged' and 'primary' are necessary to give meaning to such a claim.

Theissen includes among the producers of the group ethic those who are only *insecure* about their position.[68] Gager himself shifts, when making another point, to the view that 'the earliest believers did not necessarily come from the lowest social and economic strata', because *relative* deprivation, i.e. 'uneven relation between expectation and the means of satisfaction . . . most often characterizes pre-millenarian conditions'.[69] In other words, even a prosperous and powerful Jew might feel deprived of, say, equestrian rank, and find himself filled with millenarian resentment.[70] The category represented by such a definition becomes absurdly inflated, and the task of assigning texts to a particular group becomes correspondingly simple: those who feel hostile are members of the hostile group. Further criticism of this method must await the next chapter; for the sake of meaningful discussion at this point, we will retain the initial caricature of Gager that 'disadvantaged' indicates deprived economic status.

Although not so subject to equivocation, the word 'primary' can be equally elusive. Quantification is implied by the use of the word in conjunction with the concept of group membership. If ideological rather than numerical strength is emphasized, there is no need so to stress the bleak economic conditions of the time—one or two dominant destitute prophets would do. Moreover, the theory requires a group whose ethic is voiced by the prophet. Quantification, then, is required. Evidence must be shown that the new faith was adopted in the main by elements in society that were economically deprived, and that these were the dominant voices in the community.

The handicap of such an enquiry is its dependence on internal data from a text that clearly does not intend a representative description of the economic conditions of the time or the economic circumstances of members of the movement. We noted above the silence of the sources with respect to widespread poverty. We can make further observations with respect to Jesus' audience and followers. To say that Jesus preached good news to the poor clearly does not necessitate a conclusion that early communities contained a dominant lower class constituency. The text does not say that poor people followed him, nor that his followers experienced general hardship. The poor are mentioned primarily as objects of charity[70] or as an object lesson of charity (Mark 12.42-44/Luke 21.1-4). In later chapters we will offer reasons to regard other instances of the word (Matt 11.5/Luke 4.18; 7.22) as formulaic designations of Israel's pious remnant. That these are not necessarily deprived economically is apparent from the solvency of some who received the preaching and followed Jesus: workers in a family business (Mark 1.20); tax-collectors (Luke 5.27-29; 19.1-8); women of independent means (Luke 8.1-3); and presumably a rich council member (Matt 27.57; cf Mark 15.43; Luke 23.50-51; John 19.38). Jesus ministered to a centurion (Matt 8.5-13) and to the ruler of a synagogue (Mark 5.22). His ethical teaching about charity assumes throughout ample means to distribute.

Looking beyond the period covered by the Gospel narratives, we observe the expansion of Christianity among primarily middle-class urban groups, with notable upper-class patrons. We are indebted here to the works of E.A. Judge, G. Theissen, and W. Meeks, who have admirably combined insights from sociology, archaeology, prosopography, and the biblical material itself to provide a picture of social constituency in the Pauline churches.[72] The accumulation of evidence for this consensus confirms the conclusion of Judge in 1960 that Christianity left the most underprivileged classes (peasants and slaves) largely untouched and experienced early growth as a 'socially well backed movement of the great Hellenistic cities'.[73]

The internal narrative evidence thus reviewed offers a picture quite to the contrary of that which includes a high or significant proportion of destitute believers. Conversely, there is no positive record of economically deprived followers as a large or influential part of the group.

Conclusions

Our consideration of the economic conditions of the period and the social constituency of early communities can be summarized by several statements:

Tris

1. The work of Theissen *et al.* involves a dangerous amount of deduction, from didactic material to SEC.
2. Evidence of general economic conditions in Palestine between AD 10 and 60 does not reveal a bad or worsening level of prosperity.
3. Taxation is not known to have increased or exceeded the ability of the population to sustain.
4. Over-population cannot be substantiated.
5. The single natural disaster recorded in the period is not known to have produced long-term effects.
6. Increase in, or degree of hardship caused by, social stratification has not been substantiated.
7. Internal narrative evidence does not suggest primary membership or influence on the part of the most economically deprived classes in the Christian groups of the period.

The last six of these statements are purposely expressed in a negative form both to emphasize the first statement and to reflect the caution warranted by the ambiguity of the data in setting forth an alternate view. We do better to say 'it is not known' than to say 'it is not so' or 'not this, but that'. And we do best of all to avoid a theory that makes of particular SEC a *sine qua non*.

In terms of the general thesis, this chapter begins a two-stage process of dissociation between SEC and texts that express hostility to wealth. The conclusions call for skepticism with respect to a causal link between particular economic conditions and Synoptic ethical teaching.

Chapter 2

SOCIO-ECONOMIC CIRCUMSTANCES
AND SOCIOLOGICAL METHOD

The evidence of economic conditions in the first century calls into question the view that HW in the Synoptics is a response to a particular economic crisis on the part of disadvantaged groups. But the weakness of the evidence in support of the view does not in itself necessitate a complete dissociation of HW from SEC. Even in the absence of strong internal or external evidence from ancient texts, similar conclusions might be maintained by appeal to models constructed from observation of modern phenomena. Sociologist-theologians use these models to fill in gaps in the evidence by extrapolation from similarities between ancient and modern data.

Sociology is a relatively young discipline, and the use of its method by NT theologians is very recent. Thus we encounter neither a consistently employed, definitive model nor a thorough treatment of both ancient and modern data by an author concerned with the Synoptics.[1] But the criticisms of method and application that follow presuppose an appreciation for the creativity and possibilities for understanding engendered by such enquiry. These criticisms should be seen as corrective rather than destructive in purpose, and that only in the limited area of economic ethics.

Sociology and Validity

One very general or preliminary concern for the theologian must be the question of validity. Sociology confines itself to more general, structured aspects of religious phenomena; and sociologists often express, either explicitly or implicitly, causal derivation of religious phenomena from social facts.[2] Although Theissen asserts in defense of the sociological approach that 'the validity of an idea is quite independent of whatever causes may have given rise to it in the first place'[3] there are implications of such an understanding that go beyond what he dismisses as 'deep and dark suspicions'.[4] If one man takes a wallet because he wants money and reckons that the owner of the wallet has money to spare, and another man takes a wallet because he knows that its owner has defrauded him of the money it contains, no responsible judge will divorce cause from validity in his evaluation of the two cases. Similarly, if HW is expressed in texts because 'this is the way the poor have always consoled themselves . . . to work off their aggression'[5] or because the poor indulge in 'the prejudiced projecting into others what they themselves are unconsciously tempted by and do not admit',[6] then our evaluation of validity will be at least partially dependent on our assessment of the applicability of the ideas in broader socio-economic, psychological, and chronological contexts.

But this kind of cause specification may be criticized as too confining. Sociologist-theologians commonly bring all energies to bear on the phenomenon of HW as an almost immediate response to a particular situation. Thus, for example, Gager remarks that 'by the second century the ideology of poverty had outlived the social conditions that had spawned it'.[7] We observed above the lack of evidence for a causal link between economic conditions, group constituency, and texts. At this point we can add the criticism that the approach is too narrow in scope. Factors such as the development of ethical thought, the sources of other HW traditions in ancient texts, and the religious reasons for adoption or adaptation of ethical tradition must be given careful consideration. In terms of validity, the idea may be viewed as unrealistic, unworkable, or token; but in any case, it must be viewed in light of its broad ideological and historical substructure.

The Model in Sociological Method

There are a number of methodological problems that confront those who use comparative material for the elucidation of the texts in question. Foremost among these problems is the absence of a consistent model. Comparative analysis intends to compensate for insufficient data in that it 'supplements and reinforces the analysis of each separate case by introducing a wider perspective'.[8] The danger is that the perspective become too wide to distinguish properly between applicable and non-applicable specifics. When this danger is realized, causation is either described in such general terms as to be meaningless, or described in terms too specific to remain true to the model.

The oft cited works which contain data about millenarian cult phenomena in the last few centuries, although possessed of provocative titles like *New Heaven, New Earth, The Pursuit of the Millennium*, and *The Trumpet Shall Sound*, actually contain no consideration of biblical data or the biblical period. To date, no NT scholar has attempted a thorough review of the relevant Synoptic texts and history in light of the comparative material. Still, those who borrow heavily from comparative material or who exercise great creativity in sociological analysis have in common a neat agreement between the models that they propose and the textual and historical data as they present them. This would give no cause for concern if it were a simple case of misinterpretation or selective presentation of the ancient data; but additional complications are caused by the disagreement among sociological theorists over the model itself.

One aspect of uncertainty with regard to the model is, as we noted in the previous chapter, the economic situation of the group. The term 'relative deprivation' is most often employed to describe the social status of a group ripe for millenarian activity. But definitions of the term and descriptions of the group to which the term applies vary from theorist to theorist. Talmon writes that

> Radical millenarism found support in all levels of society at one time or another but essentially it is a religion of the *deprived groups*—oppressed peasants, the poorest of the poor in cities and towns, populations of colonial countries.[9]

This, the primary characteristic of millenarian group constituency, is coupled with *cataclysmic change* as the primary catalyst to millenarian activity. Wilson explains that

> Such conditions are present particularly in times of rapid social change. Wars, famines, climatic changes, national economic reversals, and the shock of sudden cross-cultural contact can all lead to unusually widespread and severe feelings of deprivation.[10]

These conditions, common to modern millenarian cult phenomena, were, as we have seen, anything but common to the early decades of the first century in Palestine. But as key elements in the sociological model, 'oppressed groups' and 'cataclysmic changes' are in danger of serving as lenses through which the available data are seen.

Sociologists do not, however, limit themselves to these primary elements in their descriptions of contemporary phenomena. Their expansion to a wider perspective in order to include variants may explain—but not excuse—the equivocation of Gager (and to a lesser extent Theissen) with regard to the groups and conditions involved in first-century phenomena. Gager takes from Talmon[11] the defining phrase 'uneven relation between expectations and the means of their satisfaction', which in both Gager's and Theissen's models makes relative deprivation apply to any group or condition provided that some threat is perceived. But apart from the criticism made in the previous chapter that such a model creates an absurdly large category, there are problems with regard to Gager's definition of relative deprivation. Gager refers the reader beyond the phrase quoted from Talmon to an article by Aberle[12] in which an important qualifier is added to the definition. In Aberle's words,

> Relative deprivation is defined as a negative discrepancy between *legitimate* [italics mine] expectation and actuality. Where an individual or group has a particular expectation and furthermore where this expectation is considered to be a proper state of affairs, and where something less than that expectation is fulfilled, we may speak of relative deprivation . . . We must furthermore consider the expectations as standards, rather than merely as prophecies of what will happen tomorrow.[13]

Moreover, Aberle recognizes that

> The discovery of what constitutes serious deprivation for particular groups or individuals is a difficult empirical problem. It requires careful attention to the reference points that people employ to judge their legitimate expectations, as well as to their actual circumstances.[14]

In other words, we cannot declare, *a priori*, that any denied expectation causes millenarian activity; or more specifically, that denied expectation causes hostility to wealth; or still more specifically, that Synoptic economic ethics are a case in point. More work needs to be done to establish legitimate expectation with regard to economic circumstances before the relevant Synoptic texts can be placed reliably in the millenarian model.

There are in fact numerous difficulties involved with the understanding that HW in the Synoptics is an aspect of early Christian millenarianism. In a general sense, there is some disagreement about whether Christianity was in fact a millenarian cult in its inception. Lanternari explains that

> Religious movements motivated by intercultural clash usually have

a different orientation from those arising from within the society. The former tend to seek salvation by immediate action through militant struggle or through direct and determined opposition to the foreign forces which beset them ... Endogenous movements, on the other hand, look for salvation through spiritual, cultural, or ethical channels ... The hope of salvation is focused on the eschaton, or end of the world, which takes on a positive meaning through the renunciation of worldly goods, whereas in the aboriginal movements it is the earthly goods which carry the greatest weight. The transcendental nature of Christianity sets it historically apart both from the messianic movements that preceded it and from those arising among primitive peoples which strive equally for human salvation on earth.[15]

The distinction of Christianity as an endogenous reform movement is more than semantic: while retaining a sociological classification of the phenomenon which avoids the connotation of singularity, it introduces a nuance of classification which conveys the connotation of dissimilarity.

The dissimilarity between the specifically economic aspects of inceptive Christianity and modern phenomena may be more striking than the similarity. Numerous authors make the point that the economic ethics of modern cults are informed by Christianity or elicited by contact with Christianity.[16] Moreover, even where modern phenomena exhibit parallels but are independent of Christianity,[17] we must ask whether the parallels justify model construction or even comparison in the economic sphere. The ancient phenomenon occurred in a complex economy, and it borrowed from long-standing precedents within an indigenous ethical tradition. The modern phenomena occur among groups experiencing little if any economic or political oppression and whose naïve beliefs about the means to power are challenged by a new ideological force.[18] Only if we ignore these important differences and limit our comparison to certain specific aspects of response (e.g. promise of reversal, abandonment of goods) or to very general conditions (e.g. concern about the meaning of money) can we find parallels. When Gager quotes Luke 6.20 and Mark 10.25 'to reveal both the economic status of believers and the deeper symbolic associations of money',[19] we must ask if a fuller picture of Synoptic economic ethics would fall as neatly into the millenarian model. And when Worsley tells us that 'the basic condition is a situation of dissatisfaction with existing social relations and of yearnings for a happier life',[20] we must ask where this condition is *not* present. This is not to say that specific comparisons are impossible, but that more work needs to be done to justify the inclusion of Synoptic economic ethics in the millenarian model.

The chronology of Synoptic economic ethics in the millenarian model presents another difficulty. The model requires not only cataclysmic changes that threaten groups but also an intermediary or prophet who voices the group concerns.[21] But if the figure must emerge c. AD 30 in order to intitiate the movement, and the events that determined the group ethic did not occur for at least another twenty years, how can economic considerations be said to play an integral part in the inception of the cult? Gager contends that, in later christological controversies, the Church used Jesus as a 'malleable symbol through which they expressed their own distinctive concerns'.[22] But he is not free to exercise such latitude with regard to the message of the prophet in the area of economic ethics, where the prophet's role is initiatory rather than symbolic.[23]

A related chronological difficulty is the confusion of sequence with regard to development in the NT period. Worsley[24] cites Paul as an example of the tendency to push millenarian beliefs into the background—in this case with the delay of the Parousia—but he fails to note that Paul was writing before the Evangelists, perhaps even before the so-called economic crisis period of the 50s and 60s. Mealand, on the other hand, attempts to distinguish between Jesus' own attitude and later HW resulting from the AD 48 famine and the crisis period of the 60s, which was quickly modified again in the redactions of the evangelists—again in direct response to a changing social situation in the Church.[25] Yet Mealand acknowledges that sayings like the Lukan woes have parallels in much earlier literature.[26] Some such parallels, as we will see in Part II, occur in wisdom writings of the upper classes, i.e. in non-millenarian contexts. Must sayings be pronounced only at the point when they best reflect SEC? Can Paul and other NT writers be allowed to push millenarian beliefs into the background—or to reintroduce them—when a theological or literary purpose dictates? Must we cluster all texts, books, and redactions hostile to wealth into the period AD 48-70 because this is possibly the greatest period of crisis? L.T. Johnson is one who recognizes the fallacy of positing SEC from NT texts:

> Where references to local situations are few and ambiguous, and where there is clear evidence of literary technique, it is hazardous

to move from the presence of a theme or *topos* to the situation of the readers .... With regard to the Gospels, then, to agree that they emerge from a life-setting does not allow us to conclude that the life-setting is determinative of the document's meaning, either as a whole or in its parts. If this is so, neither can we move directly from the concerns of the text to its life-setting, or the attitudes of its readers. Without the clear and unequivocal indication by the author in his text, we cannot establish the connection between the presence of a particular motif and the stance of the readers.[27]

Conclusions

By way of summary, it may be helpful to list in more concise form the methodological criticisms that should elicit corrections or modifications in subsequent treatments of the sociology of inceptive Christianity.

1. The middle decades of the first century are too narrow a scope of inquiry to allow for adequate consideration of ideological and historical background.
2. Relative deprivation is too broad a category to serve a meaningfully descriptive function in discussions of social constituency and economic conditions.
3. Significant differences between Synoptic economic ethics and modern phenomena warrant caution with regard to the inclusion of the former in a millenarian model.
4. Chronological difficulties relative to the role of the prophet and development within the NT period expose the fallacy of positing SEC from NT texts.

It is not the aim of this study to go beyond acknowledgment of the value of sociological study by theologians and the suggestion of certain limitations and corrections of past approaches. But the criticisms offered, coupled with the consideration of textual and historical data in the previous chapter, provide sufficient cause to reject the theory of Theissen *et al.* as a valid explanation of the phenomenon of HW in inceptive Christianity.

PART II

HOSTILITY TO WEALTH AS A DEVELOPING TRADITION

Chapter 3

ANCIENT NEAR EASTERN MATERIAL

The most useful review of ancient Near Eastern social justice is F.C. ~~Fensham~~
Fensham's article, 'Widow, Orphan, and the Poor in Ancient Near
Eastern Legal and Wisdom Literature'.[1] The title reveals the
character of the material: the wealthy are criticized only to the extent
that they violate justice due to these groups. But the religious-ethical
norm reflected by this tradition warrants consideration as the logical
starting point of HW.

We encounter almost exclusively in ancient Near Eastern sources the
point of view of the aristocracy. We should not expect, therefore, to find
direct evidence of oppression and social unrest. We may, however, infer
such from the charity of the rich, who achieve thereby psychological
reassurance of legitimacy.[2] Given this possibility, we should note
carefully any available details of socio-economic circumstances which
may illuminate early development or later parallels.

Origins of the tradition

Since the oldest pertinent written material dates from c. 2400 BC, we
must speculate about the origin of a tradition of social justice in a time
over which we have virtually no historical control. In a primitive
subsistence economy, worth is measured not by the possession of
wealth, but by the performance of allotted functions whose value is
measured in qualitative terms.[3] In this type of economy

> food and other necessities are provided by related families as gifts,
> these imposing on the recipients the obligation to give similar aid
> when it may be required.[4]

In such a reciprocative economy, the chief is obligated by his position to
provide for members of the community who are victimized by disaease
or by the death of the husband or parents. The ideal is not

that all should be equal, but that all should have adequate provision.[5] Religious sanction is realized by reference to the god(s), who provides for all men, and in whose place the chief acts.[6] Since the chief's position is not threatened by widows, orphans, and the debilitated, his action need not be ascribed to guilt about his relative position in the community. It is more likely that he fears reprisal by other leaders who resent violations of community values (including support for the poor),[7] or that his conduct is a simple function of the principle of reciprocation; he wishes to insure similar care should disaster strike his own person or family.[8]

We observe in this primitive pattern of behavior the origin of a concept of social justice. As society becomes more complex, the behavior continues, even with the advent of highly structured and moneyed economies. Thus, although the scope of the problem may increase during periods of social upheaval or decay,[9] we should not consider such periods as the original cause either of the problem itself or of the behavior offered as a solution to the problem. In addition, we should take note of the concomitant developments of legal requirement for aid and religious-ethical principles which sanction such aid as 'justice' and condemn its neglect.[10] These factors can be summarized in a single statement: without threatening social structures and without regard to changes in general economic conditions, charitable behaviour toward the poor began in primitive subsistence economies as a religious-ethical duty of those in power.

Development

The statement above is significant to the extent that the development of social justice can be traced from this origin to the concept of HW. Parallels to later sources increase in importance as we appreciate their occurrence (1) among the aristocracy, (2) of separate extra-biblical cultures, (3) during periods of relative calm and prosperity, (4) as a distinctly religious-ethical development.

Use of the word 'development' is not meant to imply a chronological sequence of thought whereby certain ideas disappear as others take their place. Although development occurs in roughly chronological sequence, different strata are found in every period and even within individual works.[11] Moreover, we should appreciate the difficulties of dating much of the material with precision, of establishing the socio-economic circumstances at the time of writing, and of determining the cause and effect of subsequent popularization of material.

Mesopotamian regal pronouncements constitute the first written *Babilonia* witness to the policy of care for orphan, widow, and poor, which we will refer to subsequently as the 'justice imperative'. Urukagina, king of Lagash c. 2400 BC, sought to reverse the corruption and heavy taxation which financed the military ambitions of his predecssors.[12] In addition to these reforms, he proclaimed that 'der Waise und der Witwe der Mächtige nichts zu Leide tat'.[13] About three hundred years later, Ur-Nammu began a relatively peaceful, building-oriented rule which led to an economically flourishing dynasty.[14] He claimed that in his reign 'the orphan did not fall prey to the wealthy', 'the widow did not fall prey to the powerful', and 'the man of one shekel did not fall prey to the man of one mina (sixty shekels)'.[15] The reign of Hammurabi of Babylon, 1728-1686 BC, occurred midway through a 300-year dynasty and was characterized by great wealth and power.[16] In the epilogue to his legal code, he includes among his purposes 'that the strong might not oppress the weak, that justice might be dealt the orphan (and) the widow', and 'to give justice to the oppressed'.[17]

Egyptian examples are numerous and occur in every period. The *Egipto* *Inscription of Nefer-seshem-re called Sheshi* from the Sixth Dynasty (2300-2150 BC) includes the claim that its author 'rescued the weak from one stronger than he as much as was in my power'; that he 'gave bread to the hungry, clothes <to the naked>'.[18] The responsibility of the god is exemplified as early as 1900 BC in the *Hymn to Hapy*, where it is said that the god 'gives bounty to the poor'.[19]

With such examples of the ideal of social justice as a starting point, we must venture beyond simple care for the poor to consider five stages of development toward HW. At the same time, we should be aware of a stratum of wisdom tradition existing alongside this development which regards wealth as a reward or gift of the god(s) or as otherwise valued.[20] Although full treatment of this stratum cannot occur within the scope of this study, both the ambivalence it suggests in some works and its relation to HW are worthy of note. Since wealth gives power, sustains life, encourages happiness, etc., it is understood in one sense as a reward. Rewards are given for virtuous behaviour; therefore, wealth=virtue, and virtue=wealth. Thus wealth can be valued as a reward for virtue and disparaged as a preclusion of virtue in the same work.[21] We even observe wealth as a reward for disparagement of wealth![22] We should not conclude that VW expresses only the viewpoint of the wealthy. It is likely that it signifies universal acceptance of an increasingly structured and/or money-oriented economy. Thus economic reversal, whether lamented by the rich or desired by the poor, is a reflection of VW rather than HW,[23] and as such should be subsumed under VW. The key distinction between this tradition and that which is the primary subject of this study is that the former assumes, and the latter challenges, wealth as a measure of worth or value.

The stages of development toward HW can be summarized in this manner:

TABLE 1
Stages of HW

STAGE	COMMAND	STRUCTURE
Justice Imperative	be just	do not be unjust
I.		injustice = greed
II.		injustice = wealth, wealth = injustice
III.	value X more than wealth	
IV.	value X	do not value wealth
V.	devalue wealth in order to value X	

One stage does not necessarily produce another, either in a logical or in a chronological sense. Frequency of occurrence of the higher stages increases in later periods, but instances of the lower stages do not at the same time decrease. Statements expressive of higher stages tend to assume or include lower stages, but this is not invariably the case; especially at stages three and five, where no negative statement is required.

The first stage in the development toward HW from the simple command of the justice imperative, 'be just/do not be unjust', is the equation of injustice with greed. This seemingly self-evident distinction is important because it serves as a transition to the consideration of wealth apart from care for the poor: implicit in the equation is a criticism of VW over the divinely sanctioned duty of justice; thus we are only a small step away from criticism of VW over *any* duty or anything divine.[24] The concept is clearly exemplified in *The Man Who Was Tired of Life*, whose author laments that 'hearts are rapacious and everyone takes his neighbour's goods'.[25] Similarly, in *The Instruction of Amenemope*, the reader is exhorted, 'Do not be greedy for a plot of land, nor overturn the boundaries of a widow'.[26] A more general reference is found in the Assyrian *Words of Ahiqar*, where the reader is told not to 'covet a wealth which is denied thee'.[27]

Related to this, but requiring distinction as a separate, second stage of development, is the equation of injustice with wealth and wealth with injustice. By definition, of course, the man who withholds his wealth from the practice of justice will be a more wealthy man than otherwise. It is the converse of this proposition that is significant: a wealthy man is necessarily an unjust man. Again, as in the first stage, there is but a thin line between injustice with regard to the poor and any disreputable behaviour or attitude. Thus, in *The Babylonian Theodicy*,[28] we encounter not only a contrast between those 'who go the way of prosperity' and those who 'are impoverished and dispossessed',[29] and between 'the heir [who] stalks along the road like a bully' and 'the younger son [who] will give food to the destitute';[30] but also references to 'the opulent nouveau rich who heaps up goods' and will deservedly be 'burnt at the stake by the king before his time',[31] to 'the godless cheat who has wealth',[32] and to 'the dregs of humanity, like the rich and opulent'.[33]

With the third stage, we leave behind any necessary link between social justice and wealth. The essence of this stage is to challenge VW by reference to a higher value; that is, to express devaluation of, or detachment from, wealth. We will refer subsequently to this stage as comparative devaluation.

Detachment can take a variety of forms, three of which we will isolate here. First, and most common, is the exhortation to value peace with God more highly than wealth. After predicting the violent fate of those who heap up goods, the writer of *The Babylonian Theodicy* challenges his readers: 'Do you wish to go the way these have gone? Rather seek the lasting reward of (your) god!'[34] Two of the *Babylonian Proverbs* remind that 'It is not wealth that is your support. It is your god', and 'Be you small or great, it is (your) god who is your support'.[35] The *Instruction of Amenemope* includes both the warning

Do not be avaricious for copper, and abjure fine clothes;
What good is a cloak of fine linen woven as mek,
    when he backslides before God?[36]

and the declaration

> Better, then, is poverty in the hand of God
>   than riches in the storehouse;
> Better is bread when the mind is at ease
>   than riches with anxiety.[37]

A second form of detachment is more directly related to justice: one should value care for the poor over wealth. The *Instruction of Amenemope* follows an exhortation to reduce a poor man's debt with a variation of the text just quoted:

> Better is the praise that comes through the love of men,
>   than wealth in the storehouse.[38]

The same work later states that

> God desires the good treatment of the poor
>   more than respect for the noble.[38]

A third form of detachment is the equation of wealth and pride. The *Maxims of Ptahhotpe* warn

> Do not (boast of) what has accrued to you in the past,
>   do not trust in your riches,
>   which have accrued to you by the gift of God.[40]

The author of the Kassite *Poem of the Righteous Sufferer* laments of men that 'in prosperity they speak of scaling heaven'. The *Words of Ahiqar* contain the admonition, '(Multiply not) riches and make not great thy heart'.[41] This last command might be construed as a transition to the next stage of development, since in its converse form it contrasts disparagement of wealth with a higher value: humility, or acceptance of one's lot.

A better example of the fourth stage, alternative devaluation, is found in the *Statue Inscription of Djedkhonsefankh* (c. 900 BC), which includes these lines:

> The people reckoned me as open-handed
> For I despised the piling up of riches.
> ... If I scattered my wealth on everybody,
> They thought <me> the equal of Hu [clothing].[42]

An instance of the fifth stage of development, teleological devaluation, occurs in the *Prayer and dedication of Simut, called Kiki*. Simut was a high official in the administration of Ramses II (c. 1300).[44] His inscription includes the following:

> Hereby I surrender to her [Mut, his god] my possessions and all
> their increase . . . . I came into my possessions through her power
> alone, because of the breath of life. (Therefore) no member of the
> household is to have a share in them; they are only to go to her in
> peace . . . . If Mut takes someone into her protection, how does the
> one whom she loves prosper![45]

It is apparent that the inscription constitutes a will of Simut's
possessions to his god after his death. Since his dedication is for the
purpose of gaining favor with the deity, and since it implies that
wealth is better used in the service of the deity than by his household,
we are able to place it in the fifth stage of development. On the other
hand, a posthumous gift hardly entails a personal sacrifice, and the
last line quoted implies that Simut enjoyed his wealth during his
lifetime.

These last few examples of alternative and teleological devaluation
are unusual or uncertain, and subsequent examples will serve better
to distinguish these stages. It is best to conclude that, in general,
ancient Near Eastern texts do not take us beyond the third stage,
comparative devaluation. Nevertheless, these three stages demonstrate
a certain amount of hostility to wealth. This hostility is based not on
a social ideal of equality, but on a tradition of active regard for the
subsistence of all members of the community. As wealth becomes
valued above this and other ethical norms, its value is attacked by
negative equations and by comparison to higher values.

Conclusions

Due to the scarcity of extant material, any attempt to trace this
development from the beginnings of civilization is necessarily
incomplete. The available evidence does, however, allow the
following summary statements:

1. Care for the subsistence of the poor originated in primitive
   economies as a religious-ethical duty of those in power,
   without challenging social structures and without regard to
   changes in general economic conditions.
2. Development occurs from this concept of justice to negative
   equations and comparative devaluation of wealth.
3. Such criticism is encountered among the aristocracy of
   separate cultures during stable and prosperous periods.

These conclusions are relevant to the general thesis in that they constitute the starting point of a religious-ethical tradition and a precedent for its occurrence in stable socio-economic circumstances.

Chapter 4

JEWISH CANONICAL MATERIAL

In the Hebrew Scriptures, if nowhere else, we encounter a tradition certain to have been both familiar and authoritative to Jesus. For this reason, we must be especially alert for concepts that find expression in Synoptic texts despite their chronological distance from the first century AD. Equally important in terms of this study are the SEC of OT authors as further evidence—and now within a Jewish milieu— of HW independent of SEC. *HW ≠ SEC*

As a preliminary to these concerns, it is necessary to delimit the subject matter to exclude, successively, the poor as an antonymic concern, property or media of exchange as uncritically regarded, the justice imperative, and the various substrata of VW. Observations of proportion and pattern derived from this delimitation process will shed light on the subsequent consideration of HW.

Rich and Poor
In terms of bulk content, history comprises 50% of the OT, prophecy *Statistical* 30%, and writings 20%. Yet by count of passages[1] relevant to this study, writings provide half the material, while history and prophecy equally divide the rest. This proportion is even more marked when we consider passages evincing some degree of HW: 80% occur in the © writings, making it clear that these books should receive particular attention. Focusing our attention for a moment on Job, Psalms, Proverbs, and Ecclesiastes, we observe that of 108 passages making reference to wealth, 27 are joint references (references to rich and poor in the same context). Of these, 13 use עשר, 2 חיל, 2 הון, and 10 miscellaneous words signifying wealth.[2] Of the 13 which use the standard word, עשר, 4 are critically positive toward wealth, 3 are neutral, and only 6 can be construed as negative.[3] Of these 6, none contain a contrast which puts poverty in a favorable light, 3 speak of injustice done to the poor (Prov 18.23; 22.7; 22.16), 2 claim consolation for poverty if accompanied by righteousness (Prov 28.6;

28.11), and one denies both poverty and riches (Prov 30.8-9). If we bring into the picture the remaining 14 joint references, we observe that 3 are positive, 2 are neutral, and 4 speak of injustice.[4] Ps 37.16, 'Better is a little that the righteous has than the abundance of many wicked', might be construed as a favorable contrast of poor over rich if indeed having 'little' is being stressed more than being 'righteous'. This is doubtful, since v. 11 promises to reward these meek with 'abundant prosperity', placing the psalm in the reversal category, and since four very similar proverbs (Prov 15.16; 16.8; 16.19; 17.1) clearly qualify poverty by some ethical distinctive which is the primary consolation or reason for reward.[5] Note also that neither עשר nor one of the words translated 'poor' (אביון, דל, עני, רוש) is used in 37.16 or in the parallels.

This glaring absence of critical contrast between rich and poor is hardly altered by reference to historical books, which, among joint references, contain only two to equality before God (Exod 30.15; 1 Sam 2.7), one to potential husbands (Ruth 3.12), and one to oppression (1 Sam 12.1-6).

Prophetic literature contains only one joint reference, and that to oppression (Jer 5.26-28).

The use of the word עשר and its equivalents, therefore, is not held in antonymic opposition to the word group 'poor'. Conversely, consideration for the poor is only rarely a context for HW. In the Psalms, for example, the word group 'poor' occurs over seventy times whereas עשר occurs only six times (of seventeen psalmic references to wealth).[6] There is no overlap;[7] indeed, the antonym of 'poor' is not 'rich' but 'violent'.[8] The poor are not necessarily so in an economic sense, whereas the rich invariably are.[9] But the most important feature in terms of this study is that sympathy with the poor does not take the form of HW: the poor are not praised for avoiding riches, and the rich are not condemned for avoiding poverty. The poor and their piety are thus a distinct concern[10] and do not have a direct relevance to the development toward HW. The occasional common context of the terms rich and poor, inevitable for two terms so naturally opposite, is the justice imperative.[11] To the extent that the poor are mentioned in that stratum as victims of the rich they are relevant to this study.

Wealth as a term

It is necessary to distinguish between the term wealth and the words or concepts used to signify it in a given context. עשר consistently denotes wealth, occurring in 65 of the 212 passages considered here.[12] חיל is second in frequency, occurring in 30 passages.[13] Silver (כסף) and/or gold (זהב and equivalents) most often denote money in a noncritical way; however, they are employed in 23 of these passages to signify wealth, 19 of which are in the HW stratum.[14] הון, which is consistently translated in terms of wealth, occurs in 21 passages.[15] טוב, which has the general meaning 'a good thing, benefit, welfare', signifies wealth in 12 passages.[16] צלח, 'prosper', is used 10 of 26 times in historical books in an economic sense, and all of these passages are in the VW stratum.[17] אוצר, 'treasure', is found in ten passages.[18] המון is found six times,[19] כבד five times,[20] בצע five times,[21] שכל five times,[22] חסן four times,[23] נכסים four times,[24] and a number of other words three times or less.[25] Clearly, this compilation is not meant to provide an exhaustive list of references to money and material possessions in the OT, but only to Hebrew words translating or connoting the term wealth. Money and possessions are normally used non-critically; i.e. without evaluation, either as illustration or in narrative.[26] Prophetic promises and curses may include wealth without mentioning it explicitly (e.g. when בזז and/or שלל are used for 'spoil'), and descriptions of goods or plunder sometimes occur without a more general word for wealth in the same context. Such instances reside in the VW stratum, and their inclusion would only accentuate proportions that can be demonstrated without reference to them.

There is no explicit delineation or consistent context in the OT that allows a precise definition of wealth in terms of a specific quantity of property or money. The fact that silver/gold is used in negative contexts more than land, possessions, or general prosperity may imply a greater suspicion attached to mobile (hoarded?) property, but this is not certain. It is not entirely tautological to say that wealth is 'that which the wealthy have', since the wealthy are a specific group understood to have 'a lot'. To be any more precise about the amount, it is necessary to assume the existence of an unnamed group between rich and poor, probably often the intended audience of a given work, who have enough to avoid classification as 'poor', but not enough to warrant classification as 'rich'. This nebulous 'middle class' may in fact represent an OT ethical ideal, since those who belong to it, according to Prov 30.8-9, avoid the dangers of both wealth (pride) and poverty (theft or profanity). The existence and at least tacit approval of such a group may signify a departure in any later literature that calls into question a greater amount, or even all, property.

The Justice Imperative

The passages containing the demand to do justice[27] do not often include references to the rich,[28] but they do merit our consieration as the continuation of the ethical tradition and the starting point of the development toward HW. The OT adds the category of גר, 'stranger', to the expected group widow, orphan, and poor as the objects of justice,[29] and it devotes special attention to usury as a particular kind of injustice,[30] but in other respects the imperative is essentially the same as that observed in other Near Eastern sources.

Possibly because of a less centralized economy,[31] the responsibility of the royal household is less important (but not absent: Prov. 29.14). Still there are a number of reasons to understand an aristocratic viewpoint in the material. The OT justice imperative assumes an audience with the financial capacity to execute justice. But even beyond that, there is a greater feeling of distance from the poor than from the rich: the rich are often addressed in the second person, especially in the justice context;[32] the poor, on the other hand, are never addressed in the second person, and they are addressed in the first person only in a few psalms where it is far from certain that economic poverty is meant.[33] We should also appreciate the high degree of literacy necessary for the production and compilation of the material. Finally, it should be noted that some measure of acceptance by ruling or influential powers was essential to the very survival of the books.

There are other similarities between the OT and Near Eastern justice imperatives. The one who executes justice acts like God (Deut 10.18) and acts in favor of those with whom God sympathizes (Exod 22.21-27; Ps 72.12-14). The imperative is present in legal and wisdom form, and in both forms the success or godliness of the individual is related to his obedience to the command (Deut 15.10; Prov 14.21). These similarities in content, source, and form suggest that in the OT we encounter not a new tradition, but the Jewish expression of a tradition common to the entire geographic region from more ancient times.[34]

Valuation of Wealth

The uniquely Jewish elements in the tradition come to the fore in the

stratum which values wealth and considers it a reward. This stratum
is certainly well-represented in the OT, and is fairly equally divided
between history, prophecy, and writings. Table 2 provides a
breakdown of the passages considered in this chapter.[35]

TABLE 2
Numerical breakdown of OT passages
according to stratum

Type	Number of passages	VW	Critical equality	HW	Reference to rich + justice imperative	Justice imperative
History	49	44	2	2	1	13
Prophecy	56	38	0	17	1	17
Writings	109	44	3	59	3	35
Totals	214	126	5	78	5	65

How can VW and HW strata exist side-by-side in a body of
literature that must, for so many, stand the test of ethical and
theological consistency? If we wish to do more than to hold the two
strata in tension or opposition, or to ignore one of the two, we must
look more carefully at the relation between wealth as a reward and
the justice imperative. One possibility of resolution is suggested by
attention to the specific subject matter of the passages. Table 3
distributes the passages in this way.[36]

TABLE 3
Numerical breakdown of OT passages
according to subject matter

Type	Number of passages	Individual wealth	Plunder	National wealth	Didactic	Overlap
History	48	32	7	4	5	2*
Prophecy	55	0	47	4	4	13**
Writings	111	1	0	0	110	0
Totals	214	33	54	8	119	15

Two of these numbers warrant special attention here: thirty-two of
forty-eight passages in historical books are narrative descriptions of
individual wealth, and forty-seven of fifty-five passages in prophetic
books describe wealth in terms of plunder. Together, these numbers
indicate that over three-fourths of the material in history and
prophecy may be either too specific or too general to imply an ethical
norm for the reader. But even assuming that the entire body of

material has personal relevance, close attention to the precise nature
of the ethical implication in each instance reveals an important
pattern. Table 4 breaks down the VW stratum into five substrata:[37]

TABLE 4

Numerical breakdown of VW stratum in the OT
according to substrata

Type	Number of passages	Related to covenant	Business advice	Noncrit- ical	Sove- reignty	Possible sarcasm
History	44	38	0	4	2	0
Prophecy	38	38	0	0	1	6
Writings	44	24	10	3	1	6
Totals	126	100	10	7	3	6

The first column of Table 4, comprising the bulk of the VW
stratum, provides the key to understanding the relation of VW to
HW in the OT. Deut 8.17-18 is the most complete statement of the
relation of wealth to covenant-keeping. After God's promise to lead
his obedient people to a rich new land comes the warning:

> Beware lest you say in your heart, 'My power and the might of my
> hand have gotten me this wealth'.
> You shall remember the Lord your God, for it is he who gives you
> power to get wealth; that he may confirm his covenant which he
> swore to your fathers, at this day.

In this and ninety-nine other passages, wealth is linked directly to
obedience to conditions of the covenant, either as a reward for
faithfulness or as plunder taken for disobedience. Of the thirty-two
passages indicated in Table 3 as referring to individuals, twenty-
seven refer to the faithful elite of OT patriarchs and kings; every one
of the thirty-eight prophetic plunder passages constitutes either a
punishment or a reward related to confirmation of the covenant.
According to 1 Sam 2.7-8, 1 Chr 29.12, and Prov 10.22, riches are
given by God alone. The wealthy man who keeps God's commandments must give God the credit for his wealth. Wealthy men who do
not attend to the conditions of God's covenant —either by neglecting
the justice imperative or by refusing to acknowledge God's sovereignty over wealth—invoke the criticism common to the prophetic
and wisdom literature. Principles of sound business practice such as
those found in Proverbs can exist side by side with statements which
devalue wealth; in either case, obedience to God is the ultimate
measure of worth. Thus it is that the OT goes some way toward a

response to Job's lamentation that the wicked 'spend their days in prosperity' (Job 21.13). It is the violation of the justice imperative—achieving the reward of God without satisfying the demand of God—that brings HW into the picture. The OT, therefore, does not contain a pure VW stratum. Instead, it contains an attempt to view wealth not as a measure of worth but as a measure of blessing—assuming the ultimate criterion of obedience to God. Ironically, as we will see below, HW can be a means to that blessing.

HW and OT Writers

The process of delimitation leaves 78 passages[38] which refer to the term wealth and reflect one or more of the five stages in development toward HW (see Table 1 above). Of this number, 2 are found in historical books, 17 in prophetic books, and 59 in the writings.

Aside from the arguments put forward above with respect to the justice imperative for an aristocratic viewpoint in the material, we have few biographical data about the authors. The data we do have, however, are almost exclusively in favor of the theory that HW came not from poor agrarian masses or movements[39] but from the political, religious, and economic hierarchy of ancient Israel. If evidence of the former is to be encountered at all, we should expect to find it in the priestly-controlled historical books and legal codes, since the priests were the most likely individuals to experience direct and extended contact with the agrarian population. But the fact of the matter is that despite the legislation to prevent over-concentration of wealth or utter destitution of the poor, we encounter in these texts by far the highest percentage of instances of VW. These priests, then, were probably members of the central religious establishment, and the criticism of wealth in their books should be understood in terms of the intent of the material and not the SEC of the writers.

The prophetic books present a greater diversity of critical evaluation, but no more support for the notion that HW is controlled by SEC. Here the situation, analogous to that of the first century AD in many ways, seems ripe for millenarian resentment:[40] colonial powers influence, threaten, or control an agrarian culture either directly or through those within the culture who co-operate with them. Corruption and oppression run rampant. Power is over-concentrated and large numbers are politically and economically disenfranchised. Mediatory figures arise to voice the desires and hopes of the people. Surely these men will exemplify and express the new values of a social revolution! Quite to the contrary, the available information indicates that generally these prophets 'had the responsibility of maintaining the stability of the social structure, and they therefore promoted orderly change and opposed anything that threatened social equilibrium'.[41]

We know, for example, that Isaiah of Jerusalem was a member of the city's upper class, and that if he was not an actual member of the royal household, his knowledge and ability gave him access to and a central role in the political establishment.[42] Ezekiel was a member of the Jerusalem priestly establishment before his exile.[43] Amos wrote his prophetic invectives as a member of the Judean upper class[44] during a time when 'externally the State was powerful and mighty, and internally flourishing and prosperous'.[45] Micah makes attacks on Jerusalem's ruling elite, possibly as one of the rural upper class.[46] Zephaniah claimed lineage from King Hezekiah, by which he 'placed himself solidly within the Jerusalemite royal establishment'.[47] Zechariah was a priest who, like these others, worked 'within the central social structure'.[48] Two other prophets contain features of the HW stratum in their writings: Jeremiah and Hosea. These two probably acted on the periphery of the political establishment, despite a measure of support from within it.[49] But even these 'peripheral' prophets were attempting to reform society according to traditional values,[50] and the parallels to 'establishment' prophets are so striking as to make it clear that the tradition was common to both.

Attention to the context of the tradition in the overall prophetic message reveals a significant feature. Material attributed to each of the prophets listed above contains not only passages in the HW stratum, but also VW passages and/or general promises ultimately to restore—even increase—the economic stature of Israel.[51] These prophets were not expressing or advocating a social change antagonistic to the rich in their own culture.[52] Theirs was the typical cultic expectation which included wealth or plunder as a reward to the nation for the return to obedience. But what of the HW tradition? It may indeed be no coincidence that the prophets listed above, for whom we have comparatively greater biographical information than for other prophets and OT writers, are the only ones who show familiarity with the tradition. Proximity to the political, economic, and religious hierarchy would allow exposure to other forms of literature circulating among the upper classes; among these, the wisdom genre is the most likely to have influenced the prophetic message.[53] Whether this historical reconstruction is accurate or not, there is no doubt that the prophetic portion of the HW stratum has a distinct wisdom flavor: two passages are in proverbial form, and nine are only to be distinguished from VW-plunder passages by the equation of wealth and pride/self-reliance —a dominant theme of proverbial wisdom.[54]

Even without biographical data, the viewpoint of the OT wisdom genre, including the psalms with which we are concerned,[55] is very clear. The writers are 'basically satisfied with the status quo and opposed to change'.[56] Their writings reveal a cosmopolitan flavor distinctive of the intellectual elite of the day.[57] Many of their ideas are adapted from aristocratic Egyptian sources.[58] Their morality is essentially utilitarian and this-worldly.[59] The evidence warrants only one conclusion: the writings are 'fundamentally the product of the upper classes in society'.[60]

This accumulation of data about the SEC of OT authors suggests that HW in its OT form was, at its most severe, an endogenous reform movement with roots in an aristocratically propagated wisdom tradition. In the main, however, the tradition reflects the value structure of a religion that attempts to relegate material success to its proper place below obedience to God—certainly a value structure not limited in relevance to particular SEC and of which the impossibility of assigning a certain date or author to the wisdom literature is an appropriate feature.

Development

The equation of injustice with greed, the first stage in the development toward HW from the justice imperative, is exemplified in Psalm 10. Although the context (vv. 2, 8-10, 18) reveals that injustice is at issue, בצע דנא רשע are equated as the cause in v. 3: 'For the wicked boasts of the desires of his heart, and the man greedy for gain curses and renounces the Lord' (cf. Prov 15.27; 21.26; Jer 6.13).

The same Psalm moves into the second stage of development when, in v. 5a, the writer equates injustice and wealth: 'His ways prosper (יחילו) at all times . . .' Ps 73.12 makes the same equation of rich and wicked independently of the justice imperative: 'Behold, these are the wicked; always at ease, they increase in riches' (cf. v. 3; Prov 18.23; 22.7; 22.16;[61] 29.13; Isa 53.9; Jer 5.26-28; 12.1; Mic 6.10-

12). In the mouths of Job's friends the equation (4.21a;[62] 15.29; 20.15; 22.20) might seem suspect, until we observe Job himself lamenting the same situation (21.7, 13, 23-36; 27.13, 19). The wealthy man is variously equated, not only with the wicked, but also with the man who 'carries out evil devices' (עשה מזמות, Ps 37.7), the violent (עריצים, Prov 11.16), the proud (גאים, Prov 15.25; 16.19; Isa 2.7, 11; 13.11, 17; Jer 51.13), the man who offers bribes (שחד, Prov 17.8), and the man who is 'wise in his own eyes' (חכם בעיניו, Prov 28.11). The author of Ecclesiastes adds the cynical warning not even to whisper against the rich, inferring that he will exert his power against those who resent him (Eccl 10.20). To his stage might be added the possible sarcasms referring to the rich (Prov 10.15; 13.8; 14.20; 18.11; 19.4; Eccl 10.19; cf. Prov 17.8; 21.14).

With the third stage of development, the valuation of some object over wealth, we see, as in the ancient Near Eastern literature, different forms of detachment proposed as alternatives to the valuation of wealth. One such form is the valuation of righteousness over wickedness when in the same context wealth is linked with wickedness (Prov 10.2; 11.28; 22.1; 28.20; cf. Ps 37.16; Prov 15.16; 16.8; 17.1; 28.6).[63] A second form extols trust in God over trust in riches. Ps 52.7 points accusingly to 'the man who would not make God his refuge, but trusted in the abundance of his riches, and sought refuge in his wealth'. Ps 62.10, similarly, warns that 'if riches increase, set not your heart on them'; instead, according to v. 8, 'trust in him [God] at all times'. This form is common elsewhere both as individual exhortation (Job 31.24-25; Ps 30.6; Prov 11.28; 28.25; 30.8-9; Jer 9.23-24), lament (Ps 49.5-6), and preface to judgment (Jer 22.21; 48.7; Ezek 28.4-5; Hos 12.7-8; cf. Deut 8.17-18). A third form of devaluation is the reminder of imminent death, as in Ps 49.16-17: 'Be not afraid when one becomes rich, when the glory of his house increases. For when he dies he will carry nothing away; his glory will not go down with him' (cf. vv. 10-14, 18-20; Prov 10.2; 27.24; 28.22; Eccl 5.13-14).[64] The eschatological 'day of wrath' should be included in this form (Prov 11.4; Isa 10.3; Ezek 7.19; Zeph 1.18). Ecclesiastes contains purely cynical statements about wealth which constitute a fourth form of devaluation (2.8, 11; 4.8; 5.10, 12; cf. 5.19). Finally, there exists a form which values, above wealth, wisdom:

> To get wisdom is better than (מה־טוב) gold; To get understanding is to be chosen rather than (מן) silver (Prov 16.16; cf. 1 Kgs 3.10-13; 2 Chr 1.11-12; Job 28.15; Prov 3.14; 8.19)

knowledge:

> There is gold, and abundance of precious stones; But the lips of
> knowledge are a precious jewel (Prov 20.15; cf. 1 Kgs 3.10-13;
> 2 Chr 1.11-12; Prov 3.14)

and the law of the Lord:

> The law of thy mouth is better to me than thousands of gold and
> silver pieces (Ps 119.72; cf. Pss 19.10; 119.14; 119.127).

There are but four OT passages that go beyond this third stage of
comparative devaluation. Three of these move into the fourth stage,
alternative devaluation, which we distinguish from the third stage as
the phrase 'instead of' is distinguished from the phrase 'better
than'.

Prov 8.10 illustrates this distinction. Although very similar in
content to the last form of stage three, which values wisdom over
wealth, it employs אל in the place of מן:

> Take my [wisdom, v. 1] instruction instead of (אל) silver, And
> knowledge rather than (מן) choice gold (cf. Prov 16.16, quoted
> above, which uses מן in both lines).

The irony of this strong statement is that the same context includes a
reward for those who pursue wisdom consisting of הון, עשר־וכבוד
להנחיל, and ואצרתיהם אמלא (vv. 18, 21)!

Prov 23.4 contains the imperative in a stronger form, since it is
isolated from elements of the VW stratum, and since it is separated
from its alternative ('seek knowledge', v. 12) by eight verses: 'Do not
toil to acquire wealth; be wise enough to desist'. The reasons given
are that wealth is deceptive and fleeting (vv. 1-3, 5-8; cf. Eccl 5.10-
12). Prov 11.4 contains a simple contrast which implies that
righteousness is the alternative to wealth: 'Riches do not profit in the
day of wrath, but righteousness delivers from death' (cf. Prov
10.2).

One passage, Job 22.23-30, moves beyond alternative devaluation
to the fifth stage, teleological devaluation. In this final stage HW
allows or is a means to a higher value. Although the speaker (Job's
'friend' Eliphaz) and the ultimate outcome (cf. 31.24-25; 42.10-12)
belie this as an expression of normative OT ethics, it is worth
observing as an example of development:

> If you return to the Almighty and humble yourself (חבנה), if you
> remove unrighteousness far from your tents, if you lay gold in the

dust, and gold of Ophir among the stones of the torrent bed, and if
the Almighty is your gold, and your precious silver, then you will
delight yourself in the Almighty, and lift up your face to God. You
will make your prayer to him, and he will hear you. You will decide
on a matter, and it will be established for you, and light will shine
on your ways. For God abases the proud (גוה), but he saves the
lowly (שח עינים).

Conclusions

The OT declares that wealth is a confirmation of God's covenant
with his people, a reward for keeping the terms of his covenant.
Among the stipulations of that covenant are the justice imperative
and the demand that man acknowledge God as the sole source of
prosperity. The OT devalues wealth accrued in violation of these
stipulations. Both VW and HW strata must, therefore, be viewed in
the light of the OT hierarchy of values. This hierarchy does not
include social or economic equalization; rather, it seeks to avoid
over-concentration of wealth that exists either at the expense of or to
the neglect of the indigent population. The data warrant these
conclusions:

1. The OT tradition of HW is similar in almost every detail to
    the religious material encountered in ancient Near Eastern
    sources.
2. Expressions of HW range from the justice imperative to
    comparative devaluation, and in a few cases alternative
    devaluation, of wealth.
3. The tradition is expressed almost exclusively from the
    viewpoint of the aristocracy and does not challenge social
    structures.
4. The different strata of references to wealth must be
    understood in terms of the ethical hierarchy which places
    reliance on God and the justice imperative above acquisition
    of property and money.

Relative to the general thesis, these conclusions suggest a
continuity in the tradition from ancient Near Eastern sources, a
Jewish precedent for HW independent of socio-economic circumstances, and the establishment of a Jewish tradition that forms the
primary ideological backdrop to the NT material.

Chapter 5

JEWISH NON-CANONICAL MATERIAL

When we consider Jewish literary production outside the Hebrew canon but before the time of Synoptic production, we make convenient distinctions which should not blind us to common or overlapping features of the material. The writings usually subsumed under the headings Apocrypha and Pseudepigrapha cover a broad spectrum of time, place, and perspective. It is helpful to distinguish from these writings the works of Philo, the rabbinic and targumic texts, and the Qumran documents. Each of these presents peculiar problems with respect to its impact on primitive Christianity. Still, the writers of all this material share with Jesus certain elements of perspective: all accept the normative ethical heritage of the Hebrew scriptures; all express an essential Jewishness coloured or at least confronted by the influx of Hellenistic ideas; all live with real or threatened subjection from without and compromise within to a foreign military and economic power. As we review the critical evaluation of wealth in this body of literature, we should observe the relation between these elements and changes in the ethical tradition; i.e. new emphases, elements, and proportions. But consideration of this material is crucial for another reason: within our limited scope of enquiry, we are attempting an excursion into the conceptual world of a first-century Jew—an excursion which will provide the immediate vocabulary of terms, phrases, and ideas from which the Synoptic material emerged.

1. *Apocrypha and Pseudepigrapha*

With some modifications, our approach to the Apocrypha and Pseudepigrapha will approximate to that of the last chapter. Among the modifications are a lack of precision about word usage due to the different languages involved, a lesser degree of control over the authors' SEC, and a cloak of caution thrown over much of the corpus because of the possibility of later Christian recension. With regard to the latter consideration, there is room for optimism: ethical content is generally an attractive element leading to the Christianization of a work, so it does not require tampering.

Included here are LXX divergences from the Hebrew text, since these reflect Jewish thinking in the centuries before Jesus. Where these embody insertions of reference to wealth, they probably indicate an increased interest in financial matters on the part of a translator, although in some cases alternate possibilities for translation suffice to explain the difference.[1] Omissions of reference to wealth are rare, and are almost always explained in terms of alternate translation possibilities.[2]

TABLE 6

Chronological categorization of apocryphal and pseudepigraphical works which contain references to wealth and/or the justice imperative.

Category A Pre-1st century AD		Category B Pre- to mid-1st century AD		Category C Late 1st century AD	
Ahiqar	500–400	1 Enoch		Pseudo-	
LXX	300–100	37-82	150-0-50	Philo	50-75
Tobit	200–150	Baruch	150-0-70	Joseph and	
Sirach	190–130	Psalms of		Asenath	50-00
1 Enoch		Solomon	70-0-60	4 Maccabees	50-100
1-36	180–150	5 Syriac		4 Ezra	50-100
Letter of		Psalms	300-0-50	2 Baruch	75-100
Aristeus	180–130	Wisdom of		Josephus	75-100
Sibylline		Solomon	110-0-50	Odes of	
Oracles III	170–140	Testament		Solomon	70-125
Jubilees	170–100	of Job	100-0-100		
1 Maccabees	170–80	Pseudo-			
2 Maccabees	170–80	Phocylides	100-0-100		
Testament		2 Enoch	100-100		
of the 12		Testament			
Patriarchs	110–50	of Abraham	0-100		
1 Enoch	170–50				
82-104					
Epistle to	300–50				
Jeremy					
1 Esdras	150–0				

Although it is difficult to date most of the literature with any degree of precision, it is possible to assign the works to chronological categories which reveal their relative importance to this study. Table 6 arranges the material in roughly chronological order[3] within three categories: works certainly predating Jesus which are likely to have been familiar to many first-century Jews; works possibly predating Jesus which reflect contemporary Jewish thought; and works of the latter decades of the first century which may reflect the ethical milieu of the Synoptic writers.

A simple list of titles can be deceiving in terms of proportion: the works placed in Category C (excluding Josephus) are as a body about 40% larger than those in Category B; if we include works and fragments not quoted, Category A comprises 50% of the content, Category B 20%, and Category C 30%. Consideration of the distribution of references within this material yields some interesting results. Although slightly larger in bulk content than the Hebrew canon, the literature yields fewer passages which make reference to wealth (199 to 214). As in the Hebrew canon, the emphasis lies heavily within wisdom/didactic writings: 145 passages occur in such material, 45 in prophetic material, and 9 in historical or narrative material.[4] The proportion of wisdom/didactic passages to prophetic passages is even greater than that in canonical books (see Table 2 above). 25 of the prophetic passages are concentrated in two books (Sib Or and 1 En); furthermore, only 22 of the prophetic references are in the HW stratum, and 12 of these are in one book.[5] The numerical breakdown of relevant passages[6] which is given in Table 7 (overleaf) reveals some noteworthy proportions seen from a chronological perspective.

Here we observe that the number of passages shrinks from 71% to 19% to 10% of the whole as we move chronologically in the literature from the Maccabean period to the aftermath of the first Jewish war. References to the justice imperative drop off even more dramatically. On the other hand, abstraction of the term wealth into figurative usage increases from occurrence in 4% of the passages in Category A to 21% in Category B to 58% in Category C.[7] All these considerations suggest that as we move into an increasingly unstable political climate—indeed, as we observe less aristocratic control over the production of texts—we encounter less attention to economic issues. Clearly, this is not what we should expect, following the logic of sociological interpretation. If the Synoptic vocabulary of terms,

TABLE 7

Numerical breakdown of apocryphal and pseudepigraphical
passages according to stratum

passages		VW	critical equality	figurative wealth	HW	justice imperative
Category A	142	42	7	6	57*	74
Category B	38	10	1	8	21**	29
Category C	19	1	0	11	7	2
Totals	199	85	8	25	85	105

* Sir 30.14-16; 1 En 103.5-6 also contain a figurative reference to wealth.
**Pss Sol 1.3-8; Wis 8.5 also contain a figurative reference to wealth.

phrases, and ideas is present in the earlier material, but this literature
does not propound millenarian economic ethics—either generally or
in the relevant particulars—we have a problem. Either we must
regard it a mere coincidence that the vocabulary in this literature
matches that of a millenarian prophet and understand that what
really matters in terms of the production of the teaching in the
Synoptics are the SEC of first-century Christians,[8] or we are left
with the alternative that Jesus' ethical vocabulary was simply
adopted or realigned traditional material that did not owe its
relevance or existence to contemporary conditions. A position
between these options, e.g. that Jesus used the vocabulary as
common ground to voice millenarian ethics, is unacceptable: we
cannot call the use of the vocabulary common ground if its
adaptation makes it uncommon (i.e. if it is no longer recognizable as
traditional); neither can we call the ethics millenarian if their
vocabulary is only recognizable as such to a twentieth-century
sociologist, and perfectly familiar as proverbial or prophetic injunction
to a first-century Jew. Within the context of delimitation and
development in the apocryphal and pseudepigraphical material, it is
to this vocabulary that we must now direct our attention.

Delimitation
As in the previous chapter, it is necessary to reduce references to
manageable proportions without neglecting important aspects of the
excluded material. We will consider in succession the relation of

wealth to poverty, the justice imperative, the VW stratum, and figurative references to wealth.

Wealth and Poverty

Of 29 joint references, i.e. to rich and poor in the same context, again we encounter no hint of comparative ethical valuation of poverty over wealth. 8 passages convey critical equality, 9 are in the VW stratum, and of the 12 in the HW stratum, all but two mention the poor only as victims of the rich.[9] Thus the poor are no more an antonymic concern here than in the Hebrew canon. There is in this literature, however, an occasional instance of regard for the poor man that may be construed as a step further than the consolation offered in some canonical texts. Although poverty is sometimes abstracted so as to become equated with righteousness,[10] as in the canonical Psalms, there are instance of praise for the economically deprived. T Gad, 7.6, for example, asserts that 'the poor man, if free from envy he pleaseth the Lord in all things, is blessed beyond all men (αὐτὸς παρὰ πάντας πλουτεῖ), because he hath not the travail of vain men'. A poor man can be honoured for his wisdom (Sir 10.23, 30) or for his fear of God (Tob 4.21; Sir 10.22 [Heb]). His poverty can be a means of testing (Sir 2.4-6; Pss Sol 18.2-3) or even of keeping him out of mischief (Sir 20.21). God does not despise the poor man (Sir 21.5; 35.13; Pss Sol 18.2-3), and neither should any man (Sir 22.25-26; Wis 2.10). The paucity of the later figurative references to poverty and the concentration of these positive statements in a few early books should prohibit any contention that an ideology of poverty is propounded in these texts.

The Justice Imperative

The objects of justice are catalogued exactly as in the ancient Near Eastern and Hebrew canonical sources: widow, orphan, poor, etc.[11] There are some minor modifications: proselytes are added (Tob 1.7), the righteous are specified (Sir 12.1-2; 2 En A 51.2); and compassion is a proper gift where money is unavailable (T Zeb 7.1-8.3). Giving should be according to means (Tob 4.5-8, 16; Sir 29.20; 2 En 51.1), and without murmuring (Tob 4.16; Sir 14.3; 35.10; 2 En 63.1-3) or hypocrisy (T Ash 2.5-7).

Of greater interest than these modifications in the command is the number of occurrences: 105, an increase of about 60% over the number found in canonical material. Given the slight decrease in the number of references to wealth, this statistic is unexpected. It is probably explained in large measure by the interest in almsgiving, which accounts for 58 of the passages, 33 of which employ ἐλεημοσύνη (see note 10 above), and not by an increase in social injustice during the period. Not only would the latter conclusion be inconsonant with the decrease in references to economic issues as we move chronologically through the literature, but it would fail to take into account the text source of the increase: the dramatic change in number occurs among the wisdom writings. 95 of the passages are found in wisdom/didactic material and only 10 in prophetic material. In terms of percentage, this ratio of 90% to 10% contrasts to that of 52% to 29% in the canonical material. In other words, justice becomes a positive and agent-oriented injunction rather than a negative and victim-oriented invective. Whether or not social injustice was on the increase during this period,[12] we observe anything but a strong response to it in the religious and ethical literature of the time.

The precise nature of the command to give alms, the newly dominant form of the justice imperative, demands closer scrutiny as a part of our search for elements of an ethical vocabulary common to the Synoptics. Among the references to ἐλεημοσύνη are a number of instances where LXX translators employ the word for צדקה or חסד,[13] four of which give alms an atoning function (Prov 15.27a; Isa 1.27; 28.17; Dan 4.27). This potent claim for the act is not unique to the LXX translators, however: the formula 'almsgiving delivers from death/sin' is found five times,[14] and similar promises occur in other passages.[15] Reward is not always other-worldly: in four places almsgiving is rewarded by material prosperity.[16] But with respect to this study, the most significant reward offered for almsgiving is not temporal reward, but 'treasure in heaven'. Tob 4.9 grounds the command to give alms in this manner: 'So you will be laying up (θέμα) a good treasure (ἀγαθὸν θησαυρίζεις) for yourself against the day of necessity (ἡμέραν ἀνάγχης).' Sir 29.11-12 follows the command with a similar promise: 'Lay up (θὲς) your treasure (θησαυρόν) according to the commandments of the Most High, and it will profit you more than gold. Store up (σύγχλεισον) almsgiving in your treasury (ταμιείοις), and it will rescue you from all affliction'.[17] Two additional features of the command should not escape notice: ὑπάρχοντα is used to indicate the resource for almsgiving,[18] and reference is made to the quality of the eye in the same context.[19]

Valuation of Wealth

There are two noteworthy differences between the canonical material and the apocryphal-pseudepigraphical works with respect to the VW stratum of tradition. The most striking of these is the small number of references to plunder and economic role-reversal, as compared to references in the Hebrew scriptures.[20] LXX Isa 16.14; 29.2; 29.5-8; and 32.14 mention plunder, but the last two translate πλοῦτος from המן, which may have economic connotations. LXX Isa 5.14 and T Jud 23.3 mention plunder, but it is the Jews who are the victims. Sib Or III 531; 638-40; and 2 Bar 70.4 predict plunder and economic reversal within the pagan nations, but not between them and the Jews. LXX Isa 32.18 and T Jud 25.4 promise eventual prosperity to Israel, but do not mention plunder as a means to it. Sib Or III 241-47 describes an ideal of justice, but it also affirms the continuation of the polarized social structure. 1 En 97.8-10 and 98.2-3 pronounce plunder as the judgement meted out upon the rich, but the writer promises the righteous a heavenly, non-economic reward (99.10; 104.6). 1 En 38.3-5 promises something like reversal: 'Then shall the kings and the mighty perish and be given into the hands of the righteous and holy'; but this is not clearly an economic change: it may mean only that the oppressed will be the instruments of punishment. Sib Or III is more clear: after making reference to the destruction of the wealth of various cities and lands (345; 388; 436; 444-48), the author predicts that 'again the people of the mighty God shall be laden with excellent wealth' (657; cf. 750; 783). Here, finally, in one Greek-styled and Egyptian-produced work, we encounter a contemporary message that approximates the canonical prophetic prediction of economic reversal. But given the impersonal and largely amoral nature of the description, we must question whether the reversal idea here is primarily economic, or religious and political. We simply do not encounter in the literature as a whole the pervasive economic resentment which is posited as the precursor of first-century millenarianism, and which is claimed for these works in the form of a 'crude desire for vengeance'[21] and a 'crude symbolism of the political and economic dream which fired the hearts of the poor and oppressed.'[22] Hearts may have been fired, and revolts certainly took place, but the direct influence of this body of literature must be considered doubtful. Granted, appeal may have been made by analogy to earlier, canonical material in an effort to justify hope for economic reversal, but even this conjecture seems inconsistent with the progressive dematerialization of later literary production.[23] Alternately, this kind of resentment may be unrecorded, and at the time it may have been unspoken, or even unconscious, as a motive for religious and political upheaval.[24] But it is not to our purpose to engage in this level of conjecture. Synoptic teaching in its relation to these texts provides adequate literary evidence to warrant our investigation of apocryphal/pseudepigraphical material as the heritage of the Gospels.

If the paucity of plunder passages is one important difference from the Hebrew canon, the appearance of a 'purer' valuation of wealth equally merits attention. Despite considerably fewer passages in the VW stratum than in the canonical books (85 to 126), this literature contains a greater number devoted to business advice,[26] and many that assume the value of wealth with no contextual reference to piety or to anything even remotely covenantal.[27] The most common argument is that every effort should be made to build economic insurance against the ultimate shame of beggary. As Ahik 26.10 [Gk] puts it,

> Every day, and for the morrow, do thou store up (ἀποταμίευου); for it is better to die and leave one's estate to enemies than to live and be dependent on friends.[28]

Normally, profligacy is the cause of this condition (Ahik 2.51 [Syr A]; Sir 18.32–19.1), but it can also be due to excessive generosity in giving (Sir 33.19) or lending (Sir 8.13).[29] Despite this high estimation of fortune-building, however, acquisition of wealth is not praised without qualification. Sir 13.24 states simply that 'Riches are good if they are free from sin', and the catalogue of sins included in similar contexts very often mentions neglect of benevolence.[30] A picture emerges of VW tempered by charity—an approach that does not emphasize righting wrongs so much as doing right. Although the action often appears token, the amount given is less significant at this point than the context: the call for charity can exist without a challenge to VW. Indeed, most of the passages in the justice imperative stratum which recommend almsgiving assume a wealthy audience, and numerous almsgiving commands occur in the VW

stratum—but hardly ever in the HW stratum.[31] Almsgiving is not
generally a way of expressing hostility to wealth; rather, it is most
often an expression of social responsibility on the part of the rich.
This qualified valuation of wealth has affinity to the canonical
literature in that justice is both pronounced and performed in large
measure by the rich. But the danger of tokenism is apparent in the
later literature, due on the one hand to the uncritical attention to
fortune-building, and on the other hand to the cautions against
excessive generosity. Justice of the rich and by the rich is in danger of
becoming justice for the rich.

Figurative References to Wealth

Another distinctive development of this period is the increased
abstraction of the term wealth.[32] Only a few canonical references can
be considered in this category.[33] In the apocryphal/pseudepigraphical
literature, however, clearly figurative references occur with increasing
frequency (note 6 above). Since these passages do not refer directly to
material wealth, it is best to regard them as comprising a new and
distinct stratum. There is no discernible pattern of usage: although
they often imply by analogy that wealth is a good thing,[34] they are
equally likely to inlcude HW in the same context or to use the
figurative term as a foil to some higher value.[35] In either case, an
influx of the Greek 'general use' of the term[36] seems the best
explanation.

HW and Apocrypha-Pseudepigrapha Writers

It is only with great caution that we place these largely anonymous or
pseudonymous works into social or religious categories, many of
which were relatively undefined during this period. Still, many of the
arguments adduced for the aristocratic viewpoint of canonical
material apply here as well. Most of the relevant material is wisdom/
didactic in character, exhibiting a cosmopolitan literary attainment
inaccessible to large segments of the population. Indeed, even the
most polemical apocalyptic

> would appear to have been written for the most part by wise and
> learned men who were thoroughly acquainted not only with the
> historic Jewish faith, but also with the 'wisdom' of that time ....[37]

The sense of comparative proximity caused by second-person
references to the rich is even stronger in this literature than in the
Hebrew scriptures,[38] and references to the wealth of individuals and

powers outside the Jewish fold are comparatively few.[39] Both these factors suggest that rich Jews were an intended audience. Fortunately, the largest amount of material (fifty-three passages referring to wealth) comes from a source for which we have relatively precise biographical data. Jesus ben Sira was a Jewish Jerusalemite who wrote in the early decades of the second century BC. He may have been a professional scribe[40] or a priest;[41] but wealthy or not, his morality is clearly expressed 'from the standpoint of the upper classes'.[42] To the extent that other authors produce ethical material consistent in content with this and earlier sources, proto-Pharisaic and Essene tendencies displayed in other matters become secondary in importance for our enquiry. In fact, such tendencies make it more clear that the tradition is continuous not only across temporal and geographical boundaries, but also across ideological barriers.

Development

The process of delimitation leaves 85 passages[43] that refer to wealth and reflect one of the five stages of development toward HW (see Table 1). The number and proportions are similar to the HW stratum in the Hebrew canon: 58 passages are found in wisdom material, 22 in prophetic material, and 5 in narrative material (cf. Table 2 and ch. 4 n. 38 above).

The first stage, comprising equations between greed and injustice, is well represented in this literature. Both sides of the equation are contained in Sib Or III: in one place the author makes reference to 'covetousness (φιλοχρημοσύνη) the corrupter of life, and ill-gotten wealth' (κακοκερσέι πλούτῳ 189; cf. 234-36); in another place he laments that 'no man of wealth will give any part to another, but miserable meanness (κακίη δεινή) shall be among all mortals' (41-42; cf. Ps-Philo 39.1). Greed leads not only to social injustice (T Dan 5.7; 4 Macc 2.8), but also to bad manners (Sir 31.12-18), treachery (2 Macc 10.20; cf. Ps-Philo 58.2), idolatry (T Jud 17.1; 19.1-2; cf. Sir 25.21), and excessive luxury (T Iss 4.2; cf. Ep Arist 211). Two features of this stage warrant special attention in relation to NT teaching: first, the setting 'at the table of a great man' for the teaching of Sir 31.12-18 about deference to fellow banqueters; second, the introduction of the term 'love of money' (φιλαργυρία: 2 Macc 10.20; T Jud 18.2; 19.1-2; 4 Macc 1.26; 2.8) as a synonym for greed.[44]

The second stage of development, which equates wealth and injustice, finds equally strong expression in apocryphal/pseudepigraphical sources. Often this equation mentions the victims directly, as in Sir 13.19: 'Wild asses in the wilderness are the prey of lions; likewise the poor are pastures for the rich'.[45] But movement occurs away from such direct links to the justice imperative. Deceitfulness is another common trait of the wealthy:

> A rich man will exploit you if you can be of use to him, but if you are in need he will forsake you (Sir 13.4; cf. 13.2-8; 10-11; 27.1-2; Jub 23.21; 1 En 94.6).

Elsewhere the wealthy are termed proud (Sir 13.20; 1 En 94.8; 97.8-9; 46.7), violent (LXX Ps 75.5; Sir 13.13), hot-tempered (Sir 28.10), and 'wanting in doctrine and wisdom' (1 En 98.2-3). Numerous sarcastic or cynical proverbs are also included in this stage, such as Ahik 2.14 [Syr A]:

> My son, the rich man eats a snake, and they say 'He ate it for medicine'. And the poor man eats it, and they say, 'For his hunger he ate it'.[46]

Two additional features relevant to Synoptic teaching appear at this stage: Sir 31.1 warns that

> Wakefulness over wealth wastes away one's flesh,
> and anxiety (μέριμνα) about it removes sleep.[47]

and 1 En 97.8 pronounces a woe in the second person (οὐαὶ ὑμῖν) upon the wicked rich.[48]

Comparative devaluation of wealth, the third stage of development, is less well represented here than in the Hebrew scriptures. One change that accounts for much of this difference is the low number of comparisons between wealth and wisdom, knowledge, or Law (Sir 1.22 [Syr]; Wis Sol 7.8-9; 8.5). Other forms of detachment parallel canonical passages, indicating an essential continuity of tradition. Trust in God, or fear of God, is often valued over wealth (Sir 5.13; 40.18-26; Bar 3.16-17; Pss Sol 1.4-6; T Job 15.7-9; Ps-Phoc 53-54; cf. Sir 10.23-24). Righteousness is valued over wickedness where in the same context wealth is linked with wickedness (LXX Prov 19.22; Tob 12.8-10). The reminder of imminent death, which in this literature is often understood to include subsequent judgment, forms another kind of devaluation (Sir 5.8; 11.18-19; 1 En 100.6; 103.5-6; 52.7; 63.10; Bar 3.16-19; Wis Sol 5.8-9; T Job 33.3-5). Cynicism about seeking riches is still expressed (Sir 11.11; cf. 31.3-4). A few new forms appear as well: friendship (Sir 7.18) and health (Sir 30.14-16) are valued above wealth; and in a radical departure from the Hebrew text, LXX Prov 23.4 advises simple detachment as an alternative to injustice:

μὴ παρεκτείνωπένης ὤν πλοθσίῳ
τῇ δὲσῇ ἐννοίᾳ ἀπόσχου

The imminence of death form is now familiar, but its expression in 1 En 97.8-10 reveals another group of terms common to Synoptic teaching and to Luke 12.16-21 in particular: the soliloquy of the doomed rich man includes the treasuring (τεθησαυρίκαμεν) of a quantity of goods (ἀγαθὰ πολλά, cf. Luke 1.53; 12.19; 16.25) in storehouses (θησαυροῖς, οἰκίαις).[49]

Eleven passages go beyond the third stage to express either alternative or teleological devaluation. It is significant that these are found in ten different works representing a variety of sectarian, chronological, and geographical positions.

The first instance of stage four is found in LXX Ps 33.11, which translates כפירים as πλούσιοι. The change could be attributed to the reading כבדים or כבירים;[50] in any case, the result is an implicit command to be one of 'those who seek the Lord' who 'lack no good thing (מוב, ἀγαθοῦ)' rather than to be rich—a thought that approximates the message of Matt 6.33.

T Benj 6.2-3 provides a second example which reveals a clear contrast between heavenly and earthly values:

Βνωι howhve
≠ riče

> And he (τοῦ ἀγαθοῦ ἀνδρὸς, v. 1) gazeth not passionately upon corruptible things, nor gathereth together riches through a desire for pleasure. He delighteth not in pleasure, he grieveth not his neighbour, he sateth not himself with luxuries, he erreth not in the uplifting of the eyes, for the Lord is his portion.

A third instance of alternative devaluation is found in Pss Sol 5.16-17, where the man with abundance in righteousness (πλησμονὴν ἐν δικαιοσύνῃ) is lauded (μακάριος), but by possessing excessive wealth (ὑπερπλεονάσῃ) a man sins (ἐξαμαρτάνει). The *economic* ideal here is not poverty but 'a due sufficiency (συμμετρίᾳ αὐταρκείας)' or 'moderate means (μέτριαν)' supplied by God.

Two passages representative of stage four, alternative devaluation, are found in T Job. In 18.8 the hero, recalling the Lord's promise of reward for obedience in suffering (4.6-9), claims that 'Thus I also now considered my possessions (τὰ ἐμά) as nothing (οὐδέν)'.[51] Later each of Job's daughters are magically transformed into hymn-singing saints so that one μηκέτι φρονεῖν τὰ τῆς γῆς (48.2), another μηκέτι ἐνθυμηθῆναι τὰ κοσμικά (49.2), and the third ἠλλοιοῦτο ἀφισταμένη ἀπὸ τῶν κοσμικῶν (50.2; cf. 33.5-9).

Ps-Philo 35.5, when describing the angel's advice to Gideon, gives a fifth instance of alternative devaluation. Gideon is told that God looks 'upon that which is upright and good, and upon meekness (*in directum bonum, et in mansuetudinem*)' whereas man looks upon 'the glory of the world and upon riches (*in gloriam seculi, et divitias*)'.

Five passages evince teleological devaluation, the fifth and final stage of development toward HW. In each of these passages, the voluntary loss of wealth reflects a higher value and results in a heavenly reward. None can be said to laud poverty; indeed, three are simply expressions of the justice imperative that allow for radical loss but do in no way condemn wealth. This nuance is significant: the motivating factor of treasure in heaven allows for—even encourages—radical loss irrespective of the need of the poor, the valuation of poverty, or the devaluation of wealth.

The first example is an apt illustration of this nuance. Sir 29.9-10 is a departure from the similar command to give alms in Tob 4.5-11, 16 only in that it places in the immediate context (cf. 29.20) no limit on giving (κατὰ τὸ πλῆθος, Tob 4.8; ὁ ἐὰν περισσεύσῃ σοι, Tob 4.16); instead, it commands the reader to

> Lose (ἀπόλεσον) your silver for the sake of a brother or a friend (or poor man, vv. 8-9), and do not let it rust (ἰωθήτω) under a stone and be lost.

Both the Tob and Sir passages promise treasure in heaven as a reward, but when the Sir passage is read as a unit, there is no check on the idea that the greater the amount given, the greater the subsequent reward. Such an understanding may ultimately have precipitated legislation such as *b. Ketub.* 50a: '. . . if a man desires to spend liberally he should not spend more than a fifth, [since by spending more] he might himself come to be in need [of the help] of people'.[52]

1 En 104.6 follows the series of woes against the wicked rich with this admonition:

And now fear (φοβεῖσθε) not, ye righteous, when ye see sinners growing strong and prospering in their ways: be not companions with them, but keep afar from their violence (πάντων τῶν ἀδικημάτων αὐτῶν).

The Ethiopic version adds 'for ye shall become companions of the hosts of heaven', echoing the thought of vv. 1-2 [Gk], and v. 13 [Gk] promises reward (ἀγαλλιάσονται) to the righteous. These factors suggest an ethical implication that goes beyond mere consolation for victims: given a choice, the righteous are to avoid wealthy men and their methods. The strong equation of wealth with wickedness in the preceding chapters makes it likely that religious purity (103.7-9), and not acquisition of wealth in a godly manner, is the recommended alternative. If an incidental result of this purity is poverty, the argument of the passage may be not far removed from the first Lukan beatitude and woe.

The third passage, similar in content to Sir 29.10-11, is 2 En 50.5:

> Whoever of you spends gold or silver for his brother's sake, he will receive ample treasure in the world to come.[53]

Again the admonition is radical only when considered as an independent saying, since 51.1 and the introduction to chapter 61 make the giving proportional.

Jos Asen 10-12 describes the heroine's repentance, the outward manifestation of which includes throwing her expensive adornments and gold and silver idols out the window τοῖς πένησι, τοῖς πτωχοῖς καὶ τοῖς δεομένοις (10.11, 13). Her subsequent prayer of repentance explains this action:

> For behold, all the goods (χρήματα) of my father Pentephres are ephemeral and uncertain; but the gifts (δώματα) of your inheritance, Lord, are incorruptible and eternal (αἰώνια, 12.12).[54]

The ethical implications of this are mitigated somewhat by the very tangible reward later given to Asenath: a rich and powerful husband with whom at one point she shares the gift of στεφάνους χρυσοῦς (21.41)! Nevertheless, for the reader who was not apt so to enjoy the best of both worlds, her action may have represented a means of happiness in the next.

The fifth passage evincing teleological devaluation is Josephus's description of the Essenes (*BJ* II 119-123; cf. 124-161). Whether Josephus had any first-hand knowledge of the group is less important here than that his description shows an awareness of such practice as a viable option for Jewish piety.[55] As part of their effort to practice holiness (δοκεῖ σεμνότητα ἀσκεῖν, 119) the Essenes 'shun pleasures as a vice (τὰς μὲν ἡδονὰς ὡς κακίαν ἀποστρέφονται, 120)' and 'despise riches (καταφρονηταὶ ... πλούτου, 122)'. The result of their κοινωνικόν (122) is that none experiences either 'abject poverty (πενίας ταπεινότητα, 122)' or 'inordinate wealth (ὑπεροχὴν πλούτου, 122; cf. 134; *JA* XVIII 18-20'). This practice has more in common with 1 En 104.6 than with the other passages cited in that it demands separation from wealth which presumably has become tainted by association with evil men and evil practice.

Conclusions

A composite statement of words, phrases, and ideas taken from apocryphal/pseudepigraphical works, and especially from the passages comprising the last two stages of development, summarizes the evidence for the claim that the Synoptic vocabulary emerged largely from this tradition:

> Give alms to the poor from your possessions, and lay up treasure
> for yourself in heaven. Do not be fearful or anxious about wealth,
> or love money, or have an evil eye. But woe to you rich.

This statement could of course be expanded by the inclusion of canonical elements that are repeated or affirmed in this literature, and we might also adduce the setting at the table of a rich man (Sir 31.12-18) and the soliloquy of the rich (1 En 97.8-10) as part of the heritage of the Gospels. These and other considerations discussed above warrant the following conclusions:

1. References to justice and material wealth decrease markedly through this period of writing.
2. The tradition is identical in almost every detail to the religious-ethical material encountered in Jewish canonical and Ancient Near Eastern sources.
3. Despite sectarian production, the conservative, even aristocratic, viewpoint expressed and the proportions between strata of the tradition are consistent with canonical sources.
4. Expressions of HW range from the justice imperative to a few instances of alternative and teleological devaluation.
5. The tradition contains elements of vocabulary common to Synoptic material.

These conclusions have important ramifications for the general thesis of this book. Not only do the apocryphal/pseudepigraphical sources fail to evince a millenarist tendency in the economic ethics of the period, but they demonstrate that much of the Synoptic teaching can be reconstructed from elements of the conservative tradition dominant in this literature and continuous with canonical literature.

2. *Philo and the Greek Influence*[56]

Philo is important to this study as an example; both in terms of the relation between his SEC and his writings, and in terms of his representation of a part of the Jewish spectrum of thought accessible to the producers of the Synoptic tradition. Given the strong Greek influence in Philo's works, it is here that we will review Greek views and practices that have particular relevance to our subject.

David Mealand's article, 'Philo of Alexandria's Attitude to Riches',[57] focuses on the influence of Greek philosophical schools in Philo's writings about poverty and wealth. Mealand documents Stoic, Cynic, Aristotelian, and Platonic ideas; and he likens Philo's aristocratic praise of poverty to that of Seneca, but concludes that the best explanation of his disparagement of wealth is 'Philo's adherence to a religion some of whose texts reflect the outlook of less privileged groups'.[58] This argument is a *non sequitur*; but it also falls prey on the one hand, as we have seen, to a misinformed conception of the 'outlook' of Jewish texts, and on the other hand, as we will see, to a misreading of Philo's use of Jewish tradition.

Mealand documents Philo's personal wealth, remarking that 'the basic puzzle is the discrepancy between his recorded statements and his personal affluence'.[59] This should come as no surprise by now; almost every source encountered thus far containing HW shows evidence of aristocratic production. Philo is in fact the example *par excellence* of this phenomenon. A member of an established and wealthy family, possessed of means sufficient to allow for substantial study and voluminous writing, influential enough to represent his community to the Emperor, Philo was hardly ripe for millenarist resentment. Yet from his pen came no less than thirty-eight passages reflecting alternative or teleological devaluation of wealth—a total nearly three times that encountered in all the literature considered thus far. Clearly there are possibilities for the production of such texts other than the author's SEC. In Philo's case, it seems likely that

philosophical ideas working in conjunction with religious-ethical
traditions produced what seems to be a theoretical position inconsistent with a socio-economic position. The religious-ethical
traditions in the philonic synthesis are of primary importance here:
as we examine his teaching in the delimitation-development format,
we must consider Philo's use of features common to other Jewish
texts.

Delimitation

Passages that make reference to wealth are common in Philo's
writings. We will consider over 200 of these, concentrating on those
using πλοῦτος, which constitute about two-thirds of the total.[60]
Other words commonly used for wealth are ἄργυρος and/or
χρύσος,[61] and χρῆμα.[62]

Figurative use of πλοῦτος occurs fifty-one times in Philo,[63]
occasionally as a foil to negatively-regarded material wealth, as in
Som. I 179: 'Of what riches can we any longer stand in need, when
we have Thee who art alone the true riches . . .?'[64] Πλοῦτος is used
nine times without critical evaluation[65] and in eight other passages
which address the justice imperative to the wealthy without giving a
contextual indication of valuation or hostility.[66]

The justice imperative is not a burning issue to Philo. Although he
praises the just laws of the Pentateuch (e.g. Spec. II 107: Virt. 97), he
does not mention ἐλεημοσύνη and only rarely refers to 'widow,
orphan, and poor' as the recipients of aid. Instead, he offers a vague
ideal of general welfare or commonality (Spec. IV 159; Virt. 169;
Praem. 168)[67] epitomized by the practice of the Essenes (Hyp. 11.4,
11). When he does approach the familiar form of the justice
imperative, Philo's aristocratic perspective and tokenism become
clear: 'You have abundance of wealth, give a share to others, for the
excellence of wealth consists not in a full purse but in succouring the
needy' (Jos. 144).

Although about 80% of the passages in question exhibit a degree of
HW, the remainder needs to be accounted for. Did Philo simply
contradict himself, did his socio-economic position at times overcome
his philosophical understanding, or is there an observable pattern
which accounts for the discrepancies? There is indeed a pattern, and
one which deals a blow to the argument that Philo's HW reflects
sympathy toward underprivileged co-religionists. For in 31 of 43
passages exhibiting VW, Philo writes of wealth belonging to Jews.[68]

Perhaps his thinking was influenced by the scriptural narratives on which he was commenting; in any case, it is clear that he distinguishes between wealth as given by God to the Jews (L.A. III 197) and wealth as an ethical subject. When he demonstrates an awareness of deprivation among the Jews it is to promise them wealth (Praem. 168). Clearly, Philo's praise of poverty and disregard for wealth are not informed by borrowed feelings of disenfranchisement.

The other twelve VW passages are instructive with respect to nuances in Philo's position, but they do not contradict his ethical teaching. When he allows for the possibility of 'good' wealth, he includes in the context a negative statement (Plant. 171; Sob. 40) or a goal more worthy of striving (Her. 286-87). In Praem. 104 he makes a statement very much like Matt 6.33:

> For those who possess store up in Heaven the true wealth whose adornment is wisdom and godliness have also the wealth of earthly riches in abundance (cf. 118).

A careful reading of the context reveals that Philo defines this abundance in terms of an ongoing provision of food and shelter (98-100), and not the superfluity of luxury which he condemns elsewhere. Six of the seven remaining references value wealth in a particular context, exemplified by Leg. 123:

> These things are horrible . . . when the rich become poor, the well-to-do destitute, suddenly through no fault of their own rendered hearthless and homeless (cf. Flacc. 58; 60; 77; Leg. 108; 343).

Leg. 9 and 343 (cf. 18-21) speak sympathetically of inherited wealth, completing the picture of valuation of *involuntarily acquired or deprived* wealth. The will is the key. Where Philo is positive toward wealth, he regards it as involuntary: a gift of God to the Jews, an inheritance, or a plundered fortune. Where he is negative, wealth represents for Philo the acquisitiveness that cannot exist side-by-side with virtue, and renunciation represents the choice for virtue. The involuntary poverty of his fellow Jews scarcely attracts Philo's notice and hardly relates to this scheme. Apparently, then, Philo does not regard his co-religionists as disinherited or plundered. It is to the extent that Jewish ethics support, or Jewish examples illustrate, his scheme of virtue in relation to wealth that Philo reveals his Jewishness.

Development

The first stage of development toward HW (see Table 1) is exemplified in Vita 17, where Philo states that 'injustice is bred by anxious thought for the means of life and for money-making'.[69] Vices other than injustice are also linked with greed,[70] and among these equations is a reference to desire/covetousness as 'that insidious foe and source of all evils' (Virt. 100). Thirteen occurrences of the Greek-borrowed term φιλαργυρία/φιλοχρηματία[71] mark 'love of money' as a standard phrase used by Philo in condemning greed.

The second stage of development is very common in Philo's writings. Here we consider not only the equation of wealth and injustice that distinguishes this stage from the last[72] but also simple disparaging statements about wealth itself. Typical of the latter is Spec. I 25-28, in which riches are described as 'blind', 'unstable', and 'idols and unsubstantial shadows'.[73] Wealth is also commonly linked with pride[74] and excessive luxury or pleasure.[75] It is the fool's desire (Conf. 112; Jos. 254) and the antithesis of virtue (Som. II 12; Mos. II 53); it is 'no true blessing, but actually a grievous evil' (Gig. 37).[76]

Comparative devaluation is the third stage of development. In Philo's writings, this usually takes the form of valuation of virtue over wealth. Abr. 24-25 is typical: 'What wealth is equal in worth to these [virtues] . . . for in very truth the wealth which is not blind but keen in sight is abundance of virtue'.[77] Related to this form are valuations of prudence[78] or right relation to God[79] over material wealth. But requiring distinction are a few passages that express comparative devaluation without truly disparaging wealth itself. Det. 122 lauds justice because of 'its complete indifference to objects on the borderline between vice and virtue, such as wealth . . . .' Gig. 38 advocates that one neither seek nor refuse wealth, but rather cultivate detachment from it.

Det. 164 recommends 'economy' and Prob. 145 'moderate livelihood' as the proper middle road. One passage defies categorization but may be included here as a way of demonstrating detachment without hostility. In Fug. 25-29 Philo suggests that one 'expose the worthless man of wealth' not by 'penury and humility and a strict unsocial mode of life'; rather, says Philo, 'do not refuse abundance of wealth', but practice generosity to such an extent that 'you will all but throw your private property into the common purse'. The exaggeration of the last line should not disguise Philo's implicit defense of (his own?)

wealth. Virtue may be above it, but virtue can also redeem it (Sob. 40). Whatever this passage may hint about Philo's underlying belief or practice, it represents only an exception to his written rule. It may be seen in terms of Jewish prerogative, and it should be noted that Philo here advocates 'not refusing' rather than 'acquiring'.

With the fourth stage of development, alternative devaluation, we encounter a strength of hostility foreign to the sources considered thus far. Up to this point most of Philo's statements find parallels in earlier semitic literature, despite the Greek caste which he gives to them.[80] But at this stage he seems to see less of a tension and more of an opposition between the delights of wealth and the demands of virtue. Eighteen passages reflect this thinking;[81] we will consider three of these as representational, giving the bulk of attention to stage five. In Gig. 15 Philo disparages

> glory, wealth, and offices, and honours, and all other illusions which like images or pictures are created through the deceit of false opinion by those who have never gazed upon the true beauty.

Ebr. 75 extols the one who has

> learnt that nothing else, neither wealth, nor glory, nor honour ... nor the whole world, but only the true cause, the Cause Supreme among causes, deserves our service and highest honour.

This mutual exclusivity of values takes its most typically philonic form in Congr 27. which states that

> (virtue) trains us to despise (καταφρονητικῶς ἔχειν) all (πάντων) that should be held of little account, reputation and wealth and pleasure ....

This opposition between the pursuit of virtue and the pursuit of wealth is taken a step further in twenty passages that evince teleological devaluation. Here, in passages containing some interesting parallels to Synoptic material, Philo makes voluntary dispossession of wealth a means or way of achieving virtue. L.A. III 142-45 is notable for the verb used to indicate the act of renunciation. Philo says of Moses that

> not only does he renounce (ἀποτάττεται) the whole belly, but with it he scours away the feet, that is, the supports of pleasure ... We must not fail to notice that Moses, when he refuses the entire belly, that is the filling of the stomach, he practically renounces (ἀποτάττεται) the other passions too.

The same verb is used in Luke 14.33. Philo usually employs ἀποτάσσω/ἀποτάττω to indicate purely mental activity,[82] and that sense may be implicit here, but it is interesting to encounter the word in such a context. A stronger statement is found in Deus 147-51:

> Have you won the Olympic crown of victory over all wealth, and so risen superior to all that wealth involves, that you accept nothing of what it brings for your use and enjoyment?... Will you see all the treasuries of wealth, one after the other, full to the brim, yet turn aside from them and avert your eyes?... For (a celestial and heavenly soul) takings its fill of the vision of incorruptible and genuine goods (ἀγαθῶν), bids farewell (ἀποτάττεται) to the transient and spurious.[83]

Here it is clear that hostility goes beyond attitude to active separation from wealth. Plant. 66 makes explicit the junction of attitude and action:

> This is the mind which, as the lawgiver insists, should be that of those who provide themselves with no property that has its place among things created, but renounce (ἀπογινώσκοντας) all these on the ground of that intimate association with the Uncreate, to possess Whom, they are convinced, is the only wealth, the only gauge of consummate happiness.

In Mos. I 152-55 Philo praises the lawgiver because 'he did not treasure up (ἐθησαυρίσατο) gold and silver'; and states that 'God rewarded him by giving him instead the greatest and most perfect wealth' (cf. Luke 12.21). Similarly, Philo advises in Spec. IV 74:

> So then let not the rich man collect great store of gold and silver and hoard it at his house, but bring it out for general use that he may soften the hard lot of the needy with the unction of his cheerfully given liberality ... (cf. Praem. 104).

Philo's descriptions of the Essenes and Therapeutae provide additional examples of teleological devaluation. He lauds the former because

> they have become moneyless and landless by deliberate action rather than by lack of good fortune, [but] they are esteemed exceedingly rich, because they judge frugality with contentment to be, as indeed it is, an abundance of wealth (Prob. 77; cf. 76).

He praises the latter, likewise, because they

> preferred magnanimity to negligence and gave away (χαρισάμενοι) their possessions (τὰς οὐσίας) instead of wasting them, benefiting both others and themselves .... (Vita 16)

The Therapeutae garner further praise from Philo in that

> when they have divested themselves of their possessions and have
> no longer aught to ensnare them they flee without a backward
> glance and leave their brothers, their children, their wives, their
> parents, the wide circle of their kinfolk, the groups of friends
> around them, the fatherlands in which they were born and reared,
> since strong is the attraction of familiarity and very great its power
> to ensnare (Vita 18).

Clearly, Philo presents these groups as contemporary examples of
the biblical figures he describes elsewhere as embodiments of his
ideal. Other examples of teleological devaluation could be given,[84]
but these suffice to complete the pictureof Philo's ideal as that of a
man who voluntarily scorns and leaves his wealth by practising
charity and frugality. Although he praises such action, he does not
make it an absolute (Fug. 25-29) or universal (Mut. 32, 39)
requirement, nor does he laud poverty. Instead, his focus is upon
virtue as an exercise of the will, of which HW is one important
form.

The Greek Influence

In order to assess more carefully Philo's severity and its relation to
previous Jewish and subsequent Christian traditions, it is useful at
this point to consider Greek attitudes toward wealth. Summaries and
numerous references are provided by Hauck/Kasch on the subject of
wealth in general;[85] and by Bolkestein, Hands, and Den Boer on the
subject of charity.[86] If we compare these works with our knowledge
of Philo, we discover that Philo's eclectic approach mirrors many
elements of Greek thought, from pre-Socratic to Stoic.[87] His
expressions of teleological devaluation, however, most closely
resemble Cynic ideals, not only in their radical extent of renunciation,
as opposed to the mere detachment of Stoics;[88] but also in their
individual point of reference, as opposed to the *polis* in Plato and
Aristotle.[89] Diogenes, Crates, and Demetrius serve as rhetorical
examples for various authors,[90] prompting doubt as to the prevalent
practice of Cynic ideals. Seneca, who in social status and teaching
can be compared to Philo,[91] exemplifies this inconsistency. In *Epist.*
62.3, praising Demetrius for renouncing his wealth, he pens the
concise maxim 'The shortest cut to [true] riches is to despise riches'.
In a later epistle he makes the fuller statement that

we must spurn wealth; wealth is the diploma of slavery. Abandon gold and silver, and whatever else is a burden on our richly-furnished homes; liberty cannot be gained for nothing. If you set a high value on liberty, you must set a low value on everything else (*Epist*. 103.34).

Yet in *Vita Beat*. 18.1-3 Seneca freely admits to neglecting the practice of his ideals, arguing that the praise of virtue is necessary despite his own lapses. It may be that Philo's scriptural and sectarian Jewish heroes correspond to these Cynic heroes, and that his practice was equally far removed from his ideals.

Another similarity between Philo and Greek authors is his lack of concern for almsgiving.[92] Despite occasional attention to the cause of the needy,[93] Philo tends to share the Greek distinctive that 'the giver's action is self-regarding'.[94] That is, he concentrates on the dangers of wealth to the individual and not on the need of it by others less fortunate. Praise or compassion for the poor are rare both for Philo and for Greco-Roman writers.[95] Generosity to society in the forms of grain doles, feasts, buildings, and other public benefits only incidentally benefited the poor as part of the general population.[96]

But if we look closer at the motivation for giving, we observe a crucial distinction that sets Philo apart from the Greeks who influenced so many aspects of his expression. The self-regarding action of the giver in the Greek world is such 'in the sense that he anticipates from the recipient some sort of return'.[97] This principle of reciprocity, which Bolkestein calls one of the *Grundlagen* of Greek society,[98] operates primarily among the upper classes[99] and brought either equivalent gifts or honour to the giver.[100] Philo's economic ethic is not informed by this dominant pagan ideal. Rather, his expression of Greek ideas is combined with a Jewish cast of characters, suggesting that he perceived a strong link between HW and Jewish tradition. If he was primarily a Cynic in orientation, he was so only to the extent that he saw a warrant or a precedent for Cynic ideas in the Hebrew scriptures and in contemporary Jewish sectarian practice.

With respect to subsequent Synoptic tradition, we must grant the possibility of familiarity with Cynic and even philonic writings among the Christians of the middle decades of the first century. But given the warrant/precedent in Jewish sources for the same ideas, the similarities in expression are perhaps best regarded in terms of coincidence and not dependence.

Conclusions

Our consideration of Philo's writings can be summarized as follows:

1. Philo writes from an aristocratic point of view.
2. Philo consistently expresses HW, including a significant number of passages exhibiting alternative and teleological devaluation of wealth.
3. Philo's HW is not informed by sympathy for oppressed Jews.
4. Philo's affinities to Greek thought, especially to that of the Cynics, are limited in scope to those that he perceives to be consistent with Jewish tradition.

These conclusions are relevant to the general thesis in that they present a contemporary Jewish example of HW independent of SEC. The 'puzzle' of Philo's position is such only for those who assume a causative relation between SEC and critical evaluation of wealth. The evidence of Philo is in fact a compelling argument that this assumption is mistaken.

3. *Rabbinic and Targumic Literature*

Our review of the literature in the previous sections has brought us ever nearer to the Synoptics in terms of chronology, geography, and/ or ideology. The ideal culmination of this approach would be an examination of the writings of Jesus' known contemporaries, i.e. those who may have been in dialogue with him. Unfortunately, our control over such sources is elusive at best.

The vast majority of Jesus' hearers were common people who left no written legacy. We surmise that they were not aligned with any one sect and that they absorbed ethical ideas from traditional/ proverbial wisdom, sectarian influence, and cross-cultural encounters. The Gospel accounts reveal that Jesus had at least limited contact with Sadducean, Gentile, and perhaps Essene elements of society. The social isolation of these groups stands in contrast to the social heterogeneity and accessibility of the Pharisees, whose practice (and perhaps teaching) often served as a foil to that of Jesus and his disciples. Whether their ideas/practices were a real, perceived, or contrived threat to the ethic of the early Christian community, their comparative accessibility at least allowed for the permeation of their ideas in the culture, and thus makes them an appropriate focus in our attempt to view the HW tradition among Jesus' contemporaries.

Similarities in ethical vocabulary suggest a strong influence upon Jesus and/or Synoptic producers of apocryphal/pseudepigraphical works in addition to the Hebrew canon. Thus, although we cannot be sure that direct familiarity was possible, or that these works were recommended or even tolerated by contemporary rabbis,[101] their partial presence in the Jesus tradition may be adduced as indirect external evidence that at least the vocabulary was tolerated by the Pharisees.

With respect to internal evidence, our enquiry is limited to the few sources likely to antedate Synoptic production. The difficulties of dating these traditions allow for only tentative conclusions.

Rabbinic Traditions

Isolation of data from pre-second generation tannaitic traditions[102] suggests that later periods saw an increase in scope and complexity of poor-relief legislation and a stronger VW stratum.[103] Although the scanty evidence from the earlier period precludes certainty, these factors may indicate a this-worldly turn in values among the survivors of the wars.

The bulk of material that can be ascribed to the period before the first Jewish war is found in the Mishaic tractate *'Abot*. One of its oldest traditions concerns Simeon the Just (219-99), who included among the three things that sustain the world 'deeds of loving kindness (חסדים 1.5)'. Jose b. Johanan (c. 160) specified hospitality to the poor (1.5) and respect for the property of others (2.12).

The influence of Hillel (c. 60-20) was fresh in Jesus' day. To him are ascribed the formulae 'the more flesh, the more worms; the more possessions (נכסים), the more care; . . . the more Torah, the more life' (*m. 'Abot* 2.7). These words amount to an alternative devaluation of wealth which is reinforced by other traditions about Hillel. His poverty did not daunt his pursuit of study (*b. Yoma* 35b);[104] instead, he set an example of generosity by giving a horse and a slave to a poor man (*t. Pe'a* 4.10; *y. Pe'a* 8.7; *b. Ketub.* 67b). He and his school were influential in legislating poor-relief.[105] Whether or not Hillel is typical of Pharisaism for the period is moot; we know that in subsequent decades radical giving was occasionally practiced[106] and wealth disparaged[107] for the sake of Torah study, and we do not observe VW in strength until later generations.[108] Poverty (presumably of the involuntary kind, given the high value placed on industry to avoid mendicance) is good for those who through poverty fear and seek the Lord;[109] indeed, Samuel (AD 219-257) quotes the adage that 'poverty suits Israel as a red bridle suits a white horse' (*b. Ḥag.* 9b).

The evidence from the early centuries is too sparse to allow for any but the most tentative conclusions. But the examples indicate some similarities to Synoptic material, and it would be reasonable to posit a measure of agreement with Jesus among his Pharisaic contemporaries.[110] But many may have been unable to see past Jesus' neglect of Torah-study as the proper alternative to acquisition of wealth, or they may have viewed his commands as impractical—however well-grounded they might be in scriptural principles of justice and trust in God. And of course, as the Gospels suggest, many may have made a simplistic equation of wealth with the blessing of God. Thus the antagonism between Jesus and his audience on the subject of wealth may well be more than exemplary of the larger controversy over his authority or the later controversy between the Synoptic audience and the Jews. Those controversies may explain the generalizations, typical of Synoptic polemical material, that will always come between us and an accurate measure of the response to Jesus' teaching by his contemporaries. It remains an interesting point of conjecture that part of the ideological background of the Synoptic material lies in the very groups whose practices and ideas on the subject are held up for contempt.

Targumic Traditions

Our other sources of information about contemporary Pharisaic economic ethics are the Targums. Targums Neofiti, Pseudo-Jonathan, Fragments, and Onqelos on the Pentateuch, and Targum Jonathan on the Prophets follow closely the Hebrew text for the passages cited in Chapter 2 above.[111] The great latitude allowed for dating the traditions contained in these works[112] should not blind us to the possibility of pre-Christian or pre-Synoptic elements.

In addition to the OT traditions preserved by accurate translation, the Targums include numerous insertions of reference to wealth. These must be considered as possible evidence of tendentious hostility toward or at least interest in wealth during the early period of targumic activity.

Of interest in terms of the Synoptic ethical vocabulary is the frequent insertion of the word ממון;[113] and more specifically, ממון דשקר.[114] Most often the former is used in a neutral sense to indicate 'civil' as opposed to 'criminal' legal cases,[115] and the latter serves as a loose translation of 'bribe (בצע)'.[116] ממון alone is often used for 'bribe' as well.[117] It is also used for 'ransom'.[118] Exod 18.21 may be indicative of the kind of development that occurred in targumic traditions for the word ממון from a neutral[119] to a negative connotative word. The Hebrew exhorts Moses to choose judges who 'hate a bribe (שניא בצע)'. Targum Neofiti translates 'who hate wealth unjustly gained (סניין ממונא דשיקרא)', but a later censor erased דשיקרא. P follows the earlier N reading, but O supports the latter: דסנן לקנלא ממון. We should not perceive in these phenomena HW; rather, we should understand an occasional synonymity between ממון and 'bribe' which obviated the modifying דשקר.

There are six additional instances where ממון occurs unmodified to indicate not 'bribe' but simply 'wealth'. O, P Gen 13.13 specify that the men of Sodom were evil 'in their wealth (בממונהון)'. N,F Deut 16.19 make ממון the modifier of 'bribe': ' . . . nor shall you receive a bribe of wealth (שחוד דממון)', whereas O has only שוחד. N Deut 23.20 specifies the prohibition of a loan 'of riches (ממון)'. *J* 1 Sam 2.5 equates those who are 'proud in wealth (נאן בעותרא)' with those who are 'great in mammon (וסגיאין בממונא)'. *J* Mic 4.13 uses ממון to translate חיל, the 'wealth' of the nations which Israel will plunder. The most interesting of these instances is Deut 6.5: ' . . . love the Lord your God . . . with all your strength (מארך)'. N, O, and P all reflect a perception of an economic connotation for מאד, which according to the context could refer either to military or economic triumphs, or to both. O renders it נכסן (cf. *J* 2 Kgs 23.25), and N, P translate ממוניכון. Since the promise is that military success leads to economic prosperity, and not vice-versa, the economic connotation is more central and these targum traditions justifiable.[120]

In addition to these references to ממון, there are in the targum traditions, especially in the latter prophets, numerous insertions of the words עתר and נכסין. Most of these should be understood not as tendentious changes, but as attempts to clarify symbolic prophetic language, especially nature images[121] or scenes of 'devouring'[122] that probably imply an economic subject matter.[123] This delimitation still leaves a number of passages making reference to wealth but entirely unsupported by the Hebrew text. These we must consider as possible evidence of Jewish resentment during the pre-Synoptic period.

O, P Gen 13.13, referred to above, specify the evil of the men of Sodom 'in their wealth (בממו נחון)'. *J* 1 Sam 2.5, referred to above, makes economic reversal explicit: 'those who are proud in wealth and great in mammon will be impoverished (אתמסכנו)', while the righteous 'who were poor will become rich (עתרן)'. *J* Isa 5.17 transforms an internally directed prophecy ('The Lord will smite with a scab the heads of the daughters of Zion . . .') into a promise of economic reversal: 'And the righteous shall be nurtured as was promised concerning them, and the riches (ונכסי) of the wicked shall the righteous possess'. In 14.8-9 the 'cedars' (Heb v. 8) and 'shades' (Heb v. 9) who exult over Israel become 'those who are rich in possessions (עתירי נכסיא)'[124]—a translation justified in part by the reference to 'leaders and kings' in v. 9. In 27.10 the symbol of a calf grazing and stripping the branches in the deserted city of the enemy is replaced by an explicit promise: 'the righteous shall war against it [the enemy city], and spoil its goods (ויבזון נכסהא)'. 30.20 transforms another internal curse ('though the Lord give you the bread of adversity and the water of affliction') into a promise of its opposite: 'And the Lord will give you the riches (נכסי) of the enemy and the spoil (וביזת) of the oppressor . . . .' In 33.4, another nature image, 'spoil is gathered as the caterpillar gathers', becomes an explicit promise: 'And the house of Israel shall gather the riches (נכסי) of the nations that hate them . . . ' The translators of 48.10 conceive of Israel as tried not 'in the furnace of affliction' but 'in the distress of poverty (מסכינו)'. 53.9 suffers a radical alteration, from the prediction of the burial of the suffering servant with a rich man to this curse: 'And he shall deliver the wicked to Gehinnam, and those that are rich in possessions (עתירי נכסיא) which they obtained by violence unto the death of destruction . . .' In 60.5 Israel is promised not 'the abundance of the sea' but 'the wealth (עותר) of the West'.[125] *J* Jer 19.13 adds to the idolatrous houses to be judged those of 'the rich in possessions (ונכסיכו נכסין)'. *J* Hos 5.11 accuses Ephraim of seeking ממון דשקר where the Hebrew reads 'vanity'.[126] *J* Joel 2.8 adds to the characteristics of the Lord's army that 'they do not take bribes (ולא מקבלין ממון)'.[127] *J* Amos 4.1 changes the poor-oppressing 'cows of Bashan' to the 'rich in possessions (עתירי נכסיא)'. 6.6 specifies that 'those who are at ease in Zion (v. 1) . . . who drink wine in bowls' drink from *silver* bowls. Where they boast, in v. 13, of having 'taken Karnaim for ourselves',[128] *J* reads 'we have taken wealth (נכסין) for ourselves'. *J* Obad 17 alters the promise that 'the house of Jacob shall possess their own possessions' to read 'the house of Jacob shall plunder (ויתמנון) the riches (נכסי) of the nations who plundered her'. *J* Mic 2.8 adds to the accusation against the wicked in Judah that they 'seek bribes (ממון יקרחון)' from the innocent. In *J* Mal 1.4, Edom's hope ('we are shattered but we will rebuild') becomes her pride: 'we have become rich (עתרנא) and prominent and we will rebuild'.

Clearly, not all of these passages exhibit resentment. The most important are *J* 1 Sam 2.5; Isa 5.17; 27.10; 30.20; 33.4; 60.5; and *J* Obad 17, which promise the enrichment of Israel at the expense of her enemies. *O, P* Gen 13.13; *J* Isa 14.8-9; 53.9; *J* Jer 19.13 may be significant to the extent that they condemn Israel's (wealthy) post-biblical enemies (or assert her poverty: *J* Isa 48.10). *J* Hos 5.11; *J* Amos 4.1; 6.6; 6.13; *J* Mic 2.8 indict Israel and only apply if we assume that in every case a rich, wicked Jew is one who has compromised himself to the Gentiles. *J* Joel 2.8 is not directly relevant.

The obvious challenge is to posit a date for these traditions. Although it is possible that editorial freedom (especially with regard to nature imagery) informed by the context guided some of the translations cited above as clarifications or insertions, their sheer number weighs against this as a convincing explanation. We must then allow for a causal relationship between the perception of events and the alteration of texts. At the same time we must appreciate the span of up to 850 years, at least 600 of which post-date our area of concern, during which these changes could have occurred.[129] Likewise, we must take into account the fact that a *pervasive* view does not necessarily lie behind an altered text. Nevertheless, these factors do not exclude all, and perhaps exclude none, of the traditions in question from formation during the early period of targumic activity. Although these traditions scarcely go beyond the Hebrew text in evincing HW,[130] they do exhibit some evidence of VW in the sense of hope for economic reversal. To the extent that this hope can be joined to that expressed in 1 En and Sib Or III, dated early, and supposed widespread, we must consider its relation to Synoptic teaching in terms of conflict or continuity.

Conclusions

We are able to posit the following conclusions on the basis of this treatment of rabbinic and targumic traditions:

1.   The difficulty of assigning an early date to the rabbinic and targumic traditions precludes certainty about the relevance of the data to this study.
2.   The few rabbinic traditions ascribed to/descriptive of the pre-Synoptic period allow for HW.

3. Most new references to mammon or wealth in targumic traditions correctly translate or clarify Hebrew texts.
4. Targumic deviations do not evince new HW in significant quantity or degree.
5. A few targumic references to wealth which are unsupported by Hebrew originals may reflect economic resentment in the pre-Synoptic period.

These conclusions are relevant to the general thesis of this book to the extent that they provide information about the attitudes of contemporary, accessible, and influential Palestinian Jews.

4. *Qumran*

Discussion of economic issues at Qumran has centered around the self-designation of the group as the Poor and the extent of the group's practice of community of goods. There is, unfortunately, very little in the data relevant to these questions that has direct bearing on the attitudes toward wealth among the Qumran sectaries. What evidence there is calls into question the description of Qumran ideas and practices as ascetic.

Economic Status

There are a number of reasons not to regard the group as poor in the economic sense. Mealand claims that at least the original group of 'breakaway Zadokites' was poor, citing self-designation texts.[131] But close examination of these texts makes it clear that economic poverty is not implied. Nearly all of the references are psalmic, and we observe in both canonical and non-canonical sources a prevalent figurative connotation for the word 'poor' in such a context.[132] The word commonly used in Qumran literature is אביון.[133] In 1QH 5.22 the אביונים are equated with those who 'hunger for righteousness'; in 4Qp Ps37 2.8-9 they are equated with 'the humble'; and in 4Qp Ps37 3.9-10 they are antonymic to 'the violent' and 'the wicked of Israel'.[134] Only in CD 6.21; 14.14 does אביון connote economic poverty, but CD never uses אביון as a self-designation of the community. Indeed, the only clear references to economic poverty in the Qumran corpus are not self-designative but instances of the justice imperative: CD 6.16 enjoins readers not to rob the poor (עני); 6.21 and 14.14 command the group to succour the poor and needy (עני אביון); and 1QH 5.20 praises God for not neglecting the fatherless and poor (רש). One reference presents a problem: CD 19.9 employs עני הצאן as a self-designation, and עני is used of the economically deprived in 6.16.[135] These 'poor of the flock', however, are equated with 'the little ones (הצוערים)' of Zech 13.7, and as such are not necessarily economically deprived, either in this passage or in the biblical passage alluded to.[136] Rather, they are 'those who watch for Him'; i.e. the pious remnant of Israel. The passages which speak of the economic arrangements of the community contain no references to 'the Poor', and those passages which speak of 'the Poor' (or the poor) do not discuss the shared life at all.[137]

There are additional, circumstantial reasons to regard the Qumran sectaries as other than poor. A breakaway group of Zadokites does not necessarily mean a rabble of destitute refugees, and may in fact have included an aristocratic high-priestly pretender. Certainly the distinction between the group and the poor (CD 6.16-19), oppressed (1QS 10.26)[138] people they support indicates a continuity with the OT justice demands for the possessing classes. More significant in this regard are the numerous legislative passages[139] describing the disposition of wealth upon entrance into the community: only substantial property brought into the community by at least some new members could necessitate such legislation. Furthermore, there is reason to believe that the community throve in its environment, removed as it was from external hostility and characterized by industry and organization. The seemingly desolate surroundings were in fact quite favorable to economic prosperity and may well have supported the community even without the benefit of substantial donations.[140] Finally, it seems unlikely that the detailed instructions for richly equipping an army and the descriptions of hidden treasure, albeit symbolic and/or hyperbolic, could so interest a group with a distaste for luxury. The combined strength of these considerations weighs against the notion that the Qumran sectaries were poor or that their economic practices should be regarded as ascetic. We do not have evidence of a practice of severe abstinence or a condition of deprivation among the members, and we do not observe a doctrine of austerity in the writings.

Community of Goods

Having set aside the image of a destitute group eking out a meager and precarious wilderness existence, we must inquire further into the extent and purpose of community of goods as it was practiced at

Qumran. There is a plethora of opinion about a small and seemingly contradictory body of data.[141] The options range from no community ownership to complete community ownership, with various interstitial positions. The principal texts in question are 1QS 1.11-13 and 1QS 6.17-23; and the principal problems are the presence of coins on the site, the variance between 1QS and CD, and the meaning of the word ערב.

1QS 1.11-13 declares that

> All those who freely devote themselves to His truth shall bring (יביאו) all their knowledge, powers, and possessions (והונם) into the Community of God, that they may purify their knowledge in the truth of God's precepts and order (לתכן) their powers according to His ways of perfection and all their possessions (וכול הונם) according to His righteous counsel.

The emphasis brought to the word כור by its repetition in the purpose clause should not be missed: it may reflect a conscious effort to secure full voluntary compliance with this demand.[142] Possessions were considered impure until under the jurisdiction of the Community.[143] 1QS 6.17-23 describes the process by which a novitiate's wealth is consigned to the Community. Initially, the new member does not have 'any share (יתערב) of the property (בהון) of the Congregation' (6.17). After a year of probation,

> his property (הונו) and earnings shall be handed over to the Bursar of the Congregation who shall register it to his account and shall not spend it for the Congregation (6.19-20).

Following a second successful probationary year, 'his property (הובו) shall be merged (ולערב) and he shall offer his counsel and judgment to the Community' (6.21-23). Although this appears to indicate a process by which the community receives both control and possession of the individual's property, some Qumran scholars contend that the word ערב pertains only to business dealings, and that the purpose of this legislation is to prohibit commercial intercourse between members of the community and impure outsiders.[144] One important factor in favor of this view is the number of coins found on the site. Discounting a hoard of 561 silver coins which was buried 10-0 BC, there is a fairly even chronological distribution of 464 coins found at all levels of occupation and in all the buildings.[145] Coins are absent from the caves, but since only a few were habitable,[146] this evidence should not weigh heavily in favor of one theory: whether or not any society is moneyed, those few who choose to live in cliffside caves are rather unlikely to possess (or to lose) a quantity of coins! If, as de Vaux maintains,[147] the living quarters in the buildings housed the leaders, while the others lived in huts and tents along the cliff bases, we would not expect to find so many coins in the living-quarters of the buildings. The leaders would have to be much more circumspect with money than these finds would indicate: if they administered the community fund of a moneyless group, it would be less than exemplary of them to walk around with jingling pockets. In any case, without access to the unrecoverable remains of the dwellings of the majority of the Qumran sectaries, any distinction between them and their leaders must be regarded as unsatisfyingly conjectural.

Mealand posits a few explanations for the coins in the buildings other than that the sectaries possessed money,[148] but these are not persuasive. To the notion that novitiates or visitors lost the money it can be countered that they would not regularly inhabit the living quarters of the main buildings. The contention that the coins evince a later, post-1QS period of relaxed standards ignores the even distribution of the coins. Mealand's strongest argument is that money was handled briefly before being handed over to the group. This seems unlikely in a strictly moneyless community where immediate relinquishment would be a more likely practice. The phenomenon is equally well-explained by the scheme which will be suggested below. But until we find reason to reject the notion of thorough community of goods at Qumran, we must regard 'temporary possession' as at least a possible explanation of the coins found on the site.

Textual evidence is a more important factor in favor of the view that Qumran sectaries possessed their own money. One important text is 1QS, which legislates against a negligent individual:

> if he has failed to care for the property of the community, thereby causing its loss (לאבדו), he shall restore it (ושלמו) in full. And if he is unable to restore it, he shall do penance for sixty days.

Mealand's sophistic method here is to regard this as relevant only to 'missing' property which must then be 'found' to avoid incurring the prescribed penalty.[149] Such an explanation disregards the full meaning of אבד[150] and the common-sense inference of a broader category of neglect (e.g. breakage, abuse, carelessness) for which such a rule would have to apply. 'Restore', therefore, must mean 'replace'; either by repair, substitution, or financial compensation. And of course, any of these options might require private property.

The most important textual evidence in favor of the view that community members held individual property is the group of passages in 1QS which appear to prohibit commercial intercourse. In 7.24 no member of the community may יתערב in purity or property with a deserter/expelled member without incurring the punishment of expulsion himself. If we understand ערב here in a literal sense—perhaps translating 'pool' or 'merge'—we must imagine two individuals, one accepted by the community and one condemned, having the same purity (or food) and property. This hardly seems possible in such a close-knit group, as it would seem to require constant proximity—if not co-habitation—under the very eyes of a hostile community. Mere business dealings, on the other hand, could take place on the periphery of the community between present and former members who still lived in the vicinity (e.g. Jericho). The legislation thus makes sense as a guard against the luring away of members either by emotional ties on the part of the sectary or by deprecation on the part of the expelled member.

8.23 demands a similar understanding. Here 'no man of holiness יתערב in his property or counsel in any matter at all' with an expelled member. Again, actual unity of property requires the nonsensical arrangement of inclusion of an expelled member. The word 'counsel' (עצה) is also important in this context, and is overlooked by commentators. The same word is used in 6.22, where full membership allows the individual to 'offer his counsel and judgment to the Community'. Clearly, this signifies a voice in the affairs of the community. Just as clearly, 8.23 is antonymic with respect to an expelled member, and the fact that here the verb ערב is allowed to govern both הון and עצה becomes significant. The prohibition with respect to counsel means that even to converse about community affairs is potentially to corrupt the community by indirect influence on the part of the expelled individual. There is no question of a 'community of counsel', as if two people, an insider and an outsider, could set up a microcosmic community which would threaten the whole under its very eyes. Indeed, the stipulated reduction in punishment for accidental transgression in this area (8.24–9.2) rules against such an understanding. We can only conclude that ערב in this context connotes 'intercourse' or 'dealings', and that property and counsel are the two specifications of the term.

The Community Rule is not quite so strict with regard to relations between sectaries and outsiders. Members are told not to consort (יוחד) with a man of falsehood 'with regard to his work or property lest he be burdened with the guilt of his sin' and to 'keep away from him in all things' (5.14-15). But interestingly, in the further specification of this prohibition, the member is told not to 'take anything from them except for a price' (5.16). Not only does this differ from the command to shun completely exchange with expelled members, but it assumes that 'a price' could be given; i.e. that individual sectaries had property. This, of course, is the inference of 7.24 and 8.23; and taken together the passages weigh against the supposition that in the case of 5.16, money was given by the community leaders for purchases from outsiders. Presumably the group was compelled by necessity to a certain amount of economic exchange with people in the area, and this type of legislation makes it clear that they perceived a tension in such exchange.

9.8 may also reflect this tension. As a general rule governing the leaders of the group, it states that 'as for the property of the men of holiness, it shall not be merged (יתערב) with that of the men of falsehood'. We cannot conceive that ערב here connotes 'pooling'. Mealand[151] makes the verse the converse of 6.22; i.e. the community should not admit the property of the unrepentant. But this understanding involves the rather glaring oversight that community property, and not outsiders' property, is the subject of the sentence. And there is no question of the sons of Aaron (9.7) 'pooling' community property with that of outsiders—such a prohibition would be too obvious to require pronouncement. We must regard the passage as a prohibition of business dealings. In this context it could refer to the special fund of capital over which the sons of Aaron have jurisdiction; and seen in conjunction with 5.16, it could simply evince the tension between a desire for complete separation and the need for goods and services from extra-community sources. Either explanation subjects the community to the charge of inconsistency. But in any case, it is once again impossible to see יתערב as an expression indicative of pooling.

There is one other instance of יתערב in 1QS: 6.17 states that a novitiate shall not 'have any share of the property of the congregation (אל יתערב בהון הרבים)'. Considered apart from the three instances of יתערב treated above, this instance could mean either that a novitiate should not (yet) engage in matters of business (and presumably counsel) with community members. He could, then, live under the protection, rule, and roof of the community without them owing him anything. This is the key, because it maintains the consistency of the purity requirement for the group while allowing the novitiate to earn his own place in it. This explanation seems most in keeping with the legislation considered above. Certainly the fact that all four of these passages employ a prohibition (אל or לא), the word הון (with the preposition ב in three cases), and an identical form of the verb ערב demands a consistent translation. The word 'mix' is too ambiguous: one can mix tea and water (literal: 'pool'); and one can mix with friends at a party (figurative: 'intercourse'). The use of ערב in these passages[152] corresponds to the figurative sense; thus, a fair rendering in each case would be 'have dealings':

6.17   he shall not have dealings in the property of the congregation
7.24   if any member of the Community has had dealings with him in purity or property
8.23   no man of holiness shall have dealings in his property or counsel
9.8   the property of the men of holiness shall not have dealings with that of the men of falsehood.

What, then, are we to make of 1QS 6.22, where ערב is used again apparently to describe the absorption of the novitiate's capital into the community? The argument that the 'bringing in' of possessions in 1.11-13 and the 'merging' in 6.22 indicate only business dealings faces significant obstacles. The bringing of possessions into the community to order them according to God's righteous counsel seems strongly to imply control, if not ownership, on the part of the sons of Zadok (1QS 5.2-3; 9.7). The 'handing over' to the Bursar and the establishment of an account (1QS 6.19-20) suggest something beyond mere recording, and the prohibition of the Bursar's spending of this property during the second year implies that he may spend it in the third year. Furthermore, we must question the purpose of this legislation if it does not lead to complete community ownership: if one's property can be maintained, but purified merely by a year of good behaviour, why should the community need to measure and handle it in the meantime? If property was held by the community for the purpose of purifying it, what was the individual to do with it in such an environment when it was returned to him, especially if it was a large amount?

These considerations may allow for an interstitial position that membership in the Qumran community (or at least that which produced 1QS) required only an initial merging of one's wealth into the common fund—an act which purified both the wealth, by giving it over to the control of 'His righteous counsel', and the individual, by separating him forever[153] from the fruit of unrighteous acquisition.[154] Subsequently, wages/money may have been received for work/goods exchanged in or near the community; percentages of these were collected for tithes, welfare, etc., and members could transact business on a limited basis within the community. Such a scheme accounts for the coin finds on the site as well as the implications of private property in the texts. Even apart from these texts, there is nothing in the writings that requires *ongoing* giving-over of money. If the emphasis of the group was on the evil of wealth itself, such a requirement would be consistent; but with the emphasis on purity, we can maintain the consistency of a system wherein money or wages earned by an individual were pure because he was pure as a member of the holy group. In this scheme ערב must mean 'merge' only in 6.22. This is not to say that the verb changes meaning, but that the context and the different form of the verb allow for a different translation than in the other four passages.

We cannot with certainty relate the evidence of CD to that of 1QS. It may be a later document, reflecting a relaxation of earlier and more strict economic practice;[155] it may be an earlier document, representing an incomplete understanding of the implications of community reflected in 1QS; and it may be a roughly contemporary document whose economic aspects were ignored by the community. We can say that the document certainly presupposes private property[156] and that a dynamic equivalent of the sons of Zadok, the Guardian (CD 13.11, 15-16), may in the exercise of his authority have narrowed some of the perceived gaps between CD and 1QS. In any case, it seems doubtful that a document that presupposes private property would comprise part of the 'canon' of a community of ascetics.

Attitudes Toward Wealth
More important for our purposes than the economic status and practice of the Qumran community is the purpose of that practice and its relation to HW. It is clear that membership reflects the novitiate's purity, but it does not purify his property. It is the control of property by the sons of Zadok (i.e. by 'His righteous counsel', 1QS 1.13) that purifies the property. This is an important distinction,

because it makes purity, not membership (i.e. renunciation), primary. Therefore, wealth is not suspect as long as the community controls it (donation) or God gives it (plunder).

Passages from, primarily, the prophetic writings illustrate this. 1QS 5.20 states simply of those outside the community that 'all their deeds are defilement before Him, and all their possessions (הונם) unclean'. 1QM 12.14 (cf 19.6; 1QSb 3.19) promises 'the riches (חיל) of the nations' to the righteous. 1QpHab 6.1 proclaims that the Lord's army, the Kittim, 'shall gather in their riches (הונם), together with all their booty, like the fish of the sea'. 'They' in this case are the wicked priestly hierarchy of Jerusalem, who receive vengeance when, 'in the last days, their riches (הונם) shall be delivered into the hands of the army of Kittim . . .' (1QpHab 9.4-6). Reversal of dominance between the righteous and their enemies is also the theme in 1QM 11.8-9, 13; 14.7; 4QpPs37 2.8-9; 3.9-10; 4QpNah 11. 1QGen Apoc 22.29-33 sees Abraham's riches grow as a result of his obedience (22.18-26).

While these passages demonstrate the hope for the ultimate prosperity of the community, others speak disparagingly of the wealth of its enemies. 1QS 11.1-2 indicts 'men of injustice . . . who are zealous after wealth (נמקני הון)'.[157] CD 8.4-5, 7 claim that the rebels from the group 'have wallowed in the ways of whoredom and wicked wealth' (בהון רשעה) and have 'acted arrogantly for the sake of riches and gain' (הון ולבצע). In 1QH 10.25 the righteous are contrasted to the worldly who 'pride themselves in possessions and wealth (ב[מ]קנה וקנין)'. 1QpHab 8.3 asserts that 'it is riches (הון) that lead the proud to betray'.[158] The Wicked Priest, the arch-enemy of the Qumran sect, exemplifies this in that

> when he ruled over Israel his heart became proud, and he forsook God and betrayed the precepts for the sake of riches (הון). He robbed and amassed the riches (הון) of the men of violence who rebelled against God, and he took the wealth (והון) of the peoples . . . (1QpHab 8.9-12).

The last phrase, coupled with the statement in 12.10 that the priests robbed הון אביון, shows that wealth is bad only in the hands of the sect's enemies.[159]

But the evidence of VW and the condemnation of the sect's enemies do not provide the whole picture. Material from apocalyptic pseudepigraphical works such as 1 En and Jub, and from wisdom literature such as Tob, Sir, and T12P formed part of the literary milieu from which the sectaries drew.[160] The former might be added to inflate the documentation of the hopes and hatreds revealed above. The latter might be adduced as evidence of an awareness of the HW tradition as expressed in those works. There are passages scattered throughout the Qumran writings themselves that reflect stages in the tradition without making direct reference to the wealth of outsiders. CD 4.15-19 calls riches one of 'the three nets of Satan with which . . . he catches Israel by setting them up as three kinds of righteousness'. The fragmentary 4Q183 i. 5 asserts that the righteous separated themselves from 'all wealth of wickedness'. In 4Q160 7.3 the writer claims not to have sought the favour of Wisdom 'with property or wealth or purchase price'. Comparative devaluation of wealth is present in CD 10.17-18; 11.15, where honouring the Sabbath precludes the pursuit of 'riches and gain' (הון ובצע); and in 1QH 14.20; 15.23, where riches are ranked below God's truth and precepts.[161] In 1QS 10.19 the covenanter promises that 'my soul shall not covet the riches of violence (הון חמס)'. But most interesting is a fragmentary passage from the Hymn Scroll in which the writer confesses his disdain for wealth. In 1QH 10.23 he disavows gain and riches (בצע ובה[ון]) as his 'support (משעני)'.[162] 10.29-30 reads: '[For the soul] of Thy servant has loathed (תעבה)[163] [riches] and gain (ובצע) and he has not [desired] exquisite delights (ערנים)'. But apart from being the sole passage in the Qumran writings that might be adduced as evidence of the kind of asceticism posited for the Essenes by Philo and Josephus,[164] these statements are effectively contradicted later in the same scroll by the promise that God 'wilt [cause him (the righteous) to reign amid] many delights (ערנים)'.

Conclusions
From the evidence available, we can form the following conclusions about the community at Qumran:

1. The self-designation of the group as 'the Poor' is not indicative of its economic status; in fact, individual members, and the group as a whole, may have been prosperous.
2. It is unlikely that the group consistently practiced community of goods, or that the acquisition of new members' possessions was motivated by HW.
3. The dominant economic themes in the writings of the community reflect VW. They are: a hope for economic reversal, and a condemnation of the wicked acquisitiveness of the group's enemies.

Although these works were written up to 250 years before the Synoptics, the continuance of the community into NT times evinces the survival and attempted application of apocalyptic ideas in the time of Jesus. In this regard, the writings are relevant to this study as an important part of the immediate background to the Gospels.

PART III

HOSTILITY TO WEALTH IN THE SYNOPTIC GOSPELS

We have observed the phenomenon of HW as it appears and develops in semitic ethical tradition and its independence from socio-economic circumstances. The tradition is expressed primarily by and for members of the upper classes, but it may have had a wider influence and appeal. It occurs most often in a religious-ethical context. To the extent that immediately contemporary material lacks the tradition, we might perceive in the Synoptic teaching a response to a prevalent attitude. Examination of NT texts will reveal extensive parallels which, together with the data concerning first-century Palestinian economic conditions and community social constituency, justify the contention that HW in the Synoptics is part of the tradition.

As we turn our attention to Synoptic texts that express HW, we focus upon that element of the thesis statement that HW is a *fundamental religious-ethical tenet consistently expressed*. Recalling the amplification of terms in the introduction, we look here for material that urges disparagement of and separation from possessions. In order to justify the label of a *fundamental religious-ethical tenet*, this material must convey an integral relation to discipleship, i.e. to conduct required of man by God. In order to justify the claim that it is *consistently expressed*, such material must recur within and between the Gospels without rescission or mitigation.

The discussion will assume Markan priority and the use of Mark plus a sayings-source Q by Matthew and Luke. Primary consideration will be given to each author's redaction, not only with respect to his creation and alteration of elements of the tradition where such activity can be demonstrated, but also with respect to his preservation of those elements which he receives. By means of this method, we hope to understand the intention of the author and the probable impact on his readers. The passage-by-passage approach is necessary to demonstrate the truth of the thesis statement, but it should not blind the reader to the comparative importance of certain passages in later Church history. The Rich Young Ruler pericope, for example, is the only extended triple tradition material on the subject, and it became a focal point for subsequent discussion and an important part of the biblical ground for an ascetic response to Jesus' call.

Form-critical reconstructions, imaginative and provocative though they may be, do not offer the degree of certainty necessary to warrant extended consideration here. Such reconstructions all too often assume the very theory of SEC for which they are subsequently adduced as evidence. The fact that elements sympathetic to or expressive of teleological devaluation appear in the sources used by all three Synoptic writers, and in material unique to Matthew and Luke, itself calls into question the need to posit a determinative situation in the life of the Church. Whether one concludes from this that the teaching goes back to Jesus or not, its similarity to earlier wisdom material demands that it be considered pertinent not only in the midst of a famine, but whenever men reflect upon the relation between wealth and personal piety. Indeed, given the importance of economic considerations in semitic literature and the timeless relevance of the subject, we would be surprised *not* to encounter evidence of Jesus' pronouncements or of his followers' efforts to convey consistently what they understood to be his teaching on the subject. It is best to focus our attention on the efforts of Mark, Matthew, and Luke to convey the tradition of HW, simply because these are to the greatest degree recoverable.

Chapter 6

HOSTILITY TO WEALTH IN THE GOSPEL OF MARK

Chapters 1 and 2 argued that neither external nor internal evidence allows us to reconstruct the life-setting of a Gospel or the attitude of its readers. We do not know how accurate was the writer's information about his intended audience nor whether his didactic content was intended to correct or to affirm his audience. On a cursory reading of the Synoptics, we might even conclude that Mark had comparatively little interest in the conduct of believers and hardly any interest in economic questions. The only explicitly 'economic' pericopae are 10.17-31 and 12.41-44; of secondary interest are 1.6; 1.16-20; 2.14; 4.19; 6.8-9; 8.34-37; and 14.3-9. But a negative conclusion about the relevance of Mark's Gospel to this study should not be hastily drawn. We may gain an understanding of Mark's economic ethical concerns by considering material he deemed worthy of inclusion and by examining his presentation of it. As an important—perhaps indirectly apostolic—voice in the mid-century Christian community, in at least some cases transmitting traditions already ascribed to Jesus, Mark offers ample and significant material for consideration. Indeed, what his Gospel lacks in volume it compensates for in intensity.

1.6

The description of John the Baptist's clothing and food in Mark 1.6 is almost certainly intended only as an allusion to 2 Kgs 1.8, i.e. in order to reveal John's affinity to the OT prophet Elijah.[1] John renounces the joys of civilization, but this does not mean that he condemns them, because he does not teach all men to imitate him.[2] In these respects he is much more like Elijah than Jesus; and as with Elijah, the text is silent about the purpose of the phenomenon. Schlatter surmises that camel's hair, leather, and locusts are easily obtainable in the desert, and that therefore the Baptist requires no gifts.[3] This too sets him apart from Jesus' disciples who, in the midst of civilization, depend on gifts from others (cf. 6.7-11). In both cases, dependence is ultimately on God. But John's particular role as a prophet sets him apart from the new people of the kingdom. Men went out to John (v. 5), but Jesus and his disciples went out to men (v. 38).

1.16-20; 2.14

The first hint that Mark perceives an integral relation between possessions and discipleship is early and powerful. The more explicit foreshadowing of Luke ('they left *all*', 5.11) should not deprive this narrative of its more subtle significance. Just after the momentous summary of Jesus' message in 1.15 comes a narrative of the initiation of his most important followers. The absence of detail concerning the activity and teaching of Jesus prior to and including contact with these men makes the simple formula 'he saw, he called, they followed' stand out in bold relief: the main point is the compelling nature of Jesus' call.[4] But incidental to the narrative is a feature whose significance should not be missed. The disciples do not *only* follow, as they and others do elsewhere in the sense of motor activity.[5] Neither do they *simply* follow in the general metaphorical sense of discipleship.[6] Rather, their following is joined by the conjunctive καί to another specific action, as in the remaining three occurrences of ἀκολουθεῖν: 8.35; 10.21; and 10.28. *They left their nets* and followed him (1.18); *they left their father Zebedee in the boat with the hired servants* and followed him (1.20); *he rose ([from] sitting at the tax office)* and followed him (2.14). The narrative is a clear foreshadowing of the fuller statements found in subsequent didactic passages. Commentators hasten to point out that Mark may be 'exaggerating the facts',[7] since the disciples later have access to boats,[8] Peter and Levi retain houses,[9] and Peter later travels with a wife (1 Cor 9.5). The owners of the various boats, however, are not named. Boat, house, and wife can be left with family. In fact, wives are not said (or prescribed: 10.29) to be abandoned. In any case, if the act of following occurred as dramatically as Mark depicts it, there would not be time to dispose of possessions thoroughly. We do not know the time-lapse between 1.18 and 1.29 or between 2.14 and 2.15; but assuming that the events are chronologically close, this is a reasonable explanation. The reader would know that the break occurred soon enough, if not instantly. The possibility that boat, house, or even trade (cf. John 21.3-11) were returned to from time to time does not in itself compromise abandonment: following Jesus may lead past—but not as a long-term or final destination—the ties of the disciples' old lives.

Whatever the subsequent details of these first followers' conduct, it is clear that Mark here portrays a sudden and thorough break at the point of following Jesus. That this is a break with possessions the reader perceives by implication from the story itself, by separate knowledge of the subsequent careers of the apostles, and by reference ahead to 8.35; 10.21; and 10.28-30. That 'this representation probably reflects a catechetical interest'[10] is the first indication that Mark perceives an important relation between possessions and discipleship.

Another incidental feature of this narrative is its indication of the disciples' social standing at the time of their call. Although we have little reason to suspect that Mark wished to draw attention to their SEC out of personal or community empathy, it is instructive to observe that the disciples are portrayed as leaving accepted—even lucrative—positions in society. They have families, homes, and presumably steady work. They are not portrayed as members of the economically or socially disenfranchised masses, the wandering victims of oppression. If this voluntary stepping down to dependence and itinerance intends any implication to readers, it may be to suggest that those in similar positions could and should respond similarly to Jesus' call.

4.19

The explanation of the Parable of the Sower (4.13-20) is usually regarded as secondary because of its 'Christian terminology' and 'looseness of interpretation'.[11] But although Taylor is correct in his statement that the words in 4.19 'are either *hapax legomena* or belong mainly to the vocabulary of the Epistles',[12] the words in these combinations, i.e. the *terms*, are unusual.

The closest parallels to αἱ μέριμναι τοῦ αἰῶνος (= Matt 13.22) are Matt 6.25 (=Luke 12.22), where the disciples are told μὴ μεριμνᾶτε τῇ ψυχῇ ὑμῶν; 1 Cor 7.33, where 'the married man is μεριμνᾷ τὰ τοῦ κόσμου'; and Luke 21.34, where the unprepared are 'weighed down with dissipation and drunkenness and μερίμνας βιωτικαῖς'. All of these refer explicitly or implicitly to concern about one's economic circumstances: the words αἰῶνος, ψυχῇ, κόσμου, and βιωτικαῖς are in this context interchangeable.[13] Although the parallels are offered in a very tentative chronological order, the Markan phrase can hardly be dated with precision. The thought is not original to any of the writers, let alone to Jesus; rather, it has its provenance in semitic ethical tradition: we observed a similar warning in Sir 31.1 (cf. Eccl 5.12) against μέριμνα πλούτου. Significantly, the use of αἰών as a designation for the world is in the NT unanimously negative:[14] the age, the world, and probably here the things of the world, are unworthy of concern if not in fact worthy of scorn.

The second phrase, ἡ ἀπάτη τοῦ πλούτου, is without parallel as a NT expression, although the thought is approximated in earlier literature.[15] Ἀπάτη occurs in the NT only five times apart from 4.19 (= Matt 13.22), and in each case it has the negative connotation of 'deception' or 'enticement'.[16] As a designation for material wealth, πλοῦτος occurs only here (= Matt 13.22) and Jas 5.2; Rev 5.12; 18.17 (from Ezek 27.27).[17] In combination, the words occur only here, and are mistranslated by the RSV as 'delight in riches', which conveys the possibility that one may possess wealth without delighting in it. The phrase should be translated, as in the KJV, as a genitive of origin: 'deceitfulness of wealth'. The proper emphasis, then, is not upon the individual's response to wealth but upon the quality attributed to wealth. It is wealth—*deceitful* wealth—that enters in and chokes the word.

The third phrase, αἱ περὶ τὰ λοιπὰ ἐπιθυμίαι, is, according to Taylor, 'a very general expression and is intended to cover all objects of desire other than riches'.[18] Ἐπιθυμίαι is common enough as a designation for (usually illegitimate) desires,[19] but the phrase περὶ τὰ λοιπά is peculiar to Mark. Significantly, Matthew omits it after following the first two expressions verbatim. This omission may be due to the fact that the phrase 'seems vague and indefinite after the specifics of worldly cares and deceitful riches; what are "the rest of the things?"'[20] Zimmerman answers this question by suggesting a misunderstanding on the part of an early translator of the Aramaic root יתר, which can carry the connotation 'remainder' but is better translated here as 'excess' or 'superfluity'.[21] Zimmerman's theory is attractive because it makes the expresion a natural complement to the previous expressions rather than a vague 'et cetera'. If correct, his view leads to the supposition of a very early provenance for this threefold radical renunciation of wealth. The danger of wealth is put on the same level as that of Satan (v. 15) and that of apostasy (v. 17). Like those formidable foes, worldly concerns, deceitful riches, and desires for superfluities are to be avoided and abhorred.

6.8-9

Among the instructions to the disciples offered in the Mission Charge (6.7-11) are stipulations about provisions for the journey that we must consider as possible expressions of HW. A phrase-by-phrase examination reveals a complex tradition with a simple but crucial principle lying behind it.

The allowance of a staff, against Matt 10.10 and Luke 9.3, has been variously explained. Wellhausen suggests the possibility that the later evangelists had access to an older Aramaic source that read אל rather than אלא.[22] Swete contends that Matthew and Luke exaggerate Mark's earlier form unnecessarily, because 'the staff was the universal companion of the traveller, whatever else he might lack; see Gen 32.10'.[23] Lane allows the possibility that 'the staff in Mk is the walking stick or shepherd's crook which became the symbol of office, while the rod prohibited by Matthew and Luke was the shepherd's club designed for protection';[24] but regards as 'especially attractive' the view that Mark's version alludes to Exod 12.11, which commands one to eat the passover with 'your loins girded, your sandals on your feet, and your staff in your hand'.[25] A more popular explanation of the disparity is that the prohibition of a staff became obsolete with the expansion of the missionary horizon beyond Palestine to the West.[26] This explanation fails to account for the retention of the other prohibitions, which must have suffered similar obsolescence by the time of writing. A combination of the last two theories is perhaps the most satisfying: the OT allusion was found to be consistent with the realities of mission.

The prohibitions of carrying bread, bag, and money are fairly straightforward. Lagrange notes that the bag is probably a begging bag, since a provision bag would be useless if the disciple was not carrying bread.[27] Swete makes the point that 'the order is ascensive: no bread, no bag to carry what they could buy, no money to buy with'.[28]

The allowance of sandals is another difference between Mark's account and Matt 10.10 / Luke 10.4, and is similarly accounted for. Gnilka makes the point that sandals are still not strong shoes, which would have been considered a luxury.[29]

The disciple is here told not to put on (ἐνδύσησθε) two tunics, but in Matt 10.10 he is not to take (κτήσεσθε) them, and in Luke 9.3 he is not to have (ἔχειν) them. It may be quibbling to perceive in this an ascendant severity, since the third expression may be implicit in the first two.[30] The essential point is that one garment suffices,[31] and that limitation to one signified an active march[32] and the renunciation of luxury.[33]

Having considered the meanings of the various prohibitions in 6.8-9, we must enquire about their purpose. One possibility is that they signify the holiness of pilgrim missionaries. Grundmann draws attention to the rabbinic injunction in *m. Ber.* 9.5 that a man 'may not enter into the Temple Mount with his staff or his sandal or his wallet . . .' and suggests that in Mark we observe pilgrims not to the Temple Mount but to Galilean villages.[34] Both Cranfield and Taylor find in the prohibitions of the mission charge a sense of 'extreme urgency'.[35] Holiness and urgency are indeed aspects of the disciples' conduct, but the overriding significance of these stipulations for this study is that they force the disciples into dependence on others; and, ultimately, into dependence on God. Obedience to these commands makes preaching worthy of belief because it renders evidence of *Gottvertrauen*—'God-trust'.[36] The concept of *Gottvertrauen* is vital to an understanding of HW in the Synoptics. It will appear again and again that *Gottvertrauen is the end to which dispossession of wealth is a way, and that heavenly reward is the end to which Gottvertrauen is the means.* The modal relationship between HW and *Gottvertrauen* is that which makes the former a 'fundamental ethical tenet'. The purposal relationship between HW and heavenly reward in the Synoptics is that which places the tradition in the category of teleological devaluation.

8.34-37

The sayings on cross-bearing and sacrifice in 8.34-9.1 are not normally regarded as relevant to HW. Both the preceding prediction of suffering (8.31) and the references to taking up a cross, losing one's life, and being ashamed of Jesus appear to signify persecution and martyrdom. But there are several reasons to regard this pericope as relevant to this study.

That Mark intends this passage as a call to discipleship and not simply a specific instruction to disciples concerning martyrdom is suggested by the reference to the crowd[37] and the inference of 9.1

that following does not necessitate death.[38] Furthermore, taking up one's cross does not denote martyrdom but *going to* the place of execution: the phrase is parallel to 'follow me'.[39] We must ask what it means for the disciple to 'deny himself'. The view that Mark intends 'not the denial of something to the self but the denial of the self itself'[40] is too abstract to remain true to the context: although it may be argued that self-denial in Christian theology involves more than renunciation of external supports, in the context of Mark's Gospel it certainly means *no less* than the severance of ties to family and/or possessions.[41] The command to follow Jesus elsewhere in the Gospel involves in its execution just such concrete severance.[42]

Verses 35-37 contain an argument for the imperative in v. 34. The chiastic v. 35 includes the phrase ἕνεκεν ἐμοῦ καὶ τοῦ εὐαγγελίου,[43] which occurs again in the NT only at 10.29. 8.35 and 10.29 also share the address to 'whoever' (ὅς) and the promise of 'life' as a reward. But what does it mean that the disciple 'loses his life?' The context suggests that the phrase signifies something more than, or prior to, martyrdom. Both the text (9.1) and the realities of a church by this time at least thirty years old attest to the possibility of survival to the Parousia or, alternately, natural death as options for the termination of a disciple's earthly career. It may be, then, that 'life' in this context refers to the external ties to possessions (perhaps including family) which precluded full devotion.

The ground of v. 35 is contained in v. 36. It makes 'the whole world' (τὸ κόσμον ὅλον) parallel to τὴν ψυχὴν in v. 35: to save one's life is to lose eternal life; to gain the whole world is to forfeit eternal life. To 'gain the whole world' can hardly mean to commit apostasy; but it can mean 'to amass possessions'.[44] We observed above the essential equivalence of the words age, life, and world as designations for personal material provision.[45] The phrases 'gain the whole *world*' and 'loses his *life*' contain the same words. The claim to interchangeability is strengthened by appeal to 12.44, where the widow gives her 'whole life' (ὅλον τὸν βίον).[46] Βίος, like ψυχή in Matt 6.25 (= Luke 12.22-23), signifies here the 'means of subsistence;'[47] and נפשׁ probably lies behind both words.[48] The possible economic connotation of 'gain . . . forfeit'[49] in v. 36 may provide a further hint of the practical implications of the verse.[50]

The ground of v. 36, contained in v. 37, offers more explicit economic imagery. Ἀντάλλαγμα is most often employed to indicate a 'price' or 'ransom';[51] the rhetorical question argues that no quantity of wealth will acquire for a man eternal life. The allusion is to Ps 49.7, which immediately follows the condemnation of 'men who trust in their wealth and boast of the abundance of their riches'. Taken together with 8.34, as a *reason* for the disciple to 'deny himself, etc.', and following the ethical connotations of vv. 35-36, the implication of v. 37 may be that eternal life and material wealth are incompatible, if not mutually exclusive. The disciple should deny himself because (v. 35) losing his life will accrue eternal reward, and because (v. 37) wealth cannot procure eternal reward.

Verse 38 is distinguished from vv. 35-37 by the repetition of ὅς ... ἐὰν (vv. 35, 38), but it is coordinate as an independent contribution to the argument. It is perhaps better in keeping with the context of Jesus' predicted death (v. 31). But this should not lead to the conclusion that vv. 35-37 are misplaced. Persecution is expected for all aspects of the believer's life, or more properly, for his total identification with Jesus (13.9). Since following 'me and my words' (v. 38) involves not only creedal affirmation (v. 29) but also exemplary conduct (10.28-30), we should not be surprised to observe an overlapping or even imprecision in this pericope.

10.17-31
The most important Markan pericope, 10.17-31, contains the narrative of a particular call to discipleship and a series of general remarks on the subject of wealth and the kingdom. Numerous conjectures as to the evolution of the passage into its present form have been offered,[52] and a complete study has been devoted just to the categorization of its schools of interpretation.[53] We can attempt here little more than a consideration of the passage in its extant form and its probable import to early readers.

The first section, vv. 17-22, culminates in the command of v. 21 that the man ὕπαγε, ὅσα ἔχεις πώλησον καὶ δὸς τοῖς πτωχοῖς, καὶ ἔχεις θησαυρὸν ἐν οὐρανῷ, καὶ δεῦρο ἀκολούθει μοί. The command is a clear example of teleological devaluation: the man will acquire eternal reward by selling what he has and giving to the poor. Gifts to the poor and treasure in heaven are already familiar elements of semitic tradition.[54] But in its radical extent, this teaching may have purposely run counter to contemporary rabbinic teaching that valued wealth and disparaged poverty,[55] or to Qumran teaching which directed giving primarily to the community.[56] In any case, this command goes beyond sympathy for the poor to the notion that the man's possessions bind his heart and preclude entrance to the kingdom.[57] The fact that possessions are to be given away and not destroyed does, incidentally, forestall the conclusion that the material world is inherently evil.[58] And the fact that the poor are mentioned as recipients demonstrates continuity with Jewish piety, thus communicating little of social-ethical import: no organized or long-term result is effected; indeed, one more is added to the number of the poor. The poor are only of secondary interest: they are not mentioned in v. 28, which reflects obedience to this command. The common element in vv. 21 and 28 is not selling or giving, but leaving. The focus of the command, then, is upon this man in relation to his wealth. It is possible that Jesus has the first commandment in mind: possessions, which have become an idol, must be dispossessed.[59] Similarly, the command may reflect a radical application of the consistent targumic tradition that reads חיל in the first commandment as 'wealth':[60] the man should love God with all his wealth.

It is necessary at this point to go beyond these considerations and to ask what the command is intended primarily to communicate to Mark's readers, i.e. what response it intends to evoke. One view which has found wide acceptance is that the command applied only to the particular case and could not (or should not) have been taken as a general prescription concerning discipleship.[61] The most obvious difficulty with this view is the clear generalization, if not universalization, contained in the subsequent verses. The similarity of 10.21 to 8.34, and in narrative form to 1.16-20; 2.14, adds further difficulties. Verse 22 does not say that the man *loved* his great possessions, but simply that he *had* them. The disciples clearly apply v. 21 to themselves (v. 28). Indeed, we might ask why the story was preserved at all if it had no universal import.

Among those who do maintain the universality of v. 21, opinions vary as to the nature of the message. One alternative is to regard the command as a challenge to obey the positive side of the law: that is, to do good to others. Ernst contends that v. 21 must be seen in light of v. 18: in order to be good like God, the man must show that he loves all men.[62] Another alternative is to consider Jesus' challenge as hyperbole, i.e. an extreme demand that requires that the disciple rely on God's grace (v. 27).[63] This can result in either 'very substantial contribution to the support of the poor among the saints'[64] or even 'complete inner detachment from worldly things, a willingness at any moment to sacrifice one's wealth, or anything else that may be required'.[65] A third alternative is to stress the general idea of following over the specific command to sell and give.[66] In this view, the command expressive of HW is secondary or even parenthetical to the ultimate answer to the man's question in v. 17: to win eternal life one must follow Jesus. All three of these alternatives, however, generalize to an extent unwarranted by the context. It is clearly the action of dispossession which accrues treasure in heaven; likewise, vv. 22 and 25 speak of salvation in relation to economic status. Following cannot be divorced from the act that precedes it as an answer to the question of v. 17.[67] Berger draws attention to Jos Asen, and to a lesser extent T Job, as evidence that the connection between salvation and giving up goods/relations is a familiar theme in Jewish-Hellenistic conversion stories.[68] Berger's view is attractive in that it allows a consistent interpretation of this passage and provides a sensible provenance for the idea in contemporary Jewish-Hellenistic thought. But the scanty parallels cannot be considered conclusive, and caution is warranted by the presence of Gospel passages where dispossession does not involve conversion: Mark 12.44; Luke 12.21; 12.22-33; 16.9 suggest that *Gottvertrauen* is more fundamental to dispossession than following/conversion. Furthermore, unlike Asenath and Job, disciples may *leave* possessions without selling them or giving them (e.g. 1.18, 20; 2.14; 10.28).

The story of the rich man's call and refusal is followed by a conversation between Jesus and his disciples concerning wealth and entrance to the kingdom (vv. 23-27).[69] Recent discussion has centered upon the combination of traditions contained in the passage in light of the ambiguities of Jesus' words and the difficulties posed by the intense response of the disciples.[70]

The disciples react with amazement (ἐθαμβοῦντο) to Jesus' generalization that all who have riches (χρήματα) will have great difficulty entering the kingdom. This reaction, and the ascendant 'they were exceedingly astonished' (οἱ δὲ περισσῶς ἐξεπλήσσαντο) in v. 26, are unexpected from a group that presumably has little cause for empathy with the rich (v. 28). Swete's suggestion, that v. 23 refers not to the rich only, but to all who have money, is consistent with NT and LXX use of χρήματα.[71] A problem with this view is that the intensified response of v. 26 follows mention of the rich (πλούσιον, v. 25). But if the disciples are in this case reacting only to v. 24b (not entirely uncharacteristically, given their focus of attention upon themselves in v. 28); or if they are taking 'rich' in v. 25 to apply to themselves as those having χρήματα (a possible explanation of the question in v. 26b), the view may be plausible. Most scholars, however, regard χρήματα in this instance as a designation for wealth, since v. 23 is a comment on the preceding story, and χρήματα is probably intended as an equivalent to κτήματα πολλά (v. 22). This understanding leads to various explanations of the thought-sequence. Wellhausen argues that, as in D, the original order of the verses was 23, 25, 24, 26; thus the passage expresses a logical order from specific to general and precipitates the disciples' question, 'Then who can be saved?'[72] As an obvious attempt to improve the sense, this view is suspect;[73] and as Cranfield points out, v. 23b (entrance is *difficult*) is less specific than v. 25 (entrance is *impossible*).[74] Verses 24b-25 should be taken together (with v. 25 as the relevant specification of the more general v. 24b) as at least equivalent to, if not harsher than, v. 23b. Attempts to 'dwarf the camel and expand the needle's eye'[75] by making the former a rope and the latter a gate have rightly been disparaged: the point of the simile is 'to place the impossibility in the strongest light'.[76] The charateristically Markan elements of looking around,[77] amazement,[78] and speech repetition[79] give further ground for consideration of the passage in its extant form.

Why, then, were the disciples surprised at Jesus' condemnation of the rich? One possibility is that although the disciples thought of themselves as special cases, they still regarded wealth as a sign of God's favor, or perceived that Jesus' teaching entailed 'the rejection of the concept of merit accumulated through the good works accomplished by the rich'.[80] It is doubtful, however, that the disciples divorced their own conduct from that of any potential follower: 8.34-37; 10.29 are addressed to 'whoever', and Peter's statement in v. 28 corresponds to the command of v. 21. Indeed, whether they were voluntarily or involuntarily poor, the disciples were likely to welcome disparagement of the rich. A more attractive proposal is that of Reploh, who argues that Mark places his own community in the place of the disciples.[81] In this view, the apparent inconsistency of the first disciples' reaction is accounted for, because Mark is merely anticipating the response of his own community. On the other hand, we should not draw quick conclusions with regard to the economic status of that community. The amazement is not self-conscious, but message-conscious: we need no more require that the hearers of this saying be rich than that the 'amazed' witnesses of Jesus' power of exorcism (1.27) be demon-possessed.

The disciples' question in v. 26 is best understood as relative to rich men, not to men in general.[82] It lies in conjunction (καί) with their foregoing astonishment over the sayings of vv. 23b and 24-25. It also anticipates their claim of obedience in v. 28.

The repetition of the phrase 'Jesus looked (ἐμβλέψας) at them' underscores the significance of v. 27.[83] Is this saying intended to mitigate the harshness of the demand on disciples[84] and to emphasize the sufficiency of grace for entrance to the kingdom?[85] To do so would run contrary to v. 21 and would take the sting out of vv. 23b and 25. It would also make irrelevant Peter's statement in v. 28, which is intended as a response to v. 27.[86] The closest parallel[87] is LXX Zech 8.6, in which the Lord describes the future 'faithful city' (v. 3) and declares:

> If it is marvellous (ἀδυνατήσει) in the sight of the remnant of the people in these days, should it also be marvellous (ἀδυνατήσει) in my sight?

In Mark, as in Zechariah, the 'possibility' of God is not divorced from the obedience of men. Just as the condition of Zechariah's prophecy is that Israel 'render true judgments, show kindness and mercy, etc.' (7.9, cf. 8.8), so in Mark the proper response to God's ability to save includes, v. 28, to have 'left everything and followed'. Thus, although v. 27 is something of a floating tradition,[88] in this context it contributes to the sequence of thought. Rich men cannot enter the kingdom, but God is able to let them in. To the implied question 'How?' v. 28 supplies the answer, and vv. 29-31 the confirmation: obedience. Only God is able to overcome the power of possessions (v. 22), a persistent demon (9.23-29), or the threat of apostasy (14.36);[89] but in every case man's obedience is involved as well.

The attention shifts in vv. 28-31 to the subject of rewards, the connection indicated by ἤρξατο.[90] Peter's statement may be in a spirit of pride, which the Matthean version (19.27) makes more explicit by adding the demand, 'What then shall we have?'[91] In any case, ἡμεῖς is emphatic: Peter sees the conduct of the disciples in contrast to that of the rich man.[92] πάντα is equivalent to ὅσα ἔχεις in v. 21; and ἀκολουθεῖν is common to both verses (contrast ἀπῆλθεν in v. 22). Thus the only constant features in command and fulfillment are 'leaving all' and 'following'.

The lists in vv. 29-30 contain a number of noteworthy elements. Attention is sometimes drawn to the disjunctive (ἤ) list in v. 29

which, in contrast to πάντα in v. 28, may suggest that *any* sacrifice will be rewarded and that Peter's claim is exaggerated.[93] But one can scarcely leave father but not mother, children but not home, etc. Furthermore, the corresponding rewards in v. 30 are joined by καί: the best explanation is to regard the difference as a literary device to 'emphasize that what is gained will far outweigh what is lost'.[94] The family ties are listed in ascending order,[95] which makes the unusual position of 'lands' (ἄγρους) at the end of the list appear to be an afterthought.[96] But it may have the connotation not of 'fields' but of 'the country as opposed to the city'.[97] In other words, the disciple is not only to abandon house and family but also to leave the very region. This may account for the position of ἄγρους and retain the ascensive order. Merx argues that the exclusion of wives from the list may be late, since one cannot leave children without leaving one's wife.[98] It is possible, however, if the reference is to grown children, or if younger children are left with other relatives. In any case, the exclusion of wives from the list is probably due to the high view of the marriage bond in the early church.[99] Fathers are omitted from the list in v. 30, presumably because only one Father (Matt 23.9) replaces the believer's earthly father.[100] The rest of the hundredfold promise of v. 30 probably refers in a general sense to the fellowship of the new community.[101] A specific reference to the 'houses and lands' (χωρίων) of Acts 4.34-37 (cf. 2.44-45)[102] is unlikely, since there property is sold and not retained for community use. If any literal application is intended, it is probably that the disciple will have a house in which to stay wherever he goes; and whatever new fields or lands to which his journeys take him will be his as they are God's. The fields could even connote the figurative sense of the world awaiting the harvest (Matt 13.38-39). The hundredfold family members undoubtedly refer to the disciples' new family in the household of God.[103]

The phrase 'with persecutions' has been a source of concern for interpreters who find unacceptable its dissonance in a list of rewards. Clement of Alexandria paraphrased the verse in this way:

> He shall receive in return a hundredfold. To what end (does he expect) to have now in this time fields and riches and houses and brothers with persecutions? But in the coming age there is eternal life![104]

Taylor rightly regards this as an incorrect attempt to spiritualize the saying, 'which is not necessary since by wide consent the items in 30 are not to be taken literally'.[105] Zimmerman suggests that the Aramaic רדיפיא lying behind the expression may be translated as 'persecutions', but more properly here as 'other things that people strive for'.[106] However, such a nonspecific reward is unnecessary if the list in v. 30 is meant figuratively, and the expression has no parallel in v. 29. It is better, therefore, to regard the expression as a reminder that despite the advantages of the new community, only heavenly reward will give unsullied satisfaction.

Opinion is divided as to whether v. 31 refers to eschatological reversal of rich and poor or to those within the community who might be tempted to pride of place. Among those who posit a simple reversal, Best rightly de-emphasizes the condemnation of 'the first' (the rich) in favour of the reward of 'the last' (the disciples).[107] This view is consistent with the immediate context and the use of δέ. Although the conjunction can have an adversative sense, it may introduce a parenthetical remark, an explanation, or an intensification.[108] Verse 31 is probably meant in one of these latter senses as a summary of vv. 28-30 is not the entire passage.[109] Those who see in the verse a warning against pride consider it a response to Peter's outburst or an allusion to the disciples' servant role (9.35; 10.43).[110] Certainly both of these interpretations are pertinent, but it is the former that is more in keeping with the theme of the entire passage and so is to be preferred.

12.41-44

The story of the Widow's Offering (12.41-44), and especially its summary statement in v. 44, has numerous parallels in other literature.[111] Thus the story has been regarded as a parable[112] or an adapted Jewish story.[113] Whatever its origin, it is certainly consistent with other Markan teaching on related subjects. Its position here is not to be accounted for simply by the reference to widows in v. 40 and the Temple setting.[114] The connection to the foregoing diatribe is more thorough; together, vv. 38-44 reveal a 'contrast between the outward meagerness and inward richness of the widow's service, and the outward ostentation and inward barrenness of the Pharisees' religion'.[115] The fact that the disciples are called together to hear Jesus' pronouncement (v. 43a) makes it clear that the story has application to Mark's readers.

Some of the specific features of the narrative deserve notice. The widow's coins are λεπτά, whose value was one-eightieth of a day's wage.[116] This was the smallest copper coin in circulation[117] and the smallest amount that could be contributed.[118] Schweizer points out that 'it is significant that she gave two *lepta*, because she could have divided them and kept one for herself'.[119] The contrast is drawn between the πολλά of the rich (v. 41) and the πάντα of the widow (v. 44).[120]

The widow's gift exceeds the others' because while they gave out of their 'abundance' (περισσεύοντος), she gave out of her 'poverty' (ὑστερήσεως). The saying could easily end with this simple contrast and remain true to the traditional piety that honoured the gifts of the poor.[121] But it goes on to make the point—and to repeat it—that she gave *all* (πάντα, cf. 10.28) that she *had* (ὅσα εἶχεν, cf. 10.21), her *whole life* (ὅλον τὸν βίον, cf. 8.36). The repetition of these expressions before the disciples is significant. The widow is clearly 'ein lebendiges Beispiel für die auf Gottes Fürsorge vertrauende Sorglosigkeit'.[122] The ultimate destination of her money is not revealed, nor is she said to have become a follower, but her *Gottvertrauen*, expressed by her gift of all, is a paradigm of true discipleship.

14.3-9

The last Markan pericope relevant to this study is the story of Jesus' Anointing at Bethany (14.3-9). This passage affords interesting insight into Jesus' own position with regard to the wealth of others. In reference to the reaction of those (the disciples are not explicitly mentioned) who perceive the costliness of the ointment, Lane remarks that

> It was natural for them to think in terms of provision for the poor, for it was customary on the evening of Passover to remember the poor with gifts (M Pesachim 9.11; 10.1; cf. Jo 13.29). It was also the practice to give as charity one part of the second tithe normally spent in Jerusalem during the feast.[123]

Does Jesus, therefore, value devotion to himself over care for the poor? Probably not. Lane argues that Jesus is in this instance 'the poor man *par excellence*', not an object of devotion in opposition to the poor: thus the contrast in v. 7 is 'not between Jesus and the poor, but between "always" and "not always"'.[124] This passage is, of course, not the first evidence against personal asceticism on the part of Jesus: in chapter two are described his meals with tax-collectors and sinners (vv. 15-16), his disdain for fasting (vv. 18-19), and even his disregard for the owners of grainfields (v. 23).[125] Jesus was willing to *enjoy* what he would not allow himself or his disciples to have.[126]

The anonymous woman is more than an incidental element in the narrative. The commendation of her action ('she has done what she could', v. 8) is reminiscent of 12.44 ('she . . . has put in everything she had'). This and the promise of reward (v. 9) may be reminders to the reader that this passage has practical implications for discipleship.

Conclusions
Examination of material in the Gospel of Mark pertaining to wealth allows the following summary statements:

1. Important elements of the Markan tradition have parallels in earlier semitic wisdom traditions.
2. The commands in 8.34; 10.21; the statements in 10.28 and 12.44; and the narrative accounts in 1.16, 18; 2.14 reveal a patterned or formulaic teleological devaluation of wealth.
3. The commands in 6.8-9; and the statements in 4.19; 8.35-37; 10.23-27, 29-31; and possibly 14.8-9 lend implicit support to dispossession of wealth.
4. Dispossession of wealth as a way of expressing *Gottvertauen* is a means to eternal life.
5. Commands to follow Jesus are bound to teleological devaluation.
6. No significant exceptions to the foregoing statements appear in the Gospel.

To these statements may be added the secondary observations that the Gospel contains little evidence of concern for the poor, that Jesus and the disciples appear to use and enjoy possessions without owning them, and that the Gospel offers no clear indication of the SEC either of the Markan community or of the situation described. The primary statements listed above can be condensed into the original thesis statement; thus they demonstrate its applicability to the Gospel of Mark.

EXCURSUS: WAS JESUS RICH?

The only explicit internal evidence that addresses this question is 2 Cor 8.9:

> For you know the grace of our Lord Jesus Christ, that though he was rich (πλούσιος), yet for your sake he became poor (ἐπτώξευσεν), so that by his poverty (πτωχείᾳ) you might become rich (πλουτήσετε).

G.W. Buchanan, in the provocative article, 'Jesus and the Upper Class',[127] contends that this and other inferences from NT data 'support the possibility that Jesus may . . . have been reared in an upper class in society'.[128] In light of what we have observed about the SEC lying behind pre-Synoptic HW material, the question is certainly worth considering.

With regard to the verse quoted above, Buchanan notes the usual interpretation that Jesus became spiritually poor so that the Corinthians might become spiritually rich, but for two reasons he favors the view that Jesus became materially poor:

> (1) Paul did not customarily refer to Christ's divine nature when urging Christians to follow a certain pattern of behavior; and (2) more than once, Paul referred to sharing material goods in exchange for spiritual benefits.[129]

Given the context of a protracted appeal for financial assistance (8.1–9.15), Buchanan's interpretation must be considered seriously.

Corroborating evidence within the Gospels is scarce. Buchanan gives examples to suggest that the work of a carpenter (τέκτων, cf. Matt 13.55) may have included supervisory work.[130] It is not hard to imagine that the founding of a Roman city nearby while Jesus was in his teens[131] and the position of Nazareth on or near major routes of trade and pilgrimage[132] provided opportunity to a family with grown sons who were presumably skilled and experienced tradesmen. Another possibility is that Jesus left his family to join some sect where he received an education and/or began to develop upper-class associations.

The most suggestive evidence, however, comes from the Gospel teachings themselves. Buchanan points out that the vast majority of Jesus' illustrations have their setting in the activities of the upper classes.[133]

Buchanan makes the further point that Jesus has numerous contacts with members of the upper classes, appears very much at home amongst them, numbers a few among his followers, and gives instructions that assume financial means to carry them out.[134] He concludes that these factors clarify the authority of Jesus to command others to leave work and possessions: at some point he had done the same himself.[135] This view is attractive. It accounts not only for the positive associations of Jesus' teaching and activities with the upper classes, but also the absence of self-designation as poor, the scarcity of sympathy for the poor, and the absence of externally directed social criticism. It leaves us with a Jesus who did not make a virtue of necessity, but made a necessity of what he considered a virtue.

Chapter 7

HOSTILITY TO WEALTH IN THE GOSPEL OF MATTHEW

Matthew's Gospel contains three passages that can be categorized as reflecting the justice imperative: 5.42; 6.3-4; 25.31-46. These three passages assume the means to give generously. In addition, Matthew includes a 'spiritualized' version of the beatitudes. Do these features constitute a relaxation of the harsh demand on disciples which is presented in Mark? Mealand concludes that Matthew's 'softening' of the tradition shows that 'the economic circumstances of Matthew's church seem to have been less harsh than those of the earlier Christian communities'.[1]

Such a conclusion is unfounded. If 5.42 assumes for some believers the means to give or lend, 25.31-46 assumes for others the lack of means. If material peculiar to and probably composed by Matthew includes the command to give alms (6.3-4), it also includes the parable of the treasure and pearl (13.44-46) in which the characters 'sell all' for the kingdom. If Matthew may be said to spiritualize the first beatitude (5.3), he may also be said to 'materialize' the eye of the body (6.22-23). If the widow's offering is omitted, so is the general reference to anyone entering with difficulty the kingdom (19.23)—in Matthew it is precisely the rich who have difficulty. The account of John's asceticism (3.4), the story of the disciples' call (4.18-22; 9.9), the interpretation of the parable of the sower (13.22), the mission call (10.9-10), the command to deny one's self (16.24-27), the story of the rich young man (19.16-30), and the anointing at Bethany (26.6-16) are all retained and in some particulars intensified. New material is added from independent sources: the third temptation (4.8-10), the saying about treasure in heaven (6.19-21), the saying about serving two masters (6.24), and the passage about anxiety (6.25-34). Any of this material could have been spiritualized or omitted in order to adapt to the situation of a richer church, but it is not.

The argument that wealth is condoned by the assumption of ample means to give alms is overly subtle, even if such passages are considered alone. The passages put no limit on the amount to be given; indeed, obedience to 5.42 would necessarily result in quick impoverishment. In each case it is not the amount given that is at issue, but the fact (5.42), manner (6.3) or recipient (25.35f.) of the gift as seen in contrast to the conduct of the unrighteous (5.38; 6.2; 25.42f.). In terms of hostility to wealth, the spiritualization of the first beatitude can scarcely deprive the destitute of his comfort or the wealthy of the sting of 6.24 and 9.23. The wealth of Joseph of Arimathea is mentioned by Matthew (27.57; cf. Mark 15.43; Luke 23.50-51) hardly as an encouragement to richer believers, but rather as an allusion to Isa 53.9.[2] In terms of the consistency of Matthew's message and its relation to Mark and Luke, it is the *retention* of teleological devaluation that must be emphasized. No limit is placed on giving, no stigma is placed on poverty, no easier way to *Gottvertrauen* is offered, and no particularization of the teaching is given. As the more detailed consideration of the relevant passages will show, HW remains a fundamental tenet in Matthew's Gospel.

4.8-10

The third temptation of Jesus, 4.8-10, is an offer of 'all the kingdoms of the world and the glory of them', which are in Satan's power to bestow. This does not imply that the world is evil in a hellenistic or gnostic sense, because the world is created by God.[3] Nor does it necessarily imply that Satan has complete control over the kingdoms and their glory: he is merely 'playing God' in the style of Gen 13.14-15; Deut 34.1-4.[4] The significance of the passage for this study is its implicit disparagement of the kingdoms and their glory.[5] The temptation is a perversion of teleological devaluation: instead of [πάντα] δὸς πτωχοῖς (19.21), we read σοι πάντα δώσω; instead of θησαυρὸν ἐν οὐρανοῖς (9.21), we read βασιλείας τοῦ κόσμου. Jesus' fall would gain for him 'the whole world' but would forfeit his soul (16.26). It would place him in the category of those choked by 'the cares of the world and the delight in riches' (13.22). This is what it would mean to follow Satan, whereas to resist will enable Jesus to call others to follow himself. Jesus' response to Satan in v. 10 demands the same exclusivity of service to God as does 6.24; and in both cases earthly wealth is the alternative 'reward'. All this is not to say that the temptation story was regarded or intended primarily as a polemic against wealth. But the fact that the possession of all possessions is portrayed as the ultimate satanic temptation and the similarities to elements of subsequent didactic passages show the importance of the issues involved to the creator—and to the conveyor—of the tradition.

4.18-22; 9.9

Matthew reproduces the stories of the call of the disciples (4.18-22; 9.9) in substantially their Markan form, but the few changes in the narrative actually serve to enhance the severity of the action. Nets are now 'their nets' (v. 21), not simply 'the nets' (Mark 1.19), making it clear that the men leave their own fishing gear, not just their father's.[6] Similarly, the mention of hired servants (Mark 1.20) is omitted, and 'in the boat' (Mark 1.20) is changed to 'the boat', leaving the bare statement that 'they left the boat and their father' in greater conformity to 19.29.[7] The rentention of the word 'immediately' (vv. 20, 22), since Matthew usually omits it, puts stress on the suddenness of the action.[8] The relation of the passage to discipleship is stressed by the repetition of ἠκολούθησαν αὐτῷ (vv. 20, 22) against Mark's ἀπῆλθον ὀπίσω αὐτου (1.20) and Matthew's preferred ἀπέρχομαι.[9] These changes are our first indication that Matthew's interest goes beyond mere repetition of sources with minor stylistic modification. They reveal an awareness of the interrelation of relevant passages and an active interest in the effective communication of the tradition.

5.3

He who dares add to the voluminous discussion of the first beatitude, much less to review thoroughly what others have written, is, without a doubt, rich in spirit. The verse is relevant to passages that reflect teleological devaluation if, in Matthew's understanding, the poor are those who, because of their experience of economic deprivation, hope only in God's provision and salvation.[10] In this case, τῷ πνεύματι may have been added in order to make clear to Greek readers the complexity of the semitic idiom.[11] Matthew does this, therefore, not because his rich community finds poverty distasteful, but because *poor* in itself is not as attractive a concept as *dependent*, and he qualifies the word to emphasize the latter.[12] A more widely accepted view, however, is that the more original Lukan beatitude is altered from its reference only to the materially poor[13] by the Matthean addition of τῷ πνεύματι in order to indicate the humble[14] or faint-hearted[15] in a non-material, religious sense—those who 'mit leeren Händen zu Gott kommen'.[16] But even in this case, Matthew should not be regarded as softening sympathy for the materially poor, much less softening disparagement of wealth. The former could be possible only if we knew (and we do not) that he, his community, or his sources were sympathetic to the materially poor. The latter could be possible only if we knew (and we do not) that his source included the Lukan woes,[17] and that both beatitude and woe were understood by Matthew to have an exclusively material sense, whose expression was required in this context. And what is more important, neither could be possible unless Matthew's readers had that earlier source for comparison. Without it, the retention of Markan material (and other Q material in the Sermon) would suffice to communicate Matthew's view of wealth. So although we must regard as a possibility the notion that Matthew here softens an earlier tradition, we should neither regard the notion as probable nor conclude that the verse alters the intended or perceived view of wealth in the Gospel.

5.42
The view that Matthew has in 5.42 softened a more radical view on the ground that the verse presupposes adequate means to lend[18] does not adequately consider the context. 5.40 demands that one forego the provision of the Law for the poor (Exod 22.25-26; Deut 24.12-13) by offering what an adversary cannot take.[19] Far from prescribing rules for financial management, therefore, the passage recommends a gesture of appeasement and patience in respose to one of violence.[20] It is an implicit statement that God is the help of the poor,[21] whether they are so involuntarily (vv. 39-41) or voluntarily (v. 42). As such, the passage has more to commend it as an *example* of HW than as an *exception* to HW.

6.3-4
Mealand contends that the saying about almsgiving in 6.3-4 'presupposes a normal capacity for giving' and so constitutes partial evidence that material peculiar to Matthew contains little severity toward wealth.[22] He fails, however, to account for the presence of 5.42, which presupposes the same capacity, from the 'comparatively severe' source Q.[23] As in that example, the issue addressed in 6.3-4

would not be served by reference to the amount that must be given. And in both cases the command can be obeyed within the context of teleological devaluation. The rich young man of 19.21 must presumably avoid making a show of his obedience; likewise the one who stores up treasure in heaven (6.20) or comes to hate mammon (6.24). Indeed, every command to give presupposes the means to give and might be addressed to a late, prosperous community. The absurdity is countered only by thorough consideration of the redactor's intent in each instance.

6.19-21

It is difficult to imagine a more succinct and poetic[24] statement of teleological devaluation than that presented in Matt 6.19-21. Verse 19 makes a clear prohibition of accumulation of possessions: 'treasures' must here refer to anything and everything put away out of anxiety for tomorrow (v. 34). The triple scourge of animal, mineral,[25] and human destructive agents is a comprehensive statement of the futility of possession for the sake of security. Not merely gold and jewels, but even spare food and clothing are in view.

The parallel list in v. 20 is ironic: the implication is that accumulation in heaven provides a better kind of security than does accumulation on earth. Although some scholars regard the command to lay up treasures in heaven as a general reference to good works,[26] it is best regarded as a specific reference to dispossession through almsgiving.[27] We need not refer forward to 19.21, much less to Luke, for confirmation. The reader would be familiar with the common equation between almsgiving and heavenly treasure in the wisdom tradition.[28] The dispossession of goods is the natural opposite and the only alternative to the accumulation of goods prohibited in v. 19.

Verse 21 may originally have been a separate proverbial saying,[29] but it fits well here both because of its backward-pointing reference to treasure and because of its more subtle forward-pointing reference to the heart—the spiritual organ of love/devotion/service (v. 24) and anxiety/seeking (vv. 25-34). To spiritualize the saying into a command to submit one's heart to God's sovereign rule[30] is to reverse the order of treasure and heart. The heart follows the treasure, or as Gundry puts it, 'the final accent falls, then, on the importance of treasure as the determinant of the heart'.[31] There is no more explicit statement in the NT of the integral relation between conduct with regard to possessions and right relation to God. The implication of heavenly reward here and in v. 20 is in fact the strongest indication of reward in the entire section 6.19-34, and thus it should probably be understood to apply to the following sayings as well.

6.22-23

Despite attempts to generalize or spiritualize 6.22-23,[32] the evidence overwhelmingly favors the standard view that the passage as placed in this context commands generosity and condems greed.[33] Matthew recognizes that 'sound' (ἁπλοῦς) and its cognates connote generosity in other contexts,[34] and that the evil (πονηρός) eye is a by-word for stinginess.[35] 20.15 is a Matthean example of this understanding. The householder reprimands workers who express jealousy over wages for having an 'evil eye' (ὀφθαλμός . . . πονηρός). In the context of 6.19-24, and as an opposite of 'generous', the evil eye may be understood as accumulation, which assumes or expresses greed. Attitude and action cannot be separated. Just as the heart follows the treasure (v. 21) and service follows the choice of master (v. 24), so the body (σωμά, v. 22) follows the eye. One's conduct with regard to possessions determines or reflects his spiritual state—perhaps even his eternal reward. Matthew does not employ 'darkness' (σκότος) in the usual NT sense of 'sinfulness'[36] except in his quotation of Isa 9.2 (Matt 4.16). He is alone among the evangelists[37] in his use of the word as a designation for eternal punishment.[38] Thus the Matthean addition of τὸ σκότος πόσον in v. 23[39] may be an inference of reward. Those who are generous are the light of the world (5.14-16); those who accumulate are consigned to darkness.

6.24

Matt 6.24 makes it clear that the service of God and the service of mammon[40] are mutually exclusive options. The question is whether one can *possess* mammon without *serving* it. Certainly one cannot 'possess' God without serving Him; in the same sense, one cannot dissociate possession of wealth.[41] The first part of v. 24 makes this explicit: given the choice between the two masters, God and mammon, one must 'hate' and 'despise' mammon, 'love' and 'be devoted to' God. As negatively and positively stated elucidations of the word 'serve' (δουλούειν), the words refer to conduct and not to attitude.[42] How then can one's conduct toward mammon express hatred? To regard 'love' and 'hate' here as comparative rather than absolute opposites, as in Gen 29.31-33; Deut 21.15, where the 'hated' wives are those who are not preferred,[43] is unacceptable. Whereas in that context (at least) two wives are retained, in this context two masters cannot be retained: any master would spurn a servant who ignored him, neglected him, or refused to serve him. We get no help from other Matthean uses of μισεῖν, which refer either to a resentful attitude toward one's neighbor (5.43) or to persecution from the world (10.22; 24.9). Instead, we must turn our attention to the numerous OT instances of 'hate' where the word connotes an action of rejection or avoidance.[44] An excellent example is Prov 1.29-30, which includes a parallel 'despise' (וַיִּנְאֲצוּ, ἐμυκτήριζον):

> Because they hated knowledge and did not choose the fear of the
>   Lord,
> would have none of my counsel, and despised all my reproof...

Corroborating evidence from the NT is found in Luke 6.22, where μισήσωσιν has as its parallel ἀφορίσωσιν ('exclude, excommunicate'[45]), and Luke 14.26 (cf. John 12.25), where the potential disciple is told to 'hate' his family. The obvious parallel in this case to Luke 5.11, 28; 18.28 makes it clear that the recommended response is not to 'love less' but to 'leave behind'.[46]

ἀντέξεσθαι occurs in the same sentence with δουλούειν and ἀγαπᾶν in Jer 8.2 and with ζητεῖν in Zeph 1.6, where it has the connotation 'to look to for support and help'.[47] If that is the sense here, the word is a striking summary of what it means to serve and love God with one's possessions, and an apt transition to the subsequent admonition to avoid anxiety and seek the kingdom.

6.25-34

The teaching about anxiety, Matt 6.25-34, begins with διὰ τοῦτο, an indication that the passage is, in the intention of the redactor, an inference from the previous sayings. In particular, the passage may be said to work out in practice the implication of 6.24.[48] Following the commands of 6.19-24, the audience would very naturally ask, 'What is to become of us if we follow this teaching literally?' 6.25 anticipates the question, 6.33 offers an answer, and everything else expounds the argument. The parallel negative imperatives of 6.25, 31, 34 are restated in positive form in 6.33. In this understanding, vv. 25-34 constitute not a shift in emphasis from a rich audience to a poor one but an apt and integral continuation of the previous sayings, notably v. 24. The master supplies the needs of the servant, so the servant need only concern himself with service. No accumulation is necessary, no anxiety about tomorrow, if only he will choose the right master and reject the wrong master.

It would be a mistake to perceive in the passage an exhortation to action only during the period of imminent eschatological crisis,[49] i.e. to isolate that crisis ethic from the moral teaching that remains relevant for as long as the coming kingdom is delayed. The preservation of the passage in its present form argues against this, as do the realities of survival: the need for food, drink, and clothing is far more immediate than that which could be assigned to a *period* extending beyond a few weeks. In the present context the need is in fact a *daily* need. Whatever the duration of the present age envisioned in the original version of this passage, then, the principle of *Gottvertrauen* expressed here had perceived relevance as moral guidance as late as Matthew's writing.

The precise meaning of μεριμνᾶν has been the subject of extensive discussion. Opinion is divided as to whether the word connotes only an attitude of anxious concern or the actual putting forth of effort. In favour of the former view are the reference to mental anxiety in the only other Matthean occurence (10.19),[50] a few similar references in Paul,[51] and the probability that μεριμνήσητε in v. 31 connotes only attitude.[52] In favour of the latter view are examples of μεριμνᾶν with the connotation of 'work',[53] the metaphors of vv. 26-30 which appear to imply a lack of labour,[54] and the interchangeability of μεριμνᾶν and ζητεῖν, the latter of which (vv. 32-33) seems to connote effort.[55] Although the normal use of the word and its other occurrence in Matthew tip the scales slightly in favor of the former view, neither word need be emphasized to the neglect of the other. On the one hand, it can be argued that effort presupposes care; on the other hand, care presupposes need, which in turn presupposes lack of effort—or its positive expression: voluntary poverty. Thus, if vv. 25-34 are intended as a development from vv. 19-24, anxiety can connote only attitude and not action—the action has already occurred.

It is clear that 6.25 has in view a concern about the most basic requirements for survival: ψυχή is here a synonymous parallel to σῶμα,[56] and food and clothing are common designations for the most fundamental necessities of life.[57] Furthermore, the metaphors in vv. 26-30 envision no more than the minimum for day-to-day survival: God will clothe and feed; God will determine one's span of life. The disciples' prayer for bread is apparently brought into conformity to this passage (esp. v. 34) by the shift from the present δίδου (Luke 11.3) to the aorist δὸς and from καθ' ἡμέραν to σήμερον: emphasis is placed on provision for this day alone.[58]

6.32 introduces ἐπιζητεῖν in one of two reasons to reject anxiety about provision; i.e., one should not imitate the Gentiles who seek these things, and one should recognize that God will provide what is needed. Dupont judges correctly that the meaning of (ἐπι)ζητεῖν is dependent on its context and that its use in v. 33, avoiding the negative connotation given to μεριμνᾶν in the passage, connotes 'préoccupation, mais sans anxiété'.[59] As a contrast to the prescribed 'seeking' of v. 33, the word in v. 32 need not have negative implications: the mention of the Gentiles suffices to discourage imitation. The general context includes explicit (7.7-8) and implicit (6.9-13) references to seeking without the connotation of active effort. Thus ζητεῖτε in v. 33 refers primarily to an attitude of the heart and only secondarily to conduct. Both are necessary, of course: one must both desire the kingdom (6.10a) and enter it (7.13); one must both desire the Father's will (6.10b) and perform it (7.21).

An understanding of the intent of πρῶτον in v. 33 is crucial to the issue of Matthew's 'softening'. A common view is that the word is employed in place of Luke's πλήν (12.31) to signify ranking: concern (or work) for food and clothing is permissible so long as, and after, one concerns himself with the kingdom.[60] But δὲ, and not πρῶτον, is an equal substitute for πλήν;[61] thus, the adversative sense is retained.[62] And although all but one of twenty-five Matthean occurrences of πρῶτος connote priority, the one exception (23.26) is the closest parallel in form to this verse: 'first cleanse the inside of the cup and of the plate, that the outside also may be clean'.[63] Furthermore, an intention to soften at this point would contradict the previous affirmation that God will provide for all needs, and it would obviate the subsequent reiteration of the command to avoid anxiety. Finally, v. 33 itself promises 'all these things' as a divine gift to those who seek the kingdom, forestalling the need for a second active 'seeking'. These considerations favor the minority view that the adverb is emphatic rather than permissive, indicating 'an action whose priority is not one of a series but all-encompassing'.[64] But even if πρῶτον does connote priority, it is not a priority of labour, as if believers could store up goods after they had served God. Rather, it signifies that in this context, given the commands of 6.11 and 7.7-11 to 'seek' provision from the Father, Matthew perceived a necessity to alter this verse to include such supplication. The addition of καὶ τὴν δικαιοσύνην is perhaps intended as a reflection of the order of the prayer in 6.10. As in that context, the question is whether God's (will or) righteousness refers to the activity of God or the activity of man. Man's conduct is clearly intended in the reference to God's will in 7.21; more importantly, Matthew links the kingdom and personal righteousness in 5.10, 20.[65] Furthermore, man's conduct, expressed in the word 'righteousness', is a dominant feature of the Sermon. It is likely, therefore, that the addition of the word to v. 33 brings an active connotation—or at least an active corollary—to the idea of seeking in an attitudinal sense.[66] καὶ may be explicative: 'Seek first his reign, that is to say here and now his righteousness'.[67] It seems more in keeping with the Beatitudes and the Lord's prayer, however, to view 'kingdom' primarily in a future sense, as the reward for present righteousness. Thus the phrase as a whole combines future promise and present responsibility.[68]

6.34 summarizes the passage with a repetition of the command not to be anxious. The reference to 'tomorrow' does not imply that Matthew relaxes the command to allow work 'today'.[69] Rather, as with πρῶτον in v. 33, it may betray a desire to accommodate to the command that one seek from God provision for the day (6.11). Anxiety about either day would not be a temptation unless one had acted upon the advice of 6.19-24. Thus the entire section 6.19-34 may be viewed as an explicit macrocosm of the metaphorical sayings in vv. 19-24: the attitude of trust (vv. 25-34) follows dispossession of goods (vv. 19-24) as the heart follows the treasure, the body follows the eye, and loyal service follows the choice of master.

10.9-10

A number of changes from Mark occur in Matthew's version of the mission charge, 10.1-15. A few of these are relevant to this study. The command to 'give without pay' (v. 8), the use of κτᾶσθαι (v. 9; cf. αἴρειν in Mark 10.8; Luke 9.3), and the advancement of money from fourth to first in the list of prohibitions emphasize the avoidance of remuneration for missionary service.[70] Matthew's addition of χρυσὸν μηδὲ ἄργυρον μηδὲ hardly points to a wealthier community;[71] on the contrary, it constitutes a climactic[72] and comprehensive prohibition of acquisition. The next four items to be avoided are arranged in ascending order of need,[73] and the prohibition of sandals and staff against Mark may signify the holiness of pilgrim missionaries.[74] In his retention of these sayings, Matthew conveys the more rigorous—and presumably earlier—Q version.[75]

13.22

Matthew preserves the explanation of the parable of the sower substantially intact, but he omits the reference to αἱ περὶ τὰ λοιπὰ ἐπιθυμίαι in 13.22 (cf. Mark 4.19). This omission may be attributed to a desire to balance the verse with v. 21, which mentions only two dangers;[76] to an avoidance of confusion over ἐπιθυμίαι, whose cognate Matthew uses in a positive sense in v. 17;[77] or to an estimation that mention of 'other things' is redundant or unnecessary.[78]

13.44-46

The parables of the treasure and pearl are a Matthean extrapolation from 13.22.[79] Surprisingly few commentators have noted the parables' striking parallel expression, 'he went and sold all he had';[80] or that such conduct is exactly the opposite of that lamented in 13.22.[81] Attention is usually focused on the high worth of the kingdom,[82] although this is at best[83] only implied, and on the joy of finding,[84] although this is stated only in the first parable.[85] The fact is that the narrator arranges the details of the parables in order to set the final action of the men in bold relief: the limits of the laborer's and merchant's wealth are set so that 'all' is the requisite amount for each.[86] The culminating phrase is determined by Mark 10.21,[87] and the reader of this Gospel could not fail to notice the similarity to 19.21. Furthermore, the relation to v. 22 suggests that universal application is intended.

One incidental feature of the pair of parables which may be instructive is the difference in economic status of the two examples. The laborer is at most middle-class, but he has sufficient assets to raise the money for the purchase of a field; the merchant is at least middle-class who presumably travels to make purchases—as opposed to a stationary, small-time trader. Thus a wide range of means may be inferred, but both men are able to pay.[88] Only the destitute (who would not be subject to the dangers of 13.22) could avoid seeing his own circumstances within the range covered by the two parables.

Thus the lesson of the parables could not have been intended either to justify the plight of the involuntarily poor or to particularize the command to dispossession only to the rich. Matthew regards the lesson as applicable to all disciples.

16.24-27

Matthew records almost verbatim Mark 8.34-37 in 16.24-27, but he moves Mark 8.38 to 10.33. The earlier context (10.26-32) is clearly relevant to persecution and apostasy, but the redactor is not averse to repetition: 16.25 appears again at 10.39. It is possible, therefore, that the separation is purposive. That is, Matthew regards vv. 24-27 as relevant more to the means of livelihood than to the physical existence, and he wishes to strengthen the impression. There exists a Matthean precedent for this meaning of ψυχή in 6.25, where life as the addressees understand it is contrasted to life as Jesus understands it. A further inference that conduct and not martyrdom is in view is the ethical connotation of the Matthean addition, 'he will repay every man for what he has done' (τὴν πρᾶξιν αὐτοῦ).[89] These considerations suggest that Matthew perceives and even strengthens the application to economic ethics in the passage.

19.16-30

The Matthean version of the story of the rich man (19.16-30) contains a number of changes from Mark's version that warrant consideration. Minear contends that in v. 17 Matthew 'reveals his contentment with the legal standard by making it completely adequate'.[90] But this can hardly be the intent, since the man's obedience to Jesus' specifications of the commandments still leaves a 'lack' (v. 20). Jesus' response in v. 21 becomes appositional to v. 17, a relation analogous to that of 5.48 and 5.20. Thus the addition, 'if you would be perfect (τέλειος, only here and in 5.48, where it is required of all) conveys not a double ethic,[91] but conduct expected of all disciples.[92] Furthermore, the man's renewed question about his 'lack' (v. 20), the reference to 'treasure in heaven' (v. 21), and the retained discussion of entrance to the kingdom (vv. 23-24) 'make it clear that we are still dealing with the question of eternal life, not the question of a special rank within it'.[93] The inserted reference to love of neighbor (cf. 22.39; Lev 19.18) may be intended to foreshadow the subsequent command to give 'to the poor'. Matthew adds ἀμὴν λέγω ὑμῖν to v. 23, underscoring the importance and universality of the subsequent sayings.[94] His change from οἱ τὰ χρήματα ἔχοντες to πλούσιος is not intended to modify the saying in order to exclude the disciples by condemning only the rich:[95] the disciples still apply the message to themselves (v. 27). Rather, the change should be regarded as a simplification which creates a parallel to the next verse. The omission of Mark 10.24, with its general statement about the difficulty of entering the kingdom, serves to focus attention on the particular issue of the use of possessions. The insertion of v. 28 influences the reduction of Mark 10.30 to the simple ἑκατονταπλασίονα λήμψεται.[96] This de-emphasis of the this-worldly aspect of the reward serves to intensify the tradition, since an exclusively future reward allows for no mercenary motive (cf. 10.9-10) or mistaken expectation of economic reward in this life.

25.14-30

The parable of the talents (25.14–30) is relevant to the question of the use of wealth to the extent that possessions are included in the symbolic meaning of τάλαντα.[97] The connection with the following passage suggests that material aid is at least partially in view in the present context. The similarity of v. 27, 'you ought to have invested my money with the bankers', to 6.20 might well suggest to the reader an economic application of the economic imagery. On the other hand, the amounts given to the servants are too high for a reader to make a direct transfer to his own economic situation: two talents, or 12,000 denarii, would hardly be considered 'a little' (v. 23). Originally, the parable was probably addressed to the scribes, represented by the third servant who is not faithful to that which has been entrusted to him.[98] The moralizing application to the community, made clear by the connection to the preceding admonition to 'watch' (v. 13), retains the general idea of a trust, but the trust now includes Jesus' teaching: the response of the worthless servant approximates the responses in 7.22 and 25.44. Therefore, we should regard the parable as primarily a general admonition to righteousness, part of which involves laying up treasure—or talents—in heaven.

25.31-46

The last relevant Matthean passage, the story of the judgment in 25.31-46, reveals the importance of doing justice to the concept of righteousness (v. 46). But in this context care is directed not to human need in general but specifically to other believers.[99] Moreover, the treatment of believers *by* believers is probably in view.[100] The passage does not, however, constitute a self-designation of the community as poor[101] any more than it depicts the community as naked, sick, or imprisoned. Verses 35-39, 42-44 are simply paraphrases of Isa 58.7, which undoubtedly reminded the community of the occasional circumstances of some of its members—particularly those who had voluntarily abandoned all (19.27). We have no way of knowing how typical any of these circumstances were, nor is the passage intended to convey such information. The point is to invoke reponse to opportunity.

Conclusions
Consideration of Matthean passages relevant to the subject of HW can be summarized in the following statements:

1. Matthew retains the Markan tradition expressive of or sympathetic to teleological devaluation in 4.18-22; 9.9; 10.9-10; 13.22; 16.24-27; 19.16-30; and 26.6-13
2. Matthew transmits similar Q material in 4.8-10; 5.3; 5.40-42; 6.19-21, 22-23, 24, and 25-34.
3. Matthew includes similar unique material in 13.44-46; 25.14-30; 25.31-46.
4. Matthean redaction appears to intensify the tradition in 4.18-22; 6.22-23, 24; 16.24-27; 19.23-24, 29.
5. Matthew does not soften the tradition, nor does the Gospel contain significant exceptions to the expression of the tradition.
6. Q material and unique Matthean material have parallels in earlier semitic wisdom traditions.

As in Mark, we observe little sympathy for the poor, enjoyment of possessions without ownership on the part of Jesus and the disciples, and no clear indication of the SEC either of the Matthean community or of the situation described. The conclusions listed above evince Matthew's appreciation for the tradition of dispossession as a way of expressing *Gottvertrauen*. Moreover, they substantiate the claim of consistent expression within the Gospel and between Mark and Matthew.

Chapter 8

HOSTILITY TO WEALTH IN THE GOSPEL OF LUKE

At this point it is clear that any amount of material expressing HW in the Gospel of Luke will supplement—but will not supplant—the tradition as it is presented in Mark and in Matthew. Luke's accurate transmission of Mark/Q passages and his lack of substantial alteration of additional sources show that material unique to his Gospel received its radical stamp prior to his compilation. We will observe that in places his redaction serves to bring clarity or internal harmony to the material. But given the great difference in quantity and character of material between the Gospel and Acts, we should not ascribe the Gospel material either to a personal bias or to a unique problem in Luke's own community.

Luke and Acts

Past treatments have attempted to account for the disparate views of wealth between Luke's two volumes in terms of continuity or development. But the fact remains that despite over twenty passages expressing HW, the Gospel does not describe community of goods; conversely, only the references to unity and lack of need among the first believers (Acts 2.44-45; 4.32-37) correspond even vaguely to the radical picture in the Gospel. The problem is not concretely met by efforts to find a common literary denominator in possessions as a symbol of acceptance/rejection[1] or in the poor as a symbol of Israel in need of salvation.[2] The fact that acceptance/rejection and salvation are still present in Acts may help us to understand one function of the relevant material, but such a focus side-steps the important question of the specific implication of the tradition for the conduct of its early readers. Equally inadequate are attempts to limit the applicability of the Gospel material either in scope to church office-holders[3] or in time to a period of persecution.[4] The evidence fails to substantiate in the former case such a specific connotation for the word μαθητής[5] and in the latter case a limitation fails to look beyond the audience to the ground of the radical imperative. If the argument of the tradition is universal, the inference from it can hardly be otherwise: when is the Rich Fool not a rich fool, or to whom among the little flock is it not the Father's good pleasure to give the kingdom?

This chapter does not offer another harmonization of Luke-Acts, or for that matter of the Synoptics and Paul, on the subject of wealth. Luke's initial statement of purpose (Luke 1.1-4) and his lack of reflective editorial comment in either volume suggest that he was more prone to arrange and to clarify than to compose. Clearly, his sources for the first volume contained nearly all the material available to him on the subject. That this results in two very different pictures there can be no doubt; that this entails two very different norms in the mind of Luke is very much open to question. Internal data do not satisfactorily explain the phenomenon. It remains an intriguing question whose answer, unfortunately, lies in the shadowy realm between Jesus and Paul, between ethics of the kingdom and ethics of the Church. For the purposes of this study, we must limit our inquiry to a description of the tradition as we encounter it in the Synoptics.

Luke and the Poor

A common misunderstanding of Luke's Gospel is the view that his is 'the Gospel of the poor', i.e. that it urges solidarity with or advocacy on behalf of the world's underprivilged people. However laudable such activity may be, it cannot be supported by direct reference to the Lukan tradition. The reference to the poor in Luke's scriptural allusions[7] cannot be understood apart from the pious dependence of the Jewish poor on God. Numerous HW passages in the Gospel make no reference whatever to the poor.[8] The fact that the poor are the recipients of aid in other passages[9] means only that the poor are the logical recipients of dispossessed wealth for a contemporary Jew. Indeed, these poor are initially the Jewish poor and perhaps subsequently the Christian poor. There is no hint of concern for regional or international social problems.[10] There can be no doubt, therefore, that for Luke as for Mark and Matthew, the evil of wealth consists not primarily in lack of care for the poor[11] but in independence from God: the opposite of *Gottvertrauen*.

1.52-53

The Magnificat contains the first evidence in Luke's Gospel of attention to economic polarity. Verses 52-53 describe in chiastic form the exercise of God's power in reversing the position of the mighty/ rich and the low/hungry. The passage contains an interesting balance of economic and spiritual connotation and should not be regarded either as evidence of apocalyptic, millenarian resentment on the part of the Christian community[12] or as evidence that 'there is nothing socio-economic or socio-religious about Luke's use of ('poor') terminology'.[13]

A careful reading of the entire psalm refutes the former view. D. Jones concludes his excellent treatment of the Lukan psalms with the verdict that they are 'the product of a highly developed tradition of psalmody'; that 'the circles in which these psalms were produced were sophisticated, even learned'; and that they were not borrowed, but produced by Jewish Christians.[14] The psalmist borrows freely from OT ideas and phrases;[15] significantly, where he borrows from the Song of Hannah (1 Sam 2.1-10), he *softens* the contrast between poor and rich.[16] The result is not a polemic against certain groups, but a promise to those who in piety and poverty are made part of the new plan of God.[17] Mary is not persecuted or oppressed. She is pious, i.e. she is dependent on God's mercy and power for her salvation. These words—mercy, power, salvation—are the dominant themes of all the Lukan psalms,[18] and vv. 52-53 must be understood in the context of those themes. Thus it is a mistake to think that we move from the religious to the political sphere in vv. 51-52[19] or from the political to the social sphere in vv. 52-53.[20] The tradition from which these verses are derived makes no such distinctions.[21] Rather, the entire psalm is a rehearsal of God's equitable actions, focusing on His action toward Mary or Elizabeth. Therefore, the passage should not be understood as primarily predictive. The aorist tense here is best understood in terms of the Hebrew perfect: this is what God ordinarily does.[22] If either the first translator or Luke had wished to emphasize the predictive aspect of the passage, ample precedent could have been taken from the context of the early chapters of the Gospel.[23]

While avoiding the extreme view that the Magnificat expresses a simple, naïve hope for future vengeance, we cannot ignore the relation of the subject matter to similar passages elsewhere in Luke. This relation suggests that, contrary to Seccombe's view, there is in fact something not purely spiritual—perhaps, stated positively, something 'religio-economic'—about Luke's use of poor terminology. Mary's poverty is depicted primarily in a spiritual sense, but it is not depicted exclusively so: at Jesus' purification, his parents offer the sacrifice of those who cannot afford a lamb (2.24; cf. Lev 12.8). Linguistic links to later passages provide the most telling evidence of a conscious connection to economic status. πεινῶντας ἐνέπλησεν is inverted in the second Lukan woe (6.25) to οἱ ἐμπεπλησμένοι νῦν... πεινάσατε. ἀγαθῶν appears again (τὰ ἀγαθά) in 12.18, 19; 16.25. πλουτεῖν occurs in the Gospels only here and in 12.21.[24] The link of vocabulary and subject matter to 6.20-26; 12.16-21; 16.19-31 is important. In all three passages, a past or present state of affairs is described with didactic intent: at the time of death or the eschaton it is too late to repent—one had better become dependent on God now. Since all three passages have implications for economic ethics, it is hard to escape the conclusion that Luke recognized a connection at least partially in economic terms between the Magnificat and the rest of the Gospel. It is best to conclude with Dupont's insightful distinction that while the later passages have in view the effects of the new situation, 1.52-53 focuses on their cause; therefore, he concludes

Il nous paraît... plus prudent de ne pas faire intervenir trop directement Lc 1, 53 dans l'interprétation de ce que les autres textes disent du malheur qui menace les riches.[25]

3.10-14

Luke omits the description of John's asceticism (Mark 1.6) in this context, perhaps because the emphasis here is on concern for one's neighbor.[26] In 7.25, however, Luke adds καὶ τρυφῇ ὑπάρχοντες (cf. Matt 11.8), thereby demonstrating his awareness of, and interest in conveying, the Baptist's ascetic mode of life.

The important question in the present context is whether the teaching in vv. 10-14 is intended as 'timeless ethical instruction'[27] or as an 'interim ethic' limited to a particular situation.[28] The teaching is hardly radical: the ethic is properly Jewish and finds expression in OT and rabbinic sources.[29] It would be strange to encounter Luke's understanding of the ordinary, everyday result of repentance for Christians[30] in the teaching of John rather than the teaching of Jesus, and stranger still to find it addressed to tax collectors and soldiers— hardly typical members of early communities. Verse 18 makes it clear that these instructions are examples from among πολλὰ... ἕτερα παρακαλῶν—an unusual phrase (cf. John 21.25) which evokes the suspicion that Luke had other examples.[31] In any case, if the passage is intended for catechetical use, it is odd to find in it examples only from the sphere of economic ethics. The examples should be understood as a foil to the radical teaching of Jesus, given to distinguish John as a *preliminary* (cf. vv. 15-16; 7.28; Acts 19.1-7) to Jesus.[32] There is in fact a close correspondence between these examples of John's advice and Jesus' teaching in 6.29-30. Where John's listener must share his extra coat, the hearer of Jesus must not withhold even his shirt; where the one must not collect more than his due, the other must distribute to everyone who asks; where one must not rob and must be content with his pay, the other must be content when he is robbed. The closest analogy to 3.10-14 may be Jesus' initial advice to the rich man (Mark 10.17-20 par.): the advice is good advice, but it falls short of the radical demand of discipleship.

4.5-8
Matthew's third temptation becomes Luke's second (4.5-8). The change in order is probably Lukan, intended to make the sequence correspond to the structure of the Gospel: the temptation to rule corresponds to 9.51-19.27.[33] Satan promises the kingdoms τῆς οἰκουμένης (v. 5) instead of τοῦ κόσμου (Matt 4.8), but this should not be regarded as a reference to the diabolical nature of the Roman empire:[34] τὰς βασιλείας is plural, and Luke uses οἰκουμένη elsewhere to refer simply to the whole inhabited earth.[35] Luke's version makes more explicit the devil's control over the kingdoms and their glory both by putting the offer of them directly in the devil's mouth and by adding the additional phrase, 'it has been delivered to me, and I give it to whom I will'.[36]

4.18
The Nazareth story mentions the poor, but not the rich, and should not be taken as an implicit comment about wealth or the wealthy. As an explicit allusion to prophetic teaching (Isa 58; 61), it groups 'captives', 'blind', and 'oppressed' under the rubric 'poor',[37] to which the rich are not antonymic.[38] Seccombe rightly explains each term as representative not of a specific group but of Israel in need of salvation.[39] This meaning is not new to the audience, and it is apparently acceptable (v. 22) until Jesus begins to apply it to

outsiders (vv. 24-28).[40] Therefore we should not understand the passage as an introduction to the economic ethics of the Gospel. The same can be said of 7.22, which also employs πτωχός to signify outsiders. Although in this last instance the economically deprived may be at least partially in view, it is important to note the common element that distinguishes all of these references to πτωχός (and 1.52-53) from others in Luke's Gospel: all occur in contexts that describe Jesus' soteriological mission and not his instruction to disciples.

5.11, 28
Luke combines Mark 1.18, 20 in 5.11. This conflation results in an emphasis on Peter and his future role, but it takes nothing away from the radical action of the men:[41] Luke inserts πάντα here and in v. 28 to make explicit what Mark implies.[42]

6.20-26
There are several reasons to distinguish 6.20 from the passages considered above that employ πτωχός. Foremost among these is the fact that the beatitude is addressed to disciples[43] at the beginning of a section of ethical instruction. Mere pronouncement is not sufficient to incur the effects of a beatitude: the hearers' conduct must conform to the description.[44] This is made clear in the present context by the command not only to hear but also to do (6.47). Thus Seccombe can document prophetic parallels to reward for the pious hope of the poor-hungry-weeping, but he is forced to admit that in this sense the fourth beatitude 'fits very badly' and that the woes force him to 'modify the initial thesis that this is simply a characterization of Israel in need of salvation ... (The passage) has begun to take on a cognitive and volitional dimension'.[45] This is confirmed by reward/ punishment allotted elsewhere in the Gospel to those who conduct themselves in the literal sense of these proclamations.[46] Therefore, whatever the original form and function of the beatitudes,[47] we cannot regard them in their present form and context as ontological, soteriological statements in the same sense as 1.52-53; 4.18; 7.22; 14.13, 21. Neither can we use them to force an ethical sense or community-consciousness into the other passages.[48]

It is important to decide precisely to whom both beatitude and woe are directed. Given that disciples are in view in 6.20-23, it is best to understand that they do not necessarily fit the fourfold description, but that they must conduct themselves in such a manner that they *will* fit the description. We noted above that Lukan beatitudes commonly have this sense. With regard to the fourth beatitude in particular, it is clear that the disciples have not yet earned the hatred of men—but they will, because their conduct as disciples will earn it.[49] Similarly, those disciples who have left all to follow Jesus (5.11, 28) certainly fit the description of the poor (and the hungry, 6.1-5), but it is doubtful that μαθητάς (v. 20a) is limited to these, since v. 17 speaks of ὄχλος πολὺς μαθητῶν.[50] Therefore, we must regard with skepticism Minear's argument that the stress on νῦν implies 'that these men have already fulfilled the demands levied against all disciples'.[51] It is best to understand νῦν as signifying the present age over against the future kingdom.[52] These factors suggest that the beatitudes are directed not only to those who already fit their description, but also to those among the great crowd of hearers (and readers) who will conform to the description.[53] Thus the beatitudes describe not a social category but a religious category whose economic manifestation is fundamental: 'to you, My disciples, poverty is a blessing, because it preserves you in your dependence on God'.[54] Rengstorf rightly remarks that

> Wenn Matthäus durch das 'im Geiste' mehr die innere Seite, Lukas mehr die äussere Seite solcher Armut hervorhebt, so nicht darum, weil es dem Einem nur auf diese, dem Andern nur auf jene ankäme.[55]

The woes in vv. 24-26 almost certainly were connected to the beatitudes prior to Luke's reception of them.[56] The audience need not be restricted to false prophets in the community,[57] since, as we noted above, the specifics listed are found in a literal sense elsewhere in the Gospel. Neither should the audience be expanded to 'outsiders', whether they be present and listening[58] or absent.[59] Verse 27 presents not a shift in audience from disciples or outsiders to 'the people'[60] but a contrast between the foregoing and subsequent types of conduct. ἀλλά introduces a contrast in action,[61] and ὑμῖν λέγω τοῖς ἀκούουσιν refers to those who hear but must also obey. 6.46-49 confirms this by distinguishing between those who hear (ἀκούων) and those who also obey (ποιεῖτε ἃ λέγω). Moreover, according to 8.21, such are *disciples* (cf. 8.11-15). The instruction that follows the woes (6.27-42) describes in detail the behavior that is antithetic to the behavior of those condemned: disciples must give, love, and show mercy. The rich and full do not give (12.21; 16.19-31); those who laugh[62] do not love (16.14-15; 11.52-54; 14.1); those who receive the praise of men do not show mercy (11.42-46; 20.46-47). Thus the woes need not be understood as addressed only to those who have already rejected Jesus. Rather, they describe the circumstances that are characteristic of rejection and by the pronunciation of woes warn against behavior that will lead to it. The woes certainly apply to those who have rejected Jesus, but their application will not be lost to those within the community who fit the description.[63] Woe to them if they do not change before it is too late. This understanding is complementary to that of the beatitudes. And as with the beatitudes, the HW, which is expressed more directly here, is fundamentally religious in nature. The rich warrant a woe because their wealth keeps them from dependence on God: instead of hoping for His kingdom (v. 20), they are mistakenly secure in their earthly reward.[64] They are addressed with ominous irony: ἀπέχετε τὴν παράκλησιν ὑμῶν (v. 24b).

6.30, 35, 38

Matt 5.42 is substantially reproduced in Luke 6.30, 35. The Lukan addition of πάντα to 6.30 and the change from Matthew's aorist δός to the present δίδου appear to generalize and sharpen the saying.[65] Verse 35 repeats the thought of Matt 5.42b. ἀπελπίζειν usually means 'despair', but it is commonly translated here as 'hope for return' despite the lack of early attestation.[66] Schwarz argues persuasively that the original read פסס, which can mean either 'doubt' or 'clap hands (in rejection)'.[67] Verse 38 is less certainly relevant to the use of wealth, since it appears in the immediate context of a warning against judging one's brother (vv. 27-42). But the repetition of δίδοτε (cf. v. 30) and the familiar concept of multiplied and/or heavenly reward for generosity (12.33; 16/11-12; 18.29-30) would undoubtedly encourage early readers to perceive here implications for economic ethics.

8.3

Luke's brief account of the support of the disciple group by several women[68] may be relevant to the view of wealth in his Gospel. The three women named, and 'many others' unnamed, are said to have served the group continuously (διηκόνουν). διακονεῖν is employed consistently by Luke to indicate table-serving,[69] but the likelihood that Luke is here borrowing from Mark 15.41 should discourage limitation to such a narrow meaning. The reader would associate the word with the common and more general sense of διακονία as 'any loving assistance rendered to the neighbor'.[70] The unlikelihood that Mary Magdalene or all of the 'many others' had substantial capital encourages a generalization of the term in this context. On the other hand, both Luke and Paul employ the word group with reference to the charitable collection.[71] This consideration carries some weight in the discernment of Luke's intention: Luke had precedent for a limited, material connotation of διακονεῖν that would allow him to understand Mark 15.41 in terms of economic provision.

Luke's addition of the phrase ἐκ τῶν ὑπαρχόντων αὐταῖς confirms the material nature of the provision.[72] ὑπάρχοντα is a 'fixed term' for 'possessions'[73] and as such may be particularly significant here. Luke uses a variety of expressions for possessions,[74] but his most common word, and that which is most characteristic of dispossession passages, is ὑπάρχοντα.[75] By the use of this word, Luke draws attention to the material, and perhaps radical, nature of the action.[76]

The precise extent of this service cannot be determined. Continual giving to such a retinue over the course of two or three years would presumably consume large amounts of capital, and we have no reason to think that the group lived frugally (5.29-35). The change from αὐτῷ (Mark 15.41) to αὐτοῖς may be intended to emphasize large-scale provision. But of course no fixed amount or percentage can be determined.

Witherington puts the passage in an historical context by documenting the contemporary practice of women supporting rabbis and their disciples with money, property, or food.[77] But Witherington's conclusion, that the passage is intended to stress sexual egalitarianism in that women are freed 'captives',[78] does not explain their service. A more mundane explanation is to be preferred. The presence of the women needed to be accounted for: they followed out of gratitude for healing (v. 2), and they stayed because they were useful (v. 3).[79] In the latter respect the passage has a message for Luke's readers, some of whom presumably were (wealthy?) women who would wonder what their role might be in the church and what their predecessors' roles had been during Jesus' earthly ministry.

8.13-14

Luke sharpens the warning against wealth indirectly in 8.13 by removing the reference to persecution. This leaves the more general word 'temptation' as the cause of apostasy. In v. 1 Luke retains μεριμνῶν . . . τοῦ βίου (cf. μέριμναι τοῦ αἰῶνος, Mark 4.19), which he uses in 21.34 in conjunction with the 'dissipation and drunkenness' that weigh men down and preclude their preparation for 'that day'. Luke then writes simply πλούτου for Mark's ἀπάτη τοῦ πλούτου. Finally, he replaces Mark's phrase περὶ τὰ λοιπά, which he uses in 12.26 to signify food and clothing, with the pejorative ἡδονῶν.[80] The effect of these changes is to make more explicit the reference to worldly prosperity. For Luke wealth does not require the ascription 'deceitful' to warrant imputation in apostasy, and ἐπιθυμίαι (Mark 4.19) have been realized in the form of ἡδονῶν. We might regard Luke's order as ascensive: worldly concerns produce riches, which produce pleasures, which preclude Christian maturity.

9.3; 10.4

Luke agrees with Matthew in prohibiting staff and sandals in his mission charges.[81] And like Matthew, he adds an explicit prohibition of money (ἀργύριον, 9.3). The result in both Lukan mission charges is essentially the same as in Mark's and Matthew's versions: proximity to the eschaton requires urgency, and credibility on the part of the messenger requires visible expressions of *Gottvertrauen*.

9.23-27; 17.28-33

Luke transmits substantially intact Mark 8.34-38. The addition of καθ᾽ ἡμέραν in the midst of an otherwise slavish reproduction of Mark 8.34-35 reveals Luke's care to stress the ongoing, as opposed to the ultimate, sacrifice of one's life.

Luke's perception of the economic implications of the passage is clearly evident in 17.28-33. Luke depicts the people of Lot's time as engaged not only in eating and drinking (cf. v. 27, Matt 24.38), but also in buying, selling, planting, and building. Luke's readers must not be like these people, who were unprepared for destruction because worldly pursuits prevented their obedience to the will of God.[82] At the critical moment they must not be so foolish as to turn back in concern for the security of their household goods or their fields (vv. 31-32).[83] So is everyone ὅς . . . ζητήσῃ τὴν ψυχὴν αὐτοῦ περιποιήσασθαι, everyone who will not ἀπολέσῃ . . . αὐτήν. Clearly, 'life' is understood here in terms of worldly goods and pursuits.

11.41

The original form and present interpretation of Luke 11.41 are subjects of some debate. Its present form may result from a misunderstanding of an Aramaic original. One variation of this view is that דכו, 'cleanse', was mistaken for זכו, 'give alms'.[84] But זכו can have either meaning, and it may not have been in current use.[85] A more attractive possibility is that עבדד צוקא, 'make right', was confused with עבדו צדקא, 'give alms'.[86] In either case, the wording of the original would approximate that of Matt 23.26.

With regard to the Lukan form of the text, there are a number of options for interpretation. τά ἐνόντα may be an adverbial accusative, 'give alms from your inner self'; an attributive accusative, 'give alms from what is within (the cup and the dish)'; or an accusative of respect, 'with respect to what is inside, give alms'.[87] The last option is to be preferred because it avoids the excessive generality of the first option[88] and the forced specificity of the second option.[89] The immediate context, which contrasts pretense with 'justice and the love of God' (v. 42), presents an appropriate setting for a command to give alms. The attitude of the heart is shown concretely by one's conduct with regard to possessions.[90] Since the saying occurs in a polemical setting, we should not place it among instructions for believers. The saying is, however, in no way inconsistent with those instructions.

12.13-21

The occasion of the Parable of the Rich Fool is a question addressed to Jesus about the division of an inheritance (vv. 13-14).[91] This verbal exchange between 'one of the multitude' and Jesus is connected to the following verses to suggest that 'there could be no dispute to bring before an arbitrator if it were not for covetousness'.[92] It is probable that the connection is Lukan. Verses 13-14 contain the non-Lukan dative αὐτῷ with verbs of speaking, whereas from v. 15 on we observe the familiar Lukan πρός with the accusative αὐτούς.[93] A number of signs of Lukan editorial work appear in v. 15. φυλάσσειν in the sense of 'guard' is unique to Luke among the Synoptics.[94] πλεονεξίας is modified by the familiar Lukan πάσης. The ambiguity of περισσεύειν[95] probably precipitates the addition of ἐκ τῶν ὑπαρχόντων to make clear that possessions are in view (cf. 8.3; 12.33).[96] Acts 4.32 contains a similar phrase, τῶν ὑπαρχόντων, preceded by the indefinite pronoun τι; and more importantly, followed by the dative αὐτῷ to signify possession. These considerations weigh against Moule's suggestion that the clumsiness of the verse is the result of a combination of two phrases: οὐκ ἐκ τῶ περισσεύειν τινὶ ἡ ζωή and οὐκ ἐκ τῶν ὑπαρχόντων τινὶ ἡ ζωή.[97]

There are nearly as many translations of the verse as there are commentators. One group stresses the fact that other things in life are more important than possessions.[98] Another nuance is that possessions will not secure one's physical life.[99] But the context demands consideration of the fuller implication of the word ζωή. Luke uses ζωή alone to indicate eternal life in Acts 3.15; 5.20; and 11.8. The sense of origination in the phrase ἔστιν ἐκ[100] is ironic, and it implies a larger sphere of comparison than the physical: no one would argue that wealth *produces* earthly life (cf. v. 23). The application of the parable in v. 21 and its parallel in v. 33 urge attention to heavenly reward. These factors suggest that a similar pun is intended here: it is not while[101] one has abundance of possessions that one has life.[102] An acceptable translation of the saying is as follows: '(it is) not while one has abundance (that) life is his—(it does not) come from his possessions'. The converse of this in the context of the chapter is that the one who dispossesses wealth has Life. Thus Derrett rightly finds implicit in the saying:

> . . . render as much as possible superfluous to you here, and dispose
> of it according to the commandments, and it will purchase for you
> a true and lasting abundance thereafter.[103]

The parable in vv. 16-20 is intended as a case in point with respect to v. 15. The view that it was originally an eschatological warning which has been subsequently moralized[104] fails to take into account the wealth of wisdom parallels portraying the futility of riches in the light of man's morality.[105] Some of these parallels extend to verbal correspondence. Especially close are 1 En 92–105 and Sir 11.18-19. The former includes the parallel expressions τὰ ὑπάρχοντα, ποιήσω μεν ποιήσω, ἀγαθά, θησαυρίζω, and the ideas of hoarding and God's judgment upon the rich.[106] The latter includes the description of rest and of others receiving the lost wealth. Each includes a soliloquy on the part of the rich. At the same time, there are significant differences between these passages and the parable before us. Both 1 En (e.g. 97.10) and Sir (σφιγγία, cf. vv. 10-11) make clear the unrighteous acquisition of the individuals in question,[107] whereas Luke's parable makes the *land* produce the wealth (v. 16) and stresses only the satisfaction of the man with the present life.[108] Conversely, the solution is in the case of 1 En to end injustice (e.g. 103.13-15) and in the case of Sir to accept one's lot (vv. 20-21), whereas Luke's parable requires an active application in terms of one's use of wealth.

In this understanding, v. 21 is an integral part of the parable. It mirrors the thought of v. 15 and anticipates v. 33. The alternative to storing the man's πολλὰ ἀγαθά (v. 19) is to give them away as alms.[109] The present tense should be preserved by translating: 'So is the one who is treasuring up for himself and is not getting rich in relation to God'.

It is difficult to determine whether or not v. 21 is a Lukan composition. Luke employs οὕτως to introduce the application of a parable in 15.7 where Matthew (18.13) lacks the adverb.[110] θησαυριζεῖν may have been taken by Luke from Matt 6.19-20/Luke 12.33.[111] The unusual phrase εἰς θεόν occurs in Acts 10.4; 20.21; and 24.15. πλουτεῖν occurs only here and in 1.53 in the Gospels.[112] None of these expressions is necessarily Lukan, and all are very natural in the context; taken together, however, they weigh in favor of Lukan composition. The effect is to bring the parable into harmony with the larger context of ch. 12, especially vv. 15 and 23.

12.22-34

In v. 22 the attention shifts from the crowd to the disciples. This is not because the disciples have already fulfilled the requirement of v. 21 (else why v. 33?),[113] but because the tradition is clearly addressed to disciples; whereas the audience of vv. 13-21 is determined by the occasion which is set out in vv. 13-14. It would be understood that disciples heard and were expected to obey all of the ethical instruction spoken by Jesus, whether they were the sole, primary, or secondary audience. The retention of διὰ τοῦτο preserves a connection identical to that of Matt 6.25: you cannot serve God and Mammon/you cannot be rich toward God and toward yourself; therefore, do not be anxious, etc.

Luke sharpens the force of the passage in several places. Verse 26 underlines the thought of the previous sentence (v. 25, cf. Matt 6.27) with another reference to the triviality of food, drink, and clothing (περὶ τῶν λοιπῶν).[114] In v. 30 ἁπάντων is removed: the Father does not know that you need *all* these things. Likewise in v. 31 πάντα (Matt 6.33) is removed: not *all* these things will be yours as well. Just as elsewhere Luke wished, by the inclusion of πᾶς, to bring attention to the radical extent of *giving*; so here he wishes, by its omission, to deemphasize the idea of *receiving* in this life. πλὴν in v. 31 is probably editorial;[115] its effect is to present an explicit alternative, of seeking the kingdom, to worldly seeking of 'these things' (v. 30). Verse 32, which is probably not Lukan,[116] restates vv. 29-31, but promises only the kingdom, not 'these things'.

The climax of the passage for Luke is a reworked version of Matt 6.19-21 which he places in v. 33.[117] The command, πωλήσατε τὰ ὑπάρχοντα ὑμῶν καὶ δότε ἐλεημοσύνην, makes explicit what Matt 6.20 (and Luke 12.1) implies: the proper alternative to hoarding and worry over possessions is dispossession and distribution to the poor. The aorist tenses are a common feature of the Lukan commands and narratives pertaining to dispossession.[118] The significance of this feature warrants consideration. The contexts in which the aorist is used stress the decisiveness of the action, whereas the contexts in which the imperfect is used emphasize the provision for the recipients of the action,[119] and the contexts in which the present is used emphasize the contrast in character between the recommended action and the disparaged action.[120] None of these tenses excludes the idea of a sudden and complete action, but neither do they require it: even the aorist can denote 'a series or aggregate of acts viewed as constituting a single fact'.[121] In the present context, the idea of contrast between worldly and heavenly seeking produces the present tense in vv. 21, 30-31; whereas the culminating imperative of v. 33 requires the decisive sense of the aorist.

14.12-24

Luke's Parable of the Great Banquet has parallels in the Gospel of Thomas (Logion 64) and in Matt 25.1-14. The master in Thomas sends his new call to 'those whom you happen to meet (in the streets)', and Matthew's master instructs his servant to go 'to the thoroughfares, and invite to the marriage feast as many as you find'. Here Luke's version is strikingly specific, in that the new call goes out to 'the poor and maimed and blind and lame' (v. 21). We must ask why this list is given and in what relation it stands to the apparently ethical import of vv. 12-14.

Since the other versions of the parable lack the list, and there is no good reason for Matthew to have omitted it, it is probable that Luke or his source inserted it in the interest of internal harmony. Examination of the vocabulary provides support for this view. ἀνάπηρος occurs only here in the NT. χωλούς occurs only here and in 7.22 (cf. Acts 3.2; 8.7; 14.8). τυφλούς is used following Q in 6.39; 7.22; 18.35 (cf. 7.21; Acts 13.11); and in 4.18. πτωχούς occurs here and in 4.18; 7.22. Conversely, the list in v. 21 includes all the constituents of 7.22 except the deaf and dead, who could not hear a call to a banquet until their circumstances changed, and lepers, who were isolated until they experienced cleansing. The striking similarities between v. 21 and the summary of Jesus' mission in 7.22 demand that the passage be understood primarily in terms of soteriology.

This understanding introduces a problem with regard to vv. 12-14. It is difficult to imagine that two proximal and identical lists must be understood so differently: that in v. 13 primarily in a literal, material sense, and that in v. 21 primarily in a figurative, spiritual sense.[122] Given the similarity of the lists to 7.22, however, it is likely that the list in v. 13 is derived from,[123] or at least sets the stage for, the parable. The action recommended to the host is similar in many respects to Jesus' teaching elsewhere: earthly reward is subtly disparaged (cf. 6.24); unlimited generosity is commanded (cf. 6.30, 35, 38); and heavenly remuneration is promised (cf. 12.33). But in two respects the dissimilarity of the passage should signal the reader that this is not just another bit of advice about the use of wealth: the setting is polemical, and the saying clearly echoes 7.22. Furthermore, vv. 15-16 make it clear that the parable has a direct connection to vv. 12-14, and the only point of connection in either form or content is the fourfold list. For these reasons, we must view the function of vv.12-14 as primarily a foreshadowing of the following parable.

In its original context, the parable may have been a midrash on Deut 20.5-7.[124] But the excuses of those invited correspond only very roughly to those given for non-participation in a holy war, and neither a war nor a king is mentioned.[125] In this context, it is better to regard the excuses as recalling or dependent on passages like 8.14; 9.57-62; 17.28-33; etc. There can be little doubt that the excuses center on worldly concerns: the ties of business and family.[126] In other words, those who are excluded are those who are unwilling to obey Jesus' call to sever ties to possessions and family. Despite the polemical setting of the parable, this element would not be lost to Luke's readers.

The primary thrust of the passage is against those who are excluded. Verses 1, 4, 6, 7, 12 and 16 all contain clear indications of mutual antagonism between Jesus and his present audience. The parable concludes with a pronouncement of judgment on the group (v. 24). The teaching of vv. 1-14 provides the specific setting for that rejection. This audience puts restrictions upon mercy (vv. 1-6). This audience exalts itself (vv. 7-11). This audience prefers reciprocity to charity (vv. 12-14). In short, this audience values earthly attachments over heavenly rewards. Therefore, they will be excluded from heaven, and the very people they undervalue will be included.[127] Thus the group in vv. 13, 21 functions primarily as a foil to the guests who hear the parable and find themselves described in it. The ethical implications of vv. 12-14 and vv. 18-20 are subordinate constituents of the argument.

14.25-35

The precise meaning of 14.33 and the relation of the verse to the previous parable have not been explained adequately by commentators. As potentially the strongest dispossession command in the Synoptics, the verse and its context demand careful consideration.

The commands in vv. 26-27, 33 share the unique and formulaic οὐ δύναται εἶναί μου μαθητής. The order and content of these sayings generate several important affirmations. The missing reference to possessions in v. 26 (cf. Mark 10.29) is supplied by v. 33; together, the verses delineate the demands of discipleship which are repeated throughout the Gospel and summarized in vv. 26b-27 (cf. 9.23-25). Since v. 33 is a specific restatement of that more general command, the parables in vv. 28-32 can serve as ground of both v. 27 (γάρ, v. 28) and v. 33 (οὖν).

The parables of vv. 28-32 require a new explanation. The majority of commentators rightly regard the tower builder and king as Jesus' audience: τίς . . . ἐξ ὑμῶν (v. 28) is clearly parallel to πᾶς ἐξ ὑμῶν (v. 33).[128] οὕτως at the beginning of v. 33 makes it doubly clear that the listeners are expected to identify with the protagonists of the parables. But interpreters wrongly refer all the way back to v. 32a and v. 28b—'counting the cost'—as the conduct to be emulated. Thus the explanation of the passage usually takes the form, 'Do not act without mature consideration, for a thing half done is worse than a thing never begun'.[129] This understanding contradicts the notion of decisive action associated with discipleship elsewhere in the Gospel, and it requires that the reader supply a great deal of material between vv. 32 and 33 if any sense is to be made of the connection. Jülicher is closer to an acceptable understanding when he stresses the necessity in both parables to sacrifice all in order to complete a task.[130] But Wellhausen rightly responds that the opposite action is urged in v. 33: instead of committing all of one's resources to the task, one must abandon one's resources.[131]

The key to a proper understanding of the passage is to be found in two elements of the parables. The first is the word δύνατος in v. 31 (cf. ἔχει, v. 29), which, as the only linguistic connection to vv. 26-27, 33, indicates that the idea of ability with respect to resources is common to the parables and their applications. The second element is the inference of failure connected to both parabolic endeavors (vv. 29, 32): both inividuals suffer when their resources prove to be inadequate.[132] The connection of this thought to the parables is made clear when we state the converse of vv. 26-27, 33: whoever remains dependent on his own (inadequate) resources cannot be my disciple. Luke puts forward a similar argument in 17.28-33: ties to family and possessions preclude readiness for the judgment day; whoever attempts to preserve these things will lose the kingdom. Similarly, 12.16-34 and 16.9-12 urge disciples to dispense with possessions because they are inadequate—indeed, encumbering—given the exigencies of the present situation. In the present context, this means that the reference of οὕτως in v. 33 is not to the beginnings of the parables, which depict cost-counting, but to the endings, which depict mockery and surrender. The argument, in summary form, is this:

> As tower-building with inadequate materials results in mockery, and as war-making with inadequate troops results in surrender, so retention of inadequate means of security results in exclusion from the kingdom.

Careful consideration beforehand is not excluded, but it does not involve calculation of the cost. Rather, it involves reflection on the realities of the situation until one comes to the point of decision and response, as in v. 35b. The half-hearted, the hearer who will not do, the one who comes to me but will not obey my words, is like salt without its saltness. Consider this well, and act accordingly.

Examination of v. 33 makes clear the radical nature of the command. Of first importance is the unusual verb ἀποτάσσεται. We observed above the use of the verb by Philo in two passages that urge renunciation of earthly goods;[133] in other contexts he employs the verb in the middle voice to denote separation from persons or things.[134] Josephus employs the verb in the middle voice three times, each of which carry the connotation 'reject' or 'part from'.[135] Of greater significance is the sole instance of ἀποτάσσεται in the LXX, Eccl 2.20:

καὶ ἐπέστρεψα ἐγὼ τοῦ ἀποτάξασθαι τῇ καρδίᾳ μου ἐπὶ παντὶ τῷ μόχθῳ, ᾧ ἐμόχθησα ὑπὸ τὸν ἥλιον

The verse not only includes the concept of departing from old ways but also presents a parallel to the structure of the Lukan passage. Eccl 2.20 restates 2.18, where the wording is:

καὶ ἐμίσησα ἐγὼ σὺν πάντα μόχθον μου, ὅν ἐγὼ μοχθῶ ὑπὸ τὸν ἥλιον

μισεῖ in Luke 14.26 can only imply the 'leaving behind' of family (cf. Mark 10.28-30; Luke 18.29);[136]and there is no reason to suppose that ἀποτάσσεται implies anything less with regard to possessions. Additional support may be gained from a consideration of ἀποτασσεῖν elsewhere in the NT. The word occurs five times, always in the middle voice, and in each instance an individual leaves another individual or group.[137] Luke 9.61 is especially significant because it is parallel in thought to 14.26, adding weight to the argument that Mark 10.28-30 elucidates the commands in Luke 14.26-33.

The tense of ἀποτάσσεται is an important element in the verse. Marshall asserts that 'the disciple must be continually ready (present tense) to give up all that he has'.[138] There are several reasons to reject this interpretation. The close parallels in structure, wording, and tense between vv. 26-27 and v. 33 prohibit a shift in the meaning of the tense. Need one only be continually *ready* to 'bear his own cross and come after'? An aoristic present is the best understanding of the tense. The context, which depicts crowds as 'accompanying' and 'coming to' Jesus but not following him in discipleship, requires 'a punctiliar act taking place at the moment of speaking'.[139] The use of the aorist in 5.11, 28; 9.61; 12.33; etc., lends further support to this view. The conative present comes closest to the idea of willingness or readiness, but even this function of the tense implies intent toward realization.[140] ἀποτάσσεται, therefore, is properly translated simply 'leave behind'. This translation conveys the concreteness required by the context and the similar commands and narratives elsewhere in the Gospel.

The phrase πᾶσιν τοῖς ἑαυτοῦ ὑπάρχουσιν should likewise be translated to reflect the concrete connotation of the vocabulary. Luke uses ὑπάρχοντα consistently to indicate possessions.[141] He employs πᾶσιν here to give emphasis to the radical extent of the command, as in 5.11, 28; 6.30; and 18.22. Clearly, then, 14.33 cannot be taken as an abstract summary of vv. 26-27 that calls for renunciation of 'self'.[142]

The elements of Lukan vocabulary in v. 33 suggest that the verse and its connection to the parables are redactional.[143] The connection is not untrue to the sense of the parable, nor are the demands of vv. 26-27, 33 unduly creative. It is only the separation of v. 33 from v. 26 and its placement as the culmination of the passage that mark the whole as evidence of Luke's own interest in the relation between wealth and discipleship.

16.1-13

The great amount of discussion that has centered on the conduct of the steward and the praise of the master need not detain us long in our enquiry as to the meaning of vv. 9-13. Whoever describes the steward's action in v. 8a,[144] and whatever the steward did,[145] he acted well by wordly standards. Thus he is not called ἄδικος, but τῆς ἀδικίας. In other words, he belongs to the world.[146] The fact that his action was in the economic sphere legitimizes the connection of the parable to the following verses. Verses 9-13 do not contain features of Lukan thought or vocabulary that require a supposition of creation on his part. On the contrary, they convey peculiarly semitic thoughts and vocabulary, which suggests that Luke found them in substantially their present form and perhaps in their present context.[147]

Although v. 9 is clearly derived from v. 4, its meaning is obscure until its constituent elements are explained. This very obscurity is an argument both for an original connection with vv. 1-8 and for an early attachment of the clarifying vv. 10-13. Together, the verses constitute yet another instance of teleological devaluation.

The phrase ἑαυτοῖς ποιήσατε φίλους opens the admonition. Although we are not told in the parable that the steward actually made friends with his master's debtors, the inference is clear enough in v. 4. His conduct with that which is entrusted to him is that which constitutes friend-making. The focus is precisely upon his action, not upon the recipients of his action. Thus there is no reason to allegorize φίλους as the recipients of alms[148] or as the alms themselves.[149] Indeed, there is no mention of alms in the entire passage. This important point has been overlooked by commentators, who assume the meaning 'use' where the verb and the context require the meaning 'act'. Since the focus of the parable is upon the steward's action (τι ποιήσω). φίλους, in the context of recommended action with a trust, can only refer to God himself.[150]

The qualifying phrase τῆς ἀδικίας attached to μαμωνᾶ recalls the identical phrase in v. 8a used to describe the steward. Both steward and mammon belong to 'this age', both are 'of darkness' (v. 8b). Mammon is opposed to that which is 'much' (v. 10); to that which is 'true' (v. 11); to that which is 'yours' (v. 12); indeed, to God himself (v. 13). Therefore, it can scarcely be limited to ill-gotten gain in v. 9.[151] ἀδικία in this context is not a juridical or ethical category, but a religious-theological category: mammon is an element of this world.[152] Especially convincing in this regard is the fact that τῷ ἀδίκῳ μαμωνᾷ in v. 11 is contrasted not to τὸ δίκαιον or to τὸ ἀγαθόν, but to τὸ ἀληθινόν.

Degenhardt explains that ὅταν ἐκλίπῃ can refer either to the time when mammon runs out, the time of death, or the time when the world ends.[153] The last two options are to be preferred, since both find parallels in similar passages.[154]

There can be little doubt that the phrase δέξωνται ... σκηνάς signifies the heavenly reward promised by God for obedience.[155] It may be that σκηνάς (cf. οἴκους, v. 4) is a Lukan touch, since God 'does not dwell in houses (κατοικεῖ) made with hands' (Acts 7.48), but in heaven (ὁ οὐρανός, v. 49).

The argument of the passage is this:

> As a prudent man of the world will act in a critical impermanent situation with that which has been entrusted to him in order to gain lasting benefits, so you must act now with the wealth which has been put into your hands in order to gain reward from God in the age to come.

Ernst remarks that

> was 12, 33 offen ausgesprochen wurde ('verkauft euren Besitz und gebt Almosen'), wird hier nur hintergründig, aber trotzdem unmissverständlich angedeutet.[156]

And Degenhardt remarks that

> er eigentlich keine Anweisung für eine kluge Verwendung des Besitzes gibt; sein Wort zielt vielmehr auf ein kluges Sich-Freimachen vom Mammon, der Hindernis ist für den ungeteilten Dienst des Jüngers (vgl. 16, 13).[157]

The emphasis here is on dispossession, not charity. If the point were simply to use money wisely, or to give alms from part of one's possessions, wealth would not be so graphically described as an impermanent trust and characterized by the words 'unrighteous', 'little', 'another's', and 'hated/despised'.[158]

Verses 10-13 should not be considered apart from the parable and its application. The sayings may have circulated independently at one time,[159] but they possess a connection to the parable itself and not merely to v. 9 and the catchword 'mammon'.[160] All of these sayings can be understood as extrapolations from the parable in business terminology. Verses 10-11 argue that small successes earn greater responsibilities; v. 12 affirms that the good manager will be rewarded; and v. 13 describes the impossibility of working well for two employers. The compilation is certainly reasonable in this context, whether or not it is original.

The faithfulness described in vv. 10-11 with regard to wealth can only be understood in light of passages like 12.21, 33; 14.33; 18.22, which speak of treasure in heaven as the reward for dispossession. The equivalent expression here is τὸ ἀληθινόν.

The usual explanation of v. 12 involves the assumption that τῷ ἀλλοτρίῳ refers to wealth that is held on trust from God.[161] If this is the case, we must acknowledge that God loans that which is consistently disparaged in the context. It may be inferred from this difficulty that wealth is unrighteous only in that it belongs to this age as opposed to the new age. But it may also be possible to view τῷ ἀλλοτρίῳ as a reference to Satan, in the sense of 4.6. In this view, wealth is more consistently and directly opposed to God. In either view, the argument is the same: if you conduct yourself properly with regard to wealth in this life, God will give you wealth in the life to come.

Verse 13 corresponds almost verbatim to Matt 6.24. οἰκέτης is probably a Lukan addition, and it fits well in the context,[162] both of the parable and of the following verses. His version makes more explicit the fact that everyone has a master.[163]

16.14-31

The story of the Rich Man and Lazarus begins not at v. 19 but at v. 14.[164] Here the attention shifts from the disciples, who are the recipients of the teaching in vv. 1-13 (v. 1), to the Pharisees, against whom the following parable is told.[165]

Although vv. 14-15 set the stage for the following story, they must be understood in light of the previous passage: it was when they heard (ἤκουον) that they mocked him. In this context, the alternative to φιλάργυρια cannot be inner detachment: vv. 1-13 disparage wealth in order to urge dispossession, and v. 13 makes 'hate' the alternative to 'love' with regard to Mammon. These men would hardly scoff at an admonition to charity or philosophical detachment. It is the radical nature of the teaching that they reject.

The connection of v. 15 to the preceding passage has been overlooked by commentators who shift the condemnation of the Pharisees' activity from the love of money to pride.[166] This shift is unwarranted. Verse 15a makes reference to the attitude of the heart, which is inextricably bound to conduct in 12.34: those who amass and value earthly treasure show that their heart and their reward are not in heaven. Verse 15 affirms a startling reversal of human values directed at this hostile audience. Both sides of the formula are important. *Pride* is not exalted among men: men become proud because they are identified with something that men exalt. It is clear that in this context, wealth is that which is exalted (φιλ-, v. 14), loved and served (v. 13). These people justify themselves by tithing and making displays of charity (11.42; 18.11-12; 21.1), but they do not depend on God. The second part of the formula is equally telling. βδέλυγμα is consistently used in the context of idolatry in the OT.[167] This connotation fits perfectly with v. 13, which makes the servant of mammon an idolater by personifying wealth as an alternative master to God. These men show by their rejection of Jesus' teaching that they are such idolaters. They hear (ἤκουον, v. 14) but they will not do—they will not be faithful with regard to possessions. Commentators have overlooked a striking parallel in T Jud 18-19 which affirms this connection. In 18.2 the reader is warned to 'beware . . . of fornication, and the love of money (φιλαργυρίας)', because the one who serves them 'is a slave (δουλεύων) to two contrary passions, and cannot obey God' (18.6). The writer goes on to declare that 'the love of money leadeth to idolatry; because, when led astray through money, men name as gods those who are no gods . . .' 16.15, then, is perhaps the strongest statement of hostility to wealth in the Gospels.

Given the integral relation between this introduction and the preceding teaching about the use of wealth, the reader cannot miss the ethical implications of the story itself. The lesson behind the story is manifested in the description of the character *following* ethical instruction, as in 12.15-20; 14.7-24; and 18.9-14. The story is a case in point of the condemnation of the mammon-serving

Pharisees.[168] For this reason, and not because the story depicts a simple role reversal,[169] we look in vain for an explicit reference to the justice imperative in the rich man's condemnation. Certainly lack of care for Lazarus is part of his condemnation, but only part: his lifestyle would not be altered appreciably by raising Lazarus from the dust. There is little question that the rich man, and not Lazarus, is the focal point here.[170] The rich man is described at the outset of the story; he engages in conversation with Abraham as Lazarus recedes into a third-party, background role; and he received the final pronouncement of judgment. When Lazarus is on the scene, he serves as a foil to the rich man. He may represent pious Jews, or even Gentiles,[171] who will be included in the kingdom rather than the Pharisees. In any case, his 'merit' is implied by his poverty as in 4.18; 7.22; 14.13, 21.[172] He depends on God for his salvation, and he receives his heavenly reward for this dependence (vv. 22a, 25).

The rich man is graphically described as one who eats, drinks, and is merry (v.19; cf. 12.19); as one who has many goods (τὰ ἀγαθά, v. 25; cf. 12.18-19); and as one who has received comfort in life (παρακαλεῖται, v. 25; cf. 6.24).[173] These allusions to what has gone before alert the reader to the rich man's foolish complacency. His circumstances are those which are exalted among men (cf. 7.25), but as long as his riches are his own and not God's, they are an abomination. The repentance envisaged in vv. 27-31 involves turning from this life of careless autonomy to one of dependence on God. Thus the story is primarily a warning to the godless rich;[174] or perhaps, given the polemical setting from v. 14 onward and the inclusion of the poor (cf. 14.21), it signifies that for this audience it is too late.[175] In either case, Luke's readers could ignore neither the polemical blow to opponents nor the ethical sting to themselves.

The vocabulary of the passage and its use of the historical present mark it as pre-Lukan.[176] Elements of the story are derived from well-known folk material,[177] but there is no reason to suppose direct dependence on or between such sources. Like the Rich Fool, the surprise in the afterlife was a common enough theme for adaptation. Our attention to this version of the story in its present context reveals it as an illustration in a polemical format of the sayings that precede it.

18.18-30

Luke makes a number of changes in the story of the rich ruler that are worthy of note. First among these is the change from γονυπετήσας

(Mark 10.17) to ἄρχων. Luke often uses ἄρχων of rulers of the Pharisees, who are seen in a negative light. This suggests that the insertion here is a polemical touch.[178] The contrast to Zacchaeus, a *chief* tax collector (ἀρχιτελώνας, 19.1), adds to this impression,[179] as does the omission of ἠγάπησεν αὐτόν (Mark 10.21). The fact that he obeys the commandments does not make him more estimable: the tax collector in the preceding parable does not, nor does the tax collector in the subsequent narrative.

Luke sharpens the command in v. 22 by adding πάντα. The change from δός (Mark 10:21) to διάδος in conformity with Acts 4.32, 35 shows that the command is intended for a wider audience than the individual to whom it is directed here.[180] The similarity of the command to 12.33, which is clearly directed to all disciples, strengthens this impression.

In v. 23, Luke changes Mark's ἔχων κτήματα πολλά to πλούσιος σφόδρα. This conforms better to v. 25, and it may also be intended as an allusion backward to 6.24, or forward to 19.1.

Luke, like Matthew, streamlines Mark in vv. 24-27. But he goes further than Matthew by removing any reference to the disciples. This is consistent with the polemical form given to the passage by Luke. He is careful not to imply that the disciples themselves are rich—indeed, they cannot be (14.33). Instead, he brings them into the scene at v. 28 as examples of the kind of conduct recommended for all readers.

Given Luke's preference for the word πᾶς, its replacement with τὰ ἴδια in v. 28 is remarkable. The reader knows from 5.28 that Peter and others left πάντα. It is possible that this change, like that in v. 22, is made in conformity to Acts 4.32.[181] The expression connotes ownership,[182] not 'homes' (RSV), and it may be that Luke recognized the insignificance of πάντα in the same context as v. 22. The effect is to avoid making Peter, who is presented as an example, look ridiculous: 'The ruler would not leave all his great wealth, but we have left what we owned—will this do?'[183]

Luke, like Matthew, reduces Mark 10.29-30 to a single list of items to be given up. His addition of γυναῖκα adds a measure of severity, while his omission of ἀγρούς removes a like measure. The latter is especially surprising given Acts 4.34. Luke may have regarded it as awkward here at the end of the list and considered οἰκίαν sufficient to convey the idea of property. Alternatively, as his reduction of Mark 10.30 suggests, he may have wished to de-materialize the list in order to preclude material expectation with regard to 'manifold more in this time'.[184]

19.1-10

Zacchaeus is quickly labelled as one for whom salvation is possible only by an act of God (18.27): he is πλουσίος.[185] Verse 8 is clear evidence that the possibility involves not only belief in Jesus but also conduct with regard to possessions. The passage sums up several of the major themes of the Gospel;[186] it is important, therefore, to consider carefully what it conveys to Luke's readers concerning the disposition of possessions.

Zacchaeus's resolution in v. 8 is stated in the present tense not because he is in the habit of doing this[187] but because he suddenly resolves to do this in the future or from this point onward.[188] Thus the tense carries a futuristic or aoristic sense. The conditional clause, εἴ τίνος τι ἐσυκοφάντησα, 'does not put the fact of extortion in doubt, but its extent'.[189] Both the amount given to the poor and the amounts given in restitution exceed the limits of Jewish piety.[190] The reader would scarcely conclude that 'Zacchaeus remains materially in a comparable situation to where he began'.[191] He retains half not in order to possess it but in order to make restitution.[192] Thus there is no implicit limit on charity but simply a balance between charity and equity. Those who had been defrauded would hardly be impressed by an action of repentance that bypassed justice to them for the sake of the poor alone. There is no way to determine what Zacchaeus would retain after making restitution; however, if we estimate that only one denarius in ten of his income was fraudulent, and allow but another one denarius for his own maintenance, five denarii in donations plus fourfold restitution of the fraudulent denarius would leave him with nothing. We should hardly expect Zacchaeus to calculate so precisely, much less to project a remainder sufficient to sustain his accustomed lifestyle. The point is his dramatic resolution. Nevertheless, it is not unreasonable to conclude that 'if he carries through, he will no longer have the status, possessions or identity of the rich'.[193]

Although the story contains many elements of Lukan vocabulary and style, there are no compelling reasons to deny its basic historicity.[194] We do not know that Zacchaeus immediately or ultimately became a disciple, but neither do we know that the rich ruler in 18.18-23 was asked to become one. In any case, given the obvious contrast between the two stories and the similarity of action and reward in them, Luke's readers would probably perceive the two stories as examples of 18.9-14: what the law-abiding ruler will not do when asked, the scorned tax-collector does willingly. He humbles himself, and he is exalted. But considered only on its own merits, the story of Zacchaeus would undoubtedly communicate the integral relation between salvation and conduct with regard to possessions.

19.11-27
Luke's Parable of the Pounds is a reworked version of Matthew's Parable of the Talents, stressing Jesus' role as king.[195] Within this context, it is evident that stewardship of possessions is a fundamental criterion for judgment: 19.17 is an unmistakable echo of 16.10-11.[196]

21.1-4
Luke's redaction of the story of the Widow's Offering reveals his care to stress the contrast between disobedience and obedience with regard to possessions. Here it is not a crowd *and* the rich who make donations (Mark 12.41) but only the rich. Luke suppresses the large amount of their gifts (πολλά, Mark 12.41) even though in Mark this feature sets up a neat contrast to the λεπτὰ δύο of the widow. This may be due to Luke's portrayal elsewhere of the rich as hoarders: he did not want their gifts here to be confused with the dispossession of Zacchaeus. This contrast is heightened in a subtle manner in v. 4, where Luke adds τὰ δῶρα. The contrast is now not only between 'abundance' and 'lack' but also between 'their gifts' and 'her whole life'. With this change, Luke distinguishes between charity and dispossession. Finally, Luke joins Mark's concluding phrases, ὅσα εἶχεν ... ὅλον τὸν βίον, to form πάντα τὸν βίον ὅν εἶχεν. Since Luke commonly employs βίος as a designation for possessions,[197] he sees no need to leave Mark's two phrases in apposition.

22.35-36
To suppose that Luke 22.35-36 rescinds all the teaching considered above for the age of the Church[198] is to transform the Gospel of Luke into the Myth of Sisyphus. As enigmatic as the passage may be, it is clear from vv. 37-38 that the focal point is the sword and the *immediate* situation. If the intent were to convey an order for the coming open-ended period of time, Luke could have written ἀπὸ τοῦ

νῦν as in vv. 18, 69, and elsewhere.[199] It is hard to imagine that future missionaries were to travel without a mantle.[200] Clearly, then, the intent is not to alter the gear of missionaries, but to depict the utter urgency of the situation. Plummer suggests that v. 36 advocates the use of the purse or bag to buy a sword; and the one who has no purse or bag should sell his mantle to buy a sword.[201] Another plausible explanation is that the dual command produces evidence of disobedience on the part of the disciples: instead of trusting in God's provision, they possess money and weapons to ensure their personal security.[202] In either case, the question, 'Did you lack anything?' in v. 33 is ironic: in the first view, they lacked in their moment of joy what will signal their moment of despair; in the second view, they reveal now that their memory of God's provision is short-lived. The precise meaning of the passage is not clear, but there is ample reason to reject the view that it comprises an exception to the teaching about possessions elsewhere in the Gospel.

Conclusion
Consideration of Lukan passages relevant to the subject of HW can be summarized in the following statements:

1. Luke transmits Markan/Q material expressive of or sympathetic to teleological devaluation in 4.5-8; 5.11, 28; 6.20-21, 30, 35; 8.14; 9.3/10.4; 9.23-26; 12.22-33; 16.13; 18.18-30; 21.1-4.
2. Luke's Gospel includes similar unique material in 6.24-25, 38; 12.13-31; 14.18-20; 16.1-12, 14-15, 19-31; 17.28-33; 19.1-10.
3. Luke appears to intensify the tradition in 4.5-8; 5.11, 28; 6.30; 8.3, 14; 12.15, 21, 26, 30-33, 45; 14.33; 18.22; 19.17; 21.1-4.
4. Material unique to Luke's Gospel has parallels in earlier semitic wisdom material.
5. Luke's Gospel does not contain rescission or mitigation of the tradition.

As in Mark and Matthew, we observe little evidence of sympathy for the poor as such an no clear indication of the socio-economic circumstances of Luke's audience or of the situation described. The statements listed above evince Luke's active interest in communicating, in a consistent manner, dispossession of wealth as a way of expressing *Gottvertrauen*. Moreover, in conjunction with the similar conclusions regarding Mark and Matthew, Luke's Gospel confirms the consistent expression of HW in the Synoptics.

CONCLUSION

The summary statements of each chapter and the argument of the three sections can now be drawn together and reviewed in terms of the thesis statement. Following that, several remarks will be offered concerning the relation of the tradition to the Synoptic situation and to the rest of the NT.

The two-stage critique of recent sociological treatments called into question both the prevalent reading of the historical evidence and certain applications of sociological method. In Chapter 1 it was argued that evidence of general economic conditions, taxation, population, natural disasters, and social stratification presents a more positive, or at least less certain, picture of early first-century conditions than is often supposed. Early Christian social constituency was mixed, and the evidence does not suggest primary membership or influence on the part of lower classes. In Chapter 2 a narrow chronological scope of enquiry, the broad category of relative deprivation, and the use of a millenarian model were viewed as serious obstacles to an accurate description of the situation. For these reasons, the efforts of the sociologist-theologians were rejected as adequate explanations of the Synoptic HW phenomenon.

In Part II, we surveyed critical evaluation of wealth from the hypothetical origin of social justice in a primitive economy to the written material of the NT period. Five logically sequential stages were distinguished to denote different levels of severity. The tradition develops and finds expression in the writings of established, upper-class groups during periods of calm and prosperity. It occurs primarily in wisdom material, and it has a religious-ethical orientation. It is distinct from apocalyptic predictions of economic reversal and from interest in, or self-designation as, the poor. These considerations support the view that HW has a history and function independent of socio-economic circumstances.

In Part III, we observed the continuity between the HW tradition in semitic religious-ethical material and in the synoptic Gospels. Evidence was presented to support the contention that teleological devaluation is consistently expressed both within and between Mark, Matthew, and Luke.

Thesis

Together, the three sections warrant the conclusion that *hostility to wealth exists independently of socio-economic circumstances as a fundamental religious-ethical tenet consistently expressed in the Synoptic Gospels.*

Based on the descriptive evidence presented in defense of the thesis statement, it may be possible to reconstruct the situation in which the tradition appears without reliance upon its socio-economic context.

A religious-ethical HW tradition is evident in many pre-Synoptic sources, and there can be no doubt that elements of this tradition were familiar to Jesus' audience. We might speculate that Jewish groups on the fringes of that element of the culture which would ultimately voice a more favorable view of wealth preserved and advanced this tradition. Given the presence of the tradition in aristocratic sources and in Philo, a case might be made for involvement on the part of Sadducees or another group influenced by Hellenistic philosophical notions. The rabbinic writings suggest that the tradition may have found support even among the Pharisees. But whatever their party alignment may have been, it is certain that the group would have claimed implicit OT support in stressing the relation of wealth to obedience. They would scorn the spiritual autonomy and social pride with which wealth had come to be equated. Their opponents, on the other hand, also claiming implicit OT support, regarded wealth as a sign of favor from God and thereby justified their token and highly visible charity. At the same time, they claimed for themselves the appellation 'Poor' by virtue of their domination by Gentiles, and they promised themselves booty at the expense of their enemies. Righteousness they assumed; revenge they craved. This mindset finds explicit expression in apocalyptic and Qumran material; elements of it appear in contemporary Jewish material and in anti-Pharisaic Synoptic polemics.

Into this scene, or some variation of it, came a teacher who offered an unusual and dramatic challenge to these ideas. By demanding dispossession as a way to express dependence on God and by promising other-worldly reward for the righteous, he dealt in a radical manner with contemporary abuses of OT imagery and ethics.

Whether or not this reconstruction is precisely accurate, there can be no doubt that the teaching is 'situation-specific'. But to speak of that situation in terms of political and economic factors is to force too much upon the document and the teacher whom it describes. The situation, for Jesus, is the state of the human heart.

The tradition appealed to members of various strata of society, perhaps for very different reasons. Members of the lower classes might find in the teaching a justification of their own existence; members of the middle classes might see it as an expression of conservative national solidarity over against the values of Hellenistic civilization; and members of the upper classes might view it as a profound expression of self-reflective cynicism.[1] We must also reckon with the possibility that the tradition and the personality behind it were compelling in and of themselves. Indeed, it is tempting to speculate that, deprived of the powerful and exemplary presence of Jesus himself, disciples were less and less likely to practice dispossession[2] but no less likely to preserve and approve the teaching. The contemporary example of the followers of Mahatma Gandhi presents some interesting parallels in this regard.[3]

This reconstruction of the situation presented in the Synoptics is necessary speculative, but it affirms the plausibility of an explanation that takes into account both the immediate and general historical situation without sacrificing the timeless religious-ethical import of the material. Weber, in refuting the notion that the Synoptic material is a product of economic resentment, concludes that

> the need for salvation and ethical religion has yet another source besides the social condition of the disprivileged and the rationalism of the middle classes, which are products of their way of life. This additional factor is intellectualism as such, more particularly the metaphysical needs of the human mind as it is driven to reflect on ethical and religious questions, driven not by a material need but by an inner compulsion to understand the world as a meaningful cosmos and to take up a position toward it.[4]

An attempt has been made throughout to limit the discussion to descriptions of events and passages directly relevant to the Synoptic Gospels. This is not only in the interest of space but also in the interest of accuracy. Efforts to harmonize the writings of Paul, or even the book of Acts, with the tradition in Mark, Matthew, and Luke force spiritualizations and inconsistencies upon the Gospels. The method and conclusions presented in this study, on the contrary, suggest disparity between the Synoptics and the rest of the NT. The notion of a late or independent development is refuted by the presence of this disparity between, in particular, Luke and Acts.

The accounts in Acts of the life or the community (2.44-45; 4.32-5.11, 6.1), the charity of individuals (10.2, 4, 31), and the Pauline collection (11.28-30; 24.17; cf. Gal 2.10; Rom 15.26, etc.) differ fundamentally in purpose and extent from the tradition described in the third Gospel.

Still, the NT is not without evidence of the tradition outside the Synoptics. Curiously, it is from Paul, whose near silence on the subject of economic ethics constitutes the most noticeable disparity, that we gather the earliest and most specific evidence of the HW tradition. We referred above to the possibility that 2 Cor 8.9 represents an extra-Synoptic tradition that Jesus himself dispossessed wealth. A still earlier and more direct reference to dispossession is 1 Cor 13.3. Paul in this context compares six activities disfavourably to love: tongues of men, tongues of angels, prophecy, faith, dispossession (φωμίσω πάντα τὰ ὑπάρχοντα μου), and martyrdom.[5] All of these activities except dispossession are praised or recommended by Paul elsewhere.[6] This suggests that dispossession was not a negatively regarded foil (e.g. a Jewish or pagan practice); rather, it was an activity, like the others listed, that was sufficiently familiar and highly-regarded to serve as a standard of comparison even to love. We might also infer from this account that since dispossession is here paired with martyrdom, it was by the early 50s regarded as a comparatively rare and even extreme occurence. At the same time, it is important to observe that it was by this time a familiar option to Corinthian believers; and presumably, therefore, it was a didactic or narrative element of the gospel that they received.

James 2.2-7; 5.1-5 certainly expressed HW and may be said to be sympathetic to dispossession. At the same time, however, the injunctions are not pronounced from the standpoint of a poor community: the rich clearly take part in the assembly, and the poor are referred to as third parties (2.2-3). Rev 3.15-18 and 18.16-20 put wealth in a negative light but possess great affinity to the prophetic tradition than to religious-ethical instruction. Indeed, extra-Synoptic instruction with regard to the use of wealth is limited to an occasional recommendation of charity (e.g. Gal 6.6-10; 2 Cor 8.1-9.15; 1 John 3.17-18) or contentment with that which one has (e.g. Phil 4.11-12; 1 Tim 6.6-10; Heb 13.5-7). Why is there such a radical difference between the teaching of Jesus and that of his first followers?

In 1 Cor 7.30, Paul advises 'those who buy (to live) as though they had no goods (κατέχοντες)'. We may surmise that, if the context were a discussion of wealth and not of marriage, Paul would advocate dispossession for the same reasons that he advocates celibacy (vv. 31-35), and perhaps he would use himself as an example (v. 8, cf. 2 Cor 6.10).[7] Conversely, it is possible that Paul's concession on the marriage issue (vv. 36-40) provides a clue to the mystery of NT disparity with regard to HW. Although the ideal ethic and examples of it remained, the delay of the end and the great difficulty of such personal sacrifice rendered compromise 'historically inevitable'.[8] Although the NT itself does not explain this transition to us, we see its roots in the disparity between the teaching of the Synoptics and the comparative silence of the rest of the NT.

Mealand rightly notes that dispossession 'has been more ofter praised than practised'[9] in the history of the Church. Perhaps the synoptic Gospels are the first instance of that phenomenon. In any case, the tradition was as shattering to any first-century hearer as it has been to those in subsequent centuries who have felt its impact.

NOTES

Notes to Introduction

1. The two most thorough surveys of pre-Synoptic material make no attempt to relate the material to a logical structure or to examine trends. F. Hauck, *Die Stellung des Urchristentums zu Arbeit und Geld* (Gütersloh, 1921) 2-37 considers only the OT, 1 En, Sir, Pss Sol, Philo, and Josephus. D.L. Mealand, 'Disparagement of Wealth in New Testament Times' (unpublished M.Litt. dissertation, University of Bristol, 1971) neglects ancient Near Eastern material, the LXX, the Targums, and several pseudepigraphical works. Thus, although both of these studies are helpful compilations of material, they cannot be considered as treatments of development.

2. See e.g. R. Scroggs, 'The Earliest Christian Communities as Sectarian Movement', in *Christianity, Judaism, and Other Greco-Roman Cults*, ed. J. Neusner, Part Two: Early Christianity (Leiden, 1975) 9-13, 17; R.J. Cassidy, *Jesus, Politics, and Society* (Maryknoll, New York, 1978) 98-113; H.C. Kee, *Christian Origins in Sociological Perspective* (London, 1980) 134-40; W.E. Pilgrim, *Good News to the Poor* (Minneapolis, Minnesota, 1981) 39-63. For older examples of the same ideas, see e.g. A. Deismann, *Light from the Ancient East* ET (London, 1927) 466; F.C. Grant, *The Economic Background of the Gospels* (Oxford, 1926) *passim*.

3. G. Theissen, *Sociology of Early Palestinian Christianity* ET (Philadelphia, 1978); D.L. Mealand, *Poverty and Expectation in the Gospels* (London, 1980); J.G. Gager, *Kingdom and Community* (Englewood Cliffs, New Jersey, 1975).

Notes to Chapter 1

1. See Grant, *Background* 10; Mealand, *Poverty* 11; Theissen, *Sociology* 45. Scroggs (*Communities* 4) maintains that sects are not aware of the economic factor in their theological expressions: 'Members may very well 'feel' the societal rejection but they may not be able to speak it'. Gager (*Kingdom* 8) puts the matter even more plainly: '... the various images of Jesus, whatever their relation to the historical Jesus of Nazareth, are in the first instance reflections of the communities that preserved and transmitted the Gospel traditions. Their world was projected onto the person of Jesus and thus given the highest form of legitimacy'.

170   *Hostility to Wealth in the Synoptic Gospels*

2. Mealand, *Poverty* 11.
3. Grant, *Background* 54.
4. Theissen, *Sociology* 40. See also Mealand, *Poverty* 7-11; Grant, *Background* 52, 101-102.
5. Werner G. Kümmel, *Introduction to the New Testament* (London, 1966) 71, 84, 106. We should bear in mind the possibility that these books were written as early as the 50s; but rather than to make an issue of dating in this context, we will assume later dates.
6. Q, for example, probably reached *written* form between 50 and 70: Kümmel, *Introduction* 56.
7. According to T. Rajak (*Josephus: The Historian and His Society* [Philadelphia, 1983] 123), 'There is no reason to postulate a drawn-out economic crisis leading up to the great revolt. Banditry was widespread, but this has many contributory causes: weak government, dislocation of populations, rapid change in a society and its values, urbanization; bad harvests simply step up its level somewhat. Banditry was also to be found in areas which played no part in the revolt . . .' Limitations of space preclude a full analysis of the causes of the war, but some important evidence should be noted. Nationalism and religious purity were the primary issues in every violent incident between AD 6 and 66: see *BJ* 2.169-261; *JA* 18.55-89; 261-309; 20.97-136; 169-88. The rallying cries of the revolutionaries were unmistakably religious (*BJ* 2.391-93; 5.402; 413; 459; 6.63; 98), despite Josephus's attempts to protect Judaism by hiding the religious motives. Thus the majority of scholars see nationalism or religious purity, not economics, as the dominant causes of the war. See David M. Rhoads, *Israel in Revolution: 6-74 CE* (Philadelphia, 1976) 44-77; 166-70; E. Mary Smallwood, *The Jews Under Roman Rule* (Leiden, 1976) 153-55; and the bibliography in Heinz Kreissig, *Die sozialen Zusammenhänge des jüdischen Krieges* (Berlin, 1970) 13. For the role of the aristocracy in the revolt, see S.J.D. Cohen, *Josephus in Galilee and Rome* (Leiden, 1979) 97-100, 230-31, 240-42. The only purely economic factor is the unemployment caused by the completion of the temple in AD 64 (*JA* 20.219). Brigandage, which developed to a flourishing state in the middle and late 50's, was by definition aimed by poor men at rich men, but the claim that such activity 'sought a redistribution of possessions within society' (Theissen, *Sociology* 38) describes Sherwood Forest better than Judaea. Similarly, refusal to pay taxes (*BJ* 2.405) and destruction of debt records (*BJ* 2.427) were *acts* of rebellion and not *causes* of rebellion (as Theissen claims: *Sociology* 38, 43).
8. *BJ* 2.86. In *BJ* 1.524, Josephus quotes Eurycles' accusation of Alexander before Herod, including among the charges one that the nation was being 'bled to death by taxation'. When removed from the context, we must regard the statement as an opinion held by Josephus himself.
9. S. Freyne, *Galilee from Alexander the Great to Hadrian* (South Bend, Indiana, 1980) 185-87.

M. Goodman ('The First Jewish Revolt: Social Conflict and the Problem of Debt', *JJS* [1982] 417-28) and Rajak (*Josephus*, 122-23) refute the idea that Herod made harsh demands on Judaea.

11. Grant, *Background* 47.

12. Tacitus, *Histories* 5.9.2.

13. We do know that Tiberius was not averse to reduction of tribute as a goodwill gesture. Cappadocia was granted such a reduction upon receipt of provincial status according to Tacitus, *Annals* 2.56.

14. Smallwood, *Jews* 156; cf. 172. See also Rhoads, *Revolution* 66.

15. M. Rostovtzeff, *The Social and Economic History of the Hellenistic World* (Oxford, 1941) 2.272; E. Bammel, 'The Poor and the Zealots', in *Jesus and the Politics of His Day*, ed. E. Bammel and C.F.D. Moule (Cambridge, 1984) 109. See also Freyne, *Galilee* 191; M. Stern, *The Jewish People in the First Century*, Vol. I (Assen, 1974) 330.

16. Freyne, *Galilee* 193; cf. 192; Hauck, *Stellung* 89.

17. *Ibid.* 194.

18. Grant, *Background* 105. Mealand (*Poverty* 8) accepts this estimate without questioning. See also Theissen, *Sociology* 44.

19. *Ibid.* 11.

20. Smallwood, *Jews* 150-51.

21. *Ibid.* 150. The tax went from 33% under the Seleucids to 12½% under Augustus and his successors. For a description of the Seleucid system, see Solomon Zeitlin, *The Rise and Fall of the Judaean State* Vol. I (Philadelphia, 1964) 312; for a description of the Augustan system, see Freyne, *Galilee* 189; Stern, *Province* 331. Grant is followed by H. Hoehner, *Herod Antipas* (Cambridge, 1972) 77-79; Scroggs, *Communities* 9. F.M. Heichelheim ('Roman Syria', in *An Economic Survey of Ancient Rome*, ed. T. Frank, Volume IV [Baltimore, 1938] 235) thinks that there may have been an additional 1% tax on the produce of the land.

22. Heichelheim, *Syria* 237; Stern, *Province* 331; G. Alon (*The Jews in Their Land in the Talmudic Age* [Jerusalem, 1980] 64) argues that the amount depended on a man's property and income. In any case, it was the psychological impact of the tribute that was of primary importance, according to Smallwood (*Jews* 153): 'The question put to Christ was not "Is the tax too heavy?" but "Is it lawful to pay the tax?"' There were also customs duties which may have been passed on in the form of higher prices for certain non-essential goods, but we do not know if these constituted an increase from similar taxes in Hasmonean times (see Zeitlin, *State* I 312). A city sales tax was remitted by Vitellius as a goodwill gesture after the recall of Pilate in AD 36 (*JA* 18.90). One other tax assessed by the Romans, and at least temporarily remitted by Agrippa I (*JA* 19.299), was a Jerusalem house tax. We do not know the amount of this tax.

23. Smallwood, *Jews* 160; cf. Heichelheim, *Syria* 231.

24. Alon, *Jews* 64.

25. Grant, *Background* 94-96: (1) sin offering, thank offering, and shewbread; (2) first fruits of fruits and grains (a token amount); (3) the best of fruits (2%); (4) tithe of agricultural products (10%); (5) one twenty-fourth of the bread dough; (6) first-born animals; (7) redemption money for a first-born child (5 shekels); (8) parts of animals slaughtered for food; (9) extraordinary dues (e.g. release from vows); (10) the annual half-shekel; (11) wood-gathering; (12) free-will offerings.

26. A. Oppenheimer, *The Am-ha-aretz: Social History* (Leiden, 1977) 71.

27. J. Jeremias, *Jerusalem in the Time of Jesus* (Philadelphia, 1969) 103; see also Oppenheimer, *History* 71.

28. *JA* 15.365; 16.64 (Herod); 17.205 (Archelaus); 18.90 (Vitellius); 19.299 (Agrippa I); *BJ* 2.273 (Albinus's increase).

29. Grant, *Background* 45 n. 3.

30. Stern, *Province* 332.

31. Theissen, *Sociology* 43.

32. A. Byatt, 'Josephus and Population Numbers in First Century Palestine', *PEQ* 105 (1973) 51-60.

33. *Ibid.* 52. See *BJ* 3.41-58 for Josephus's description of the land and the dense population of Galilee.

34. Grant, *Background* 86.

35. *Ibid.* 84-85

36. Theissen, *Sociology* 40.

37. See G.S. Gibson, 'The Social Stratification of Palestine in the First Century of the Christian Era' (unpublished PhD dissertation, University of London, 1975) 268-72.

38. Byatt, *Population* 51.

39. R.J. Cassidy, *Jesus, Politics, and Society* (Maryknoll, New York, 1978) 100.

40. S. Applebaum, *The Jewish People in the First Century*, Vol. II (Assen, 1976) 691.

41. D. Sperber, 'Costs of Living in Roman Palestine', *Journal of the Economic and Social History of the Orient* 8 (1965) 248-71; and 'Costs of Living in Roman Palestine II', *Journal of the Economic and Social History of the Orient* 9 (1966) 182-211. See esp. 2.190. This does not mean that only Palestine had high prices: 'In Rome, however, prices of wheat appear to have been as much as twice as high as those of Palestine' (2.190).

42. Theissen, *Sociology* 40.

43. Mealand, *Poverty* 10.

44. Jeremias, *Jerusalem* 140-44. Jeremias does not mention the potential man-made disaster caused by neglect of agriculture in protest against Caligula's statue (*JA* 18.274). We do not know if this protest resulted in any real hardship; it appears to be more of a threat.

45. Alternately, Mark may be employing 'famine' and 'earthquake' as common elements in predictions of judgment. See e.g. famine: Isa 51.19; Jer

11.22; Pss Sol 15.7; 4QpPs37 1, 1; earthquake: Isa 29.6; Ezek 38.19.
Although the two words do not occur together in apocalyptic predictions,
their similarity in nature and form (רעב, רעש) make them an appropriate
pair.
46. Theissen, *Sociology* 40.
47. Jeremias, *Jerusalem* 142-43. See also K.S. Gapp, 'The Universal
Famine Under Claudius', *HTR* 28 (1935) 258-60. Gapp documents an
Egyptian famine in 45-46, caused by a Nile flood, which may have
compounded the problem of grain scarcity just prior to the Palestinian crop
failure.
48. The context is an account of priestly piety in adverse circumstances, so
we should expect some embellishment of the situation. As to the date,
Josephus gives the high priest as Ishmael (AD 59-61), but he gives the
emperor as Claudius (AD 41-54). The mention of Ishmael and the phrase
'shortly before the recent war' suggest that a later date (perhaps immediately
prior to the war) is correct.
49. Cf the rabbinic accounts in *y. Pe'a* i.I.15b (53); *b. B. Bat.* 11a; *t. Pe'a*
iv.18(24); *Pesiq. Rab.* xxv.
50. Keith F. Nickle, *The Collection* (London, 1966) 22-32.
51. See A.R. Hands, *Charities and Social Aid in Greece and Rome* (Ithaca,
New York, 1968) 89-115; S.J. Case, *The Social Triumph of the Ancient
Church* (Chicago, 1923) 15-20.
52. Mealand, *Poverty* 9.
53. Theissen, *Sociology* 41.
54. Kreissig, *Krieges* 36-54; 92-110. See also H.G. Kippenberg, *Religion
und Klassenbildung im antiken Judäa* (Göttingen, 1978) 106-33.
55. Applebaum (*People* II 662) explains that Kreissig's 'entire theory rests
on the assumption of a countrywide price-structure, or at least of a large
urban market. In effect anything like a large market was restricted to
Jerusalem and some of the larger coastal cities such as Caesarea, Gaza, and
Ascalon; transport-restrictions made the long distance transfer of bulk-
produce difficult and unprofitable.'
56. *Ibid.* 662.
57. Kreissig, *Krieges* 51-54. See Chapter 5.3 below: an increase in rabbinic
legislation does not necessitate, much less pinpoint, an increase in the
problem.
58. *Ibid.* 51. He also cites Luke 14.16-24, which can hardly substantiate his
claim 'Da die Armen einen sehr hohen Prozentsatz der Gesamtbevölkerung
ausmachen', even if it does refer to the economically deprived.
59. See Chapter 5.3 below, on Targum Jonathan to Ezek 34.3.
60. See e.g. A.H. McNeile, *The Gospel According to St. Matthew* (London,
1915) 130; M.J. Lagrange, *Évangile selon Saint Matthieu* (Paris, 1948) 192;
P. Gaechter, *Das Matthäus Evangelium* (Innsbruck, 1962) 314; P. Bonnard,
L'Évangile selon Saint Matthieu (Paris, 1963) 142.

61. Mealand, *Poverty* 16.

62. *BJ* 2.233-46; 254; 271; 273; *JA* 20.118-36; 165; 215. Significantly, Josephus ascribes political and mercenary motives to these groups, but he does not speak of their economic condition. Cf Rajak, *Josephus* 123-26.

63. Theissen, *Sociology* 41. Theissen also complains of land sales by the Romans of Archelaus's estates (*JA* 17.355; 18.2), but they may well have been bought by Jews and ultimately of benefit to Jews.

64. See H. Kreissig's discussion of *Tagelöhnern* in 'Die Landwirtschaftliche Situation in Palästina vor dem Judäischen Krieg', *Acta Antiqua* 17 (1969) 239-51.

65. B. Malina, *The New Testament World: Insights from Cultural Anthropology* (Atlanta, 1981) 85.

66. Cf. W. Meeks, *The First Urban Christians* (New Haven, 1983) 53-55.

67. Gager, *Kingdom* 24; cf 96, 106. See also G. Theissen, *The Social Setting of Pauline Christianity* (Philadelphia, 1982) 220 n. 36.

68. Theissen, *Sociology* 39-40, 46.

69. Gager, *Kingdom* 27.

70. See J.G. Gager, 'Robert M. Grant, *Early Christianity and Society: Seven Studies*; Abraham J. Malherbe, *Social Aspects of Early Christianity*; and Gerd Theissen *Sociology of Early Palestinian Christianity*', *RelSRev* 5 (1979) 180.

71. Matt 19.21/Mark 10.21/Luke 18.22; Matt 26.9/Mark 14.5; Matt 26.11/Mark 14.7; Luke 14:13, 21; 19.8. See also Rom 15.26, τοὺς πτωχοὺς τῶν ἁγίων τῶν ἐν ˙Ιερουσαλήμ. This may be an epexegetical self-designation of the community (so K. Holl, 'Der Kirchenbegriff des Paulus in seinem Verhältnis zu dem der Urgemeinde', in *Gesammelte Aufsätze zur Kirchengeschichte*, II: Der Osten [Tübingen, 1928] 59-60; E. Bammel, 'πτωχος', *TDNT* 6.909), although many commentators argue that it refers to the materially poor within the group (e.g. L.E. Keck, 'The Poor Among the Saints in the New Testament', *ZNW* 56 [1965] 100-129; Nickle, *Collection* 23-24; 100-102; E. Käsemann, *Commentary on Romans*, ET [Grand Rapids, 1980] 401; C.E.B. Cranfield, *The Epistle to the Romans* [Edinburgh, 1979] 272-73). In the latter case, the question remains open of the extent and duration of the poverty, and whether it was voluntary or involuntary in nature (cf. Paul's own poverty: 1 Cor 4.11; 2 Cor 6.10; Phil 4.11-13). Even granting that it was involuntary, it may have begun with the famine and ended with the receipt of the collection. In any case, the argument for determination of Synoptic ethical material is not greatly strengthened by appeal to a reference as ambiguous as this. The theological significance of the collection (see Nickle, *Collection* 103-43) is in the last analysis more certain—and more important— than the socio-economic circumstances deduced from the verse.

72. E.A. Judge, *The Social Pattern of Christian Groups in the First Century* (London, 1960), *Rank and Status in the World of the Caesars and St. Paul* (Christchurch, New Zealand, 1982), 'Cultural Conformity and Innovation in

Paul: Some Clues from Contemporary Documents', *TynBul* 35 (1984) 3-24;
G. Theissen, *The Social Setting of Pauline Christianity* (Philadelphia, 1982);
W. Meeks *The First Urban Christians* (New Haven, 1983) esp. 51-73. For
references indicating the possibility of higher social strata, cf. Acts 10.1;
16.14; 16.33; 17.4; 18.8; 19.31; Rom 16.1; 16.3-5; 16.13; 16.21-23; 1 Cor 1.11;
1.16; 16.15. The fact that 'not *many*' Corinthians were 'powerful' or 'of noble
birth' (1 Cor 1.26) allows for significant exceptions, and the social
pretensions for which the group is criticized (1 Cor 4.8-10; 11.20-22) may
suggest a claim to a degree of gentility from the whole group (see Judge,
Pattern 59-60; Meeks, *Urban* 67-72). The appeal to the Corinthians based on
the 'poverty' of the Macedonians (2 Cor 8.2) is probably hyperbole, since
2 Cor 9.2-4 suggest that Paul used the same sort of argument with the
Macedonians in reverse (Meeks, *Urban* 66). The obvious presence of
believers higher than the bottom of the social scale is explained, according to
Scroggs, (*Communities* 12-13; cf. Gager, *review* 179) by reference to modern
revolutionary movements which must be led from a higher class 'when the
protest group is too abject to produce its own leadership'. That the presence
appears *common* is due, asserts Gager (*review* 179), to the fact that '90 per
cent of our information concerns this small, though important minority'. He
continues, 'Thus we must not draw hasty generalizations about the majority
of believers from what we can conclude about their leaders'. Gager's
arbitrary percentage seems to fall prey to his own charge and to exemplify
the control of theory over data.
   73. Judge, *Pattern* 61. See also A.J. Malherbe, *Social Aspects of Early
Christianity* (Baton Rouge, Louisiana, 1977) 31, 86.

Notes to Chapter 2

   1. T.F. Best ('The Sociological Study of the New Testament: Promise
and Peril of a New Discipline', *SJT* 36 [1983] 181-94) has contributed an
excellent essay in which he explains this problem and outlines a program for
NT sociologists. Judge and Meeks have, in my opinion, done the most
thorough and helpful work in the Pauline area.
   2. Theissen, *Sociology* 4-5.
   3. *Ibid*. 5.
   4. *Ibid*.
   5. *Ibid*. 13.
   6. David Mealand, *Disparagement* 9.
   7. Gager, *Kingdom* 106.
   8. Yonina Talmon, 'The Pursuit of the Millenium: The Relation Between
Religious and Social Change', *European Journal of Sociology* 3 (1962) 128.
   9. Talmon, *Pursuit* 136. See also N. Cohn, *The Pursuit of the Millennium*
(London, 1970) 282; P. Worsley, *The Trumpet Shall Sound*, 2nd edn

(London, 1968) 225; R.R. Wilson, *Prophecy and Society in Ancient Israel* (Philadelphia, 1980) 77.

10. Wilson, *Prophecy* 78. See also D.F. Aberle, 'A Note on Relative Deprivation Theory as Applied to Millenarian and Other Cult Movements', in *Millenarian Dreams in Action*, ed. S.L. Thrupp (New York, 1970) 210; Theissen, *Sociology* 40; Cohn, *Pursuit* 59-60; 282; 284; Wilson, *Prophecy* 78.

11. Talmon, *Pursuit* 137 quoted by Gager, *Kingdom* 27 n. 33. See also S.R. Isenberg, 'Millenarianism in Greco-Roman Palestine', *Religion* 4 (1974) 35.

12. See n. 10 above.

13. *Ibid.* 209. See also C.Y. Glock, 'The Role of Deprivation in the Origin and Evolution of Religious Groups', *Religion and Social Conflict*, ed. R. Lee & M. Marty (New York, 1964) 27.

14. Aberle, *Note* 209.

15. V. Lanternari, *The Religions of the Oppressed* (London, 1963) 311-12. We might infer a measure of agreement on the part of Worsley, who distinguishes as 'at another pole altogether from activist millenarism . . . movements (that) blame the world's evils not on the rulers of society or a dominant Church or a foreign government, but on the people themselves as worldly sinners' (*Trumpet* 232). In another place, however, Worsley reveals his belief that inceptive Christianity was an activist movement (*Trumpet* 12).

16. K. Burridge, *New Heaven, New Earth* (Oxford, 1969) 113; B.R. Wilson, *Magic and the Millennium* (London, 1973) 1; Worsley, *Trumpet* 245; Lanternari, *Religions* 306; Talmon, *Pursuit* 139-40.

17. For example, when Europeans entered an area without or before conducting missionary ventures.

18. Wilson, *Magic* 466-67. Talmon (*Pursuit* 140) explains that 'The prevalence of millenarianism in Melanesia and the importance of expectations of cargo in its view of the millennium are, it would seem, due to the strong and almost exclusive emphasis which the indigenous religion puts on ritual activity oriented to the acquisition of material goods . . . (and) elaborated into full-fledged millenarian conceptions only under the impact of the new situation and after the contact with Christianity'.

19. Gager, *Kingdom* 24.

20. Worsley, *Trumpet* 243.

21. See, e.g., Wilson, *Prophecy* 31; 79; Worsley, *Trumpet* 251; Gager, *Kingdom* 28-31.

22. Gager, *Kingdom* 28.

23. See Burridge, *Heaven* 14; 155; 164; Wilson, *Prophecy* 31; Worsley, *Trumpet* 251; H.C. Kee, *Christian Origins in Sociological Perspective* (London, 1980) 78.

24. Worsley, *Trumpet* 226.

25. Mealand, *Poverty* 29; 38-41; 89-91.
26. *Ibid.* 45-46.
27. L.T. Johnson, 'On Finding the Lukan Community: A Cautious Cautionary Essay', *SBLASP* 16 (1979) 89-91.

Notes to Chapter 3

1. *ANET* 21 (1962) 129-39. See also J.H. Breasted, *The Dawn of Conscience* (London, 1934) 115-222.
2. Mealand, *Disparagement* 4.
3. See Burridge, *Heaven* 42-46, 144-46.
4. R.L. Beals and H. Hoijer, *An Introduction to Anthropology* (New York, 1965) 459-60; cf. M.J. Schwarz and D.K. Jordan, *Anthropology: Perspective on Humanity* (New York, 1976) 484-88.
5. P. Einzig, *Primitive Money*, 2nd edn (Oxford, 1966) 335; cf. M. Weber, *General Economic History*, ET (London, 1927) 24-50.
6. R.D. Patterson, 'The Widow, the Orphan, and the Poor in the Old Testament and the Extra-biblical Literature', *BibSac* 130 (1973) 232-33.
7. Einzig, *Money* 492.
8. M. Weber, *The Sociology of Religion*, ET (London, 1965) 212.
9. Fensham, *Widow* 132.
10. *Ibid.* 129.
11. Attention should be drawn in this regard to such works as the Egyptian *Maxims of Ptahhotep* and *The Babylonian Theodicy*. A thousand years separate the documents, yet each contains a spectrum of thought from 'wealth as a reward for virtue' to detachment from or even hostility toward wealth. See examples below.
12. S.N. Kramer, *History Begins at Sumer* (London, 1958) 86-90; cf. W.W. Hallo and W.K. Simpson, *The Ancient Near East: A History* (New York, 1971) 50.
13. P. Diemal, 'Die Reformtexte Urukaginas', *Orientalia* 2 (1920) 9; cf. 6-9 for the entire text in German translation.
14. Hallo & Simpson, *History* 77-79.
15. Translated by Kramer, *History* 77-79.
16. Hallo & Simpson, *History* 100-102.
17. Lines xxiv. 60-61, 178; cf. i. 30-31, 164 (*ANET* 178). For further Mesopotamian examples see *Daily Prayer of the King* (Hittite, 1620-1595 BC) line 59 (*ANET* 397); *Akkadian invocation to Ishtar* (1500 BC) line 25 (*NERT* 110); *Counsels of Wisdom* (Babylonian, 1500-1200 BC) lines 57-65 (*BWL* 101); *Hymn to Ninurnta* (Babylonian, c. 1100 BC) lines 11-13 (*BWL* 119); *Babylonian Proverbs* (c. 1000 BC) lines 8-15 (*BWL* 271); *Advice to a Prince* (Babylonian, 1000-700 BC) lines 15-18 (*BWL* 113); *Counsels of Wisdom* (Akkadian, before 700 BC) lines ii.12-14 (*ANET* 426); *Prayer of Ashurbanipal*

to Ninlil (c. 650) *passim* (*BPP* 73). Cf *The Keret Epic* (Ugaritic, before 1200 BC; *NERT* 224); *The Epic of Aqhat* (West Semitic, before 1400 BC) line v. 7-8 (*ANET* 151).

18.   (*AEL* 1.17).

19.   *Hymn to Hapy* xii, 6 (*AEL* 1.206). For further Egyptian examples see *The Autobiography of Harkhuf* (2300-2150 BC; *AEL* 1.24); *Stela of the Steward Seneni of Coptus* (2135-2040 BC; *AEL* 1.90); *The Tale of the Eloquent Peasant* (2135-2040 BC) lines B1.62-63, 120, 145, 204, 231 (*LAE* 35-43); *The Maxims of Ptahhotep* (2135-2040 BC) nos. 5, 6, 19, 20, 30 (*AEL* 1.64-71); *The Teaching for Merikare* (2135-2040 BC) lines 46-48 (*LAE* 183); *Stela of Intef Son of Sent* (c. 1950 BC) column 16 (*AEL* 1.122); *The Instruction of King Amenemhet I for his Son Sesostris I* (c. 1950 BC) line 6 (*AEL* 2.136); *Stela of the Priest Horemkhauf* (c. 1650 BC; *AEL* 1.130); P. Boulag 17, IV, 3-5 (c. 1400 BC; *NERT* 14); *Hymn to Amun* (c. 1300 BC; *NERT* 41); *Votive Stela of Nebre with Hymn to Amen-Re* (1550-1080 BC; *AEL* 2.105); *P. Anastasi* II.6, 5-7 (1550-1080 BC; *AEL* 2.111); *P. Anastasi* II.8, 5-9, 1 (1550-1080 BC; *AEL* 2.111); *P. Anastasi* II.9, 2-10, 1 (1550-1080 BC; *AEL* 2.112); *The Book of the Dead* (1550-1080 BC) Chapter 125 (*AEL* 2.125-28); *Hymn of Mer-Sekhmet* (c. 1300 BC) 8, 2 (*NERT* 26); *The Poetical Stela of Merneptah* (c. 1200 BC; *AEL* 2.76); *The Instruction of Amenemope* (1085-945 BC) lines 14.4, 26.9 (*LAE* 253, 264); *Statue Inscription of Djedkhonsefankh* (c. 900 BC; *AEL* 3.17); Statue Inscription of Nebneteru (c. 900 BC; *AEL* 3.22) *Statue Inscription of Harwa* (750-650 BC; *AEL* 3.26-28); *The Instruction of Papyrus Insinger* (100-0 BC; *AEL* 3.197-98). See also J.H. Breasted, *Development of Religion and Thought in Ancient Egypt* (London, 1912) 353-54; Fensham, *Widow* 133.

20.   See e.g. *Lamentation Over the Destruction of Ur* (Mesopotamian, 2000-1500 BC) lines 275-81 (*ANET* 460); *The Babylonian Theodicy* lines 22, 70-77 (*BWL* 71-77); *Samas Hymn* (c. 1100 BC) lines 118-120 (*BWL* 133); *Counsels of Wisdom* (Akkadian) lies i.20, ii.35 (*ANET* 426); *The Maxims of Ptahhotep* nos. 10, 11, 31 (*AEL* 1.66-72); *The Teaching for Merikare* lines 43-44 (*LAE* 83); *The Admonitions of an Egyptian Sage* (2100-1800 BC) 2.5, 2.10–4.5, 5.10, 7.10-8.10 (*LAE* 210-29); *The Prophecies of Neferti* (2000-1900 BC) line 57 (*LAE* 239); *The Instruction of Amenemope* 25.12 (*LAE* 263).

21.   Cf. notes 12, 20 above; see also examples in Prov and Sir, Chapters 4 and 5.1.

22.   See e.g. 1 Kgs 3.10-13; 1 Chr 1.11-12; Job 42.10-12; Ps 37.11; Prov 11.24-25; 22.4; 28.25; Sir 31.11; T Zeb 6.4-6; T Job 4.4-7; 44.7; Jos Asen 10-12, 21, 29.

23.   See e.g. *The teaching of a man for his son* (1990-1785 BC; *NERT* 47); *The Admonitions of Ipuwer* (c. 1700 BC) 2, 4-5; 8, 2 (*AEL* 1.151).

24.   Greed is said to motivate not only oppression, but cheating in business: see e.g. *The Instruction of Amenemope* 17.19–18.9 (*LAE* 256); *The Šamas Hymn* lines 103-21 (*BWL* 133).

25. Line 105 (*LAE* 206).

26. 7.14 (*LAE* 247).

27. (*ANET* 429); cf. *The Maxims of Ptahhotep* no. 20 (*LAE* 167); *The Instruction of Amenemope* 10.10 (*AEL* 1.69); *The Babylonian Theodicy* line 133 (*BWL* 77).

28. According to Lambert (*BWL* 67), this was written during the 'uneventful and largely peaceful' centuries of Kassite rule in Babylonia; see also Hallo & Simpson, *History* 108. Lichteim (*AEL* 1.149-50) maintains that such laments were purely literary, not historical-political laments.

29. Lines 70-71 (*BWL* 75); cf. lines 271-75, 281-83 (*BWL* 87-89).

30. Lines 249-50 (*BWL* 85).

31. Lines 63-64 (*BWL* 75).

32. Line 237 (*BWL* 85); cf. lines 221-23 (*BWL* 83-85).

33. Line 253 (*BWL* 87).

34. Lines 65-66 (*BWL* 75).

35. ii. 42-45 (*BWL* 232).

36. 18.8-12 (*LAE* 256-57).

37. 9.5-9 (*LAE* 249); cf. 9.10-10.15 (*LAE* 249-50). Another minor but noteworthy instance of this form is *The Maxims of Ptahhotep* no. 35 (*AEL* 1.72), which calls 'character' or 'reputation' greater than riches.

38. 16.10-14 (*LAE* 255); the stanza that follows is identical to that quoted above, p. 53.

39. 26.12-14 (*LAE* 264); cf. *The Instruction of Ani* (1100-800 BC) line viii.4-5 (*ANET* 421), where charity is extolled over greed because 'a man is nothing'.

40. No. 30 (*LAE* 170).

41. Tablet II, line 46 (*BWL* 41).

42. (*ANET* 429).

43. (*AEL* 3.15).

44. See J.A. Wilson, 'The Theban Tomb (No, 409) of Si-Mut, Called Kiki', *JNES* 29 (1970) 187.

45. (*NERT* 38-39).

Notes to Chapter 4

1. The word 'passage' is used throughout rather than 'verse', 'occurrence', etc., to indicate a distinct argument in a given work. This is done to avoid distortion in the tables, where mere verse count or word count would not be an accurate measure of proportion. At times the judgment was made that consecutive sentences or paragraphs should be considered separately where they indicate a distinct argument. Thus, for example, Eccl 5.10, 11, 12, and 13 are considered as separate passages, as are Ps 49.5-6, 10-15, and 16-20.

2. Note: Although consideration is given in the order History —Prophecy—

Writings, the contents of these divisions and the listing of references will follow the scheme and order of the English Bible. Parentheses which occur in lists of passages indicate overlap with passages using עשר; double parentheses indicate overlap with passages using חיל; square brackets indicate overlap with passages using other words, and these words are given within the brackets. Joint references using עשר: Ps 49.2; Prov 10.15; 13.7; 13.8; 14.20; 18.23; 21.17; 22.2; 22.7; 22.16; 28.6; 28.11; 30.8; using חיל: Job 20.15; Ps 10.5-18; using הון: (Prov 10.15); (13.7); 19.4; 28.8; using other words: Job 20.10 (און); 29.11-16 (describing Job's former prosperity); 34.19 (שוע); Ps 37.16 (המון); Prov 15.16 (אוצר); 15.25 (גאים); 16.8 (תבואה); 16.19 (גאים); 17.1 (מלה).

3. Positive: Prov 10.15; 13.8; 14.20; 21.17; neutral: Ps 49.2; Prov 13.7; 22.2; negative: see text.

4. Positive: Job 20.10; Prov 19.4; 28.8; neutral: Job 21: 23-26; 34.19; injustice: Job 20.15; 29.11-16; Ps 10.5-18; Prov 15.25.

5. Cf Prov 28.6; 28.11, which use עשר, and 19.1: 'Better is a poor man who walks in his integrity, than a man who is perverse in speech, and is a fool'.

6. Psalmic references using עשר: 45.13; 49.2; 49.5-6; 49.16-20; 52.7; 112.3; other words: 10.3-5; 19.10; 30.6-7; 37.7; 37.16; 49.10-15; 62.9-10; 73.3-12; 119.14; 119.72; 119.127.

7. Only Ps 49.2 contains both עשיר and אביון, but it equates them rather than contrasting them.

8. Bammel, πτωχός 888; A. Kuschke, 'Arm und Reich im Alten Testament mit besonderer Berucksichtigung der nachexilischen Zeit', *ZAW* 57 (1939) 44-57. This is significant in that while רשע and עשר and equivalents are occasionally equated or used interchangeably (Job 27.13, 19; Pss 37.7; 49.5-6; 73.3, 12; Prov 10.2; 11.16), עשר as רשע only occurs twice in joint psalmic references: 10.3-18 and 37.16 (cf. Job 20.10, 15-20; 21.23-25; Jer 5.26-28). For other words used interchangeably with 'rich', see Prov 11.16; 15.25; 16.8; 16.19; 28.6; 28.11.

9. H. Birkeland ('The Evil-doers in the Book of Psalms', *Auhandlinger Det Norske Videnskaps-Akademi* 2 [1955] 1-96) argues that the wicked are Gentiles in Pss 10, 37, 49, and 73, and 'in all cases when a definite collective body or its representatives are meant' (93), but he allows that individual Israelites may also be included in these attacks (60, 93). Since each of the psalms in question uses description or more than one word for wealth, there is no reason to deprive the passages of their material and very specific ethical content. In other words, the inclusion of the rich among the wicked does not make 'rich' a figurative term antonymic to 'poor'. English usage of the words illustrates the point. A 'poor man' can be without money, worthy of sympathy, or inadequate—but only in the first instance would 'rich man' be the proper antonym.

10. Literature on the subject is extensive. Mealand, *Poverty* 101-102, 127,

gives a summary and recent bibliography.

11. Jer 5.26-28; Job 20.15-20; cf. Prov 15.25; 16.8; 16.19.

12. עשר: Gen 14.23; 31.16; Exod 30.15; 1 Sam 2.7; 12.1-6; 17.25; 1 Kgs 3.10-13; 10.23; 1 Chr 29.12; 29.28; 2 Chr 1.11-12; 9.22; 17.5; 18.1; 32.27; Ruth 3.10; Esth 1.4; 5.11; Job 15.29; 27.19; Pss 45.13; 49.2; 49.6; 49.16; 52.7; 112.3; Prov 3.16; 8.18; 10.4; 10.15; 10.22; 11.16; 11.28; 13.7; 13.8; 14.20; 14.24; 18.11; 18.23; 21.17; 22.1; 22.2; 22.4; 22.7; 22.16; 23.4; 28.6; 28.11; 28.20; 30.8; Eccl 4.8; 5.12; 5.13; 5.19; 6.2; 9.11; 10.6; 10.20; Isa 53.9; Jer 5.27; 9.23; 17.11; Hos 12.8; Mic 6.12; Zech 11.5.

13. חיל: Gen 34.29; Deut 8.17-18; Ruth 2.1; 1 Sam 9.1; Job 5.5 (15.29); 20.15; 21.7; 31.25; Pss 10.5; (49.6); 49.10; 62.10; 73.12; Prov 13.22; Isa 8.4; 10.13-14; 30.6; Isa 60.5; 60.11; 61.6; Jer. 15.13; 17.3; Ezek 26.12; 28.4-5; Obad 11; 13; Mic 4.13; Zech 9.4; 14.14. Elsewhere חיל has a military connotation: see BDB 298-99.

14. כסף and/or זהב and equivalents: Job 3.15; 22.23-25; 28.15; ((31.24-25)); Pss 19.10; 119.72; 119.127; Prov 3.14; 8.10; 8.19; 16.16; 20.15; Eccl 2.8; 5.10; 10.19; Isa 2.7; 13.17; 60.17; Ezek 7.19; 16.13; Nah 2.9; Zeph 1.18; Hag 2.6-9. Of these, Job 3.15; Ezek 16.13; Nah 2.9; and Hag 2.6-9 are part of the VW stratum.

15. הון: (Ps 52.7 variant); (112.3); 119.14; Prov 3.9-10; (8.18); (8.21); (10.15); 11.4; (13.7); 13.11; (18.11); 19.4; 19.14; 24.4; 28.8; 28.22; 29.3; Ezek 27.12; 27.18; 27.27; 27.33.

16. טוב: Deut 23.6; 28.11; 1 Kgs 10.7; Ezra 9.12; Esth 10.3; ((Job 20.20)); ((21.13)); 36.11; Prov 17.20; Eccl 5.11; 7.14; Zech 1.17. Cf *BDB* 373-376.

17. צלח in an economic sense: Gen 39.2-3; 39.23; Deut 28.29; Josh 1.8; 1 Chr 22.13; 29.23; 2 Chr 14.7; 26.5; 31.21; 32.30; cf Ps 37.7; Jer 12.1, the only two instances outside historical books. צלח in a figurative sense: Gen 24.21; 24.40; 42.46; Judg 18.5; 1 Kgs 22.12; 22.15; 1 Chr 22.11; 2 Chr 7.11, 13.12, 18.11; 18.14; 20.20; 24.20; Neh 1.11; 2.20.

18. אוצר: Judg 18.7; Prov 10.2; 15.16; 21.20; Isa 33.6; 45.3; Jer 48.7; 50.37; 51.13; (Mic 6.10).

19. המון: Ps 37.16; [Eccl 5.10, כסף]; Ezek 7.11; 29.19; 30.4; 30.10.

20. כבד: Gen 13.2; 31.1; (Ps 49.17-18); Isa 10.3; ((61.6)).

21. בצע: Josh 5.19; ((Ps 10.3)); 119.36; Prov 15.27; Jer 6.13.

22. שכל: Deut 29.9; [Josh 1.7, צלח]; 1 Kgs 2.3; 2 Kgs 18.7; Prov 17.8.

23. חסן: Prov 15.6; 27.24; Jer 20.5; Ezek 22.25.

24. נכסים: Josh 22.8; (Eccl 5.19); (6.2); ((Isa 61.6)).

25. און: Job 22.10; (Hos 12.8); Nah 2.2; יחרם: Job 4.21a; 22.20; Jer 48.36; שבע: (Prov 3.10); 20.13; (30.9); שלום: ((Ps 73.3)); Prov 3.2; Jer 33.6; גאים: Prov 15.25; 16.19; גרל: Gen 26.3; 1 Sam 25.2; יתרה: Prov 14.23; Isa 15.7; יגיע: Isa 45.14; (Hos 12.8); שלו: Ps 30.6; Jer 22.21; אבו: Job 18.12; בעצם: ((Job 21.23)); ברד]: Job 42.12; ירש: Prov 28.25; כח: Prov 5.10; מלה: Prov 17.1; עשה: Ezek 27.16; רנוסף עוד: Prov 11.24; רחב: [Prov 28.25, ירש]; רש: Prov 29.13; [21.20, אוצר]: שוע: Job 34.19; שפע: Deut 33.19; תאוה: Prov 21.26;

182   *Hostility to Wealth in the Synoptic Gospels*

תבואה: Prov 16.8; anti-poverty but without reference to wealth: Prov 13.18; 23.21; 24.33-34: 28.19.

26. E.g. 'He took his goods to a new country', 'He bought a field with money', or 'The Lord refines his people like gold'; such usage generally assumes the usefulness of property/money, but does not assess its value in quantity or its worth as a measure of value.

27. Note: I include only clear references to material provision for widow, orphan, and/or poor. Exod 22.21, 25-27; 23.6-12; Lev 19.9-10, 13, 15, 35-37; 23.22; 25.35-38; Deut 10.18; 15.1-14; 24.10-15; 2 Sam 12.1-6; Job 22.6-9; 24.4; 24.9; 29.11-16; 31.19-21; Pss 10.12-18; 37.21; Prov 10.2; 11.1; 13.25; 14.21; 14.31; 15.27; 17.5; 19.17; 20.10; 20.17; 20.21; 20.23; 21.6; 21.13; 22.7; 22.9; 22.16; 22.22; 22.27; 25.3; 28.8; 28.16; 28.27; 29.7; 29.14; 30.14; 31.5-9, 20; Isa 1.17, 23; 3.14-15; 10.1-2; 58.6-7; Jer 5.26-29; 17.11; 22.13-17; Ezek 16.49; 18.10-17; 22.29; Amos 2.6-7; 4.1; 5.12; 8.4-6; Mic 2.2; Zech 7.10. See note 29 below for גר, note 30 below for usury. For a fuller explanation of justice in canonical literature, see B.V. Malchow, 'Social Justice in the Wisdom Literature', *BTB* 12 (1982) 122-23; N.W. Porteous, 'The Care of the Poor in the Old Testament', in *Living the Mystery* (Oxford, 1967) 146-55.

28. Only Prov 22.7; 22.16; 28.8; 29.14; Jer 5.26-29.

29. According to S.R. Driver (*A Critical and Exegetical Commentary on Deuteronomy* [Edinburgh, 1902] 126), the stranger was a man of another tribe or district who, coming to sojourn in a place without kin's protection, was liable to be a victim of injustice and oppression. Warnings against this include Exod 22.20; 23.9; Deut 1.16; 10.19; 16.11, 14; 24.14, 17, 19-21; 26.11-13; 27.19.

30. Although the prohibition of usury appears originally intended to safeguard the poor and thus becomes relevant at this point, it may be more relevant to a discussion of the Jewish work ethic (usury constitutes accumulation without labour). Since usury is neither directly linked with HW nor a concern in the NT, it does not merit extended consideration here. See Exod 22.25; Lev 25.35-38; Deut 23.19-20; Neh 5.1-13; Ps 15.5; Prov 28.8; Jer 15.10; Ezek 18.8, 13, 17; 22.12; R.P. Maloney, 'The Old Testament Teaching on Usury', *Colloquium* 5 (1973) 42-49.

31. D.L. Peterson (*The Roles of Israel's Prophets* [JSOTS, 17, Sheffield: 1981] 74-75) describes the very different economies of Israel (diffuse, heterogeneous) and Judah (central control). But Jewish religion may have worked with the economic factors; although good kings executed justice (n. 36), the entire nation shared the responsibility (n. 27, esp. passages in Deut, Lev, and Jer).

32. Deut 8.17-18; 28.11; 1 Kgs 3.10-13; 2 Chr 1.11-12; Job 22.23-30; Prov 27.23-24; Isa 10.1-3; 58.6-7; Jer 22.13-17; 22.21; Ezek 16.49; 27.27; Amos 4.1; 5.12; 8.4-6. Proverbial advice, especially against poverty (Prov 13.18; 23.21; 24.33-34; 28.19) is often clearly directed to the rich without using the second person.

33. Pss 34.6; 40.17; 69.29; 86.1-2; 109-22. None of these psalms give any contextual indication that economic poverty is meant; indeed, the parallelism of 69.29, 86.1-2, and 109.22 clearly imply a figurative meaning.

34. See G.E. Bryce (*A Legacy of Wisdom: The Egyptian Contribution to the Wisdom of Israel* [London, 1979] 57-133), who discusses the adaptation, integration, and assimilation of Egyptian wisdom by Israel, especially *The Instruction of Amenemope* (cf. Prov 22.17-24:22).

35. See note 37 for a list of the passages in the VW stratum, note 38 for a list of the passages in the HW stratum, and note 27 for a list of passages containing the justice imperative. Critical equality of rich and poor: Exod 30.14-15; Ruth 3.10; Ps 49.2; Prov 13.7; 22.2. Reference to the term wealth in the context of a justice imperative: 2 Sam 12.1-6; Prov 15.27; 22.16; 28.8; Jer 17.11.

36. Individual wealth: Gen 13.2; 14.23 (Abraham); Gen 26.13 (Isaac); Gen 30.43-31; 31.16 (Jacob); Gen 39.2-3, 23 (Joseph); Josh 1.7-8 (Joshua); 1 Sam 9.1 (Kish); 1 Sam 17.25; 1 Chr 29.28 (David); 1 Sam 25.2 (Nabal); 1 Kgs 2.3; 3.10-13; 10.7: 10.23; 1 Chr 22.13; 29.23; 2 Chr 1.11-12; 9.22 (Solomon); 2 Chr 14.7 (Asa); 2 Chr 17.5; 18.1 (Jehoshaphat); 2 Chr 24.20 (Zechariah); 2 Chr 26.5 (Uzziah); 2 Kgs 18.7; 2 Chr 31.21; 32.27; 32.30 (Hezekiah); Ruth 3.10 (any man); Esth 1.4 (Ahasuerus); Esth 5.11 (Haman); Ps 45.13 (the princess, v. 14). Plunder: Gen 34.29; Deut 23.6; 28.11; Josh 22.8; Judg 5.19; 18.7; Ezra 9.12; Isa 2.7; 8.4; 10.3; 10.13-14; 13.17; 15.7; 30.6; 45.3; 45.14; 60.5; 60.11; 60.16-17; 61.6; Jer 5.26-28; 6.13; 12.1; 15.13; 17.3; 20.5; 22.21; 48.7; 48.36; 50.37; 51.13; Ezek 7.11; 7.19; 22.25; 26.12; 27.12; 27.16; 27.18; 27.27; 27.33; 28.4-5; 29.19; 30.4; 30.10; Hos 12.7-8; Obad 11.13; Mic 4.13; 6.10-12; Nah 2.9; Zeph 1.18; Hag 2.6-9; Zech 9.4; 11.4-5; 14.8. National wealth: Deut 28.29; 29.9; 33.19; Esth 10.3; Jer 33.6-9; Ezek 16.13; Nah 2.2; Zech 1.17. Didactic: Exod 30.14-15; Deut 8.17-18; 1 Sam 2.7-8; 2 Sam 12.1-6; 1 Chr 29.12; Isa 33.6; 53.9; Jer 9.23; 17.11. Overlap: 1 Kgs 3.10-13; 2 Chr 1.11-12; Isa 2.7; 10.3; 13.17; Jer 5.26-28; 22.21; 48.7; 51.13; Ezek 7.19; 28.4-5; Hos 12.7-8; Mic 6.10-12; Zeph 1.18; Zech 11.4-5.

37. Covenant-related: Gen 13.2; 14.23; 26.13; 30.43-31.1; 31.16; 34.29; 29.2-3; 29.23; Deut 8.17-18; 23.6; 28.11; 28.29; 29.9; 33.19; Josh 1.7-8; 22.8; Judg 5.19; 18.7; Ruth 2.1; 1 Sam 17.25; 1 Kgs 2.3; 10.7; 10.23; 2 Kgs 18.7; 1 Chr 22.13; 29.23; 29.28; 2 Chr 1.11-12; 9.22; 14.7; 17.5; 18.1; 26.5; 31.20; 32.27; 32.30; Ezra 9.12; Esth 10.3; Job 5.5; 18.12; 20.10; 36.11; 42.10-12; Ps 112.3; Prov 3.2; 3.9-10; 3.16; 5.10; 8.18; 8.21; 10.22; 11.24-25; 13.18; 13.22; 14.24; 15.6; 17.20; 21.20; 22.4; 24.4; 29.3; Eccl 5.19; Isa 8.4; 10.13-14; 15.7; 30.6; 33.6; 45.3; 45.14; 60.5; 60.11; 60.16-17; 61.6; Jer 15.13; 17.3; 20.5; 33.6-9; 48.36; 50.37; Ezek 7.11; 16.13; 22.25; 26.12; 27.12, 27.16; 27.18; 27.27; 27.33; 29.19; 30.4; 30.10; Obad 11; 13; Mic 4.13; Nah 2.2; 2.9; Hag 2.6-9; Zech 1.17; 9.4; 14.14. Business advice: Prov 10.4; 13.11; 14.23; 20.13; 21.17; 23.21; 24.33-34; 28.19; Eccl 9.11; 10.6. Noncritical: 1 Sam 9.1; 25.2; Esth 1.4; 5.11; Job 3.15; Ps 45.13; Prov 19.14. Sovereignty: 1 Sam 2.7-8; 1 Chr 29.12;

Eccl 7.14. Possible sarcasm: Prov 10.15; 13.8; 14.20; 18.11; 19.4; Eccl 10.19.

38. 1 Kgs 3.10-13; 2 Chr 1.11-12; Job 4.21; 15.29; 20.15-20; 21.7-26; 22.20; 22.23-30; 27.19; 28.15; 31.24-25; Pss 10.3-5; 19.10; 30.6; 37.7; 37.16; 49.5-6; 49.10-15; 49.16-20; 52.7; 62.9-10; 73.3, 12; 119.14; 119.36; 119.72; 119.127; Prov 3.14; 8.10; 8.19; 10.2; 11.4; 11.16; 11.28; 15.16; 15.25; 16.8; 16.16; 16.19; 17.1; 18.23; 20.15; 21.26; 22.1; 22.7; 23.4; 27.23-24; 28.6; 28.11; 28.20; 28.22; 28.25; 29.13; 30.8-9; Eccl 2.8-11; 4.8; 5.10; 5.11; 5.12; 5.13; 6.2; 10.20; Isa 2.7; 10.3; 13.17; 53.9; Jer 5.26-28; 6.13; 9.23; 12.1; 22.21; 48.7; 51.13; Ezek 7.19; 28.4-5, Hos 12.7-8, Mic 6.10-12; Zeph 1.18; Zech 11.4-5.

39. See esp. N. Gottwald, *The Tribes of Yahweh* (Maryknoll, New York, 1979) 210-19, for the summary of his view that the very rise of Israel was due to a 'a group of outsiders who entered Canaan with enthusiastic adherence to the deliverer God Yahweh and who supplied a militant stimulant to revolution among the native Canaanite underclasses' (210).

40. Cf. the description in Gager, *Kingdom* 23-32.

41. B.R. Wilson, *Prophecy and Society in Ancient Israel* (Philadelphia, 1980) 302; cf. 286.

42. *Ibid.* 215, 271; C. Kuhl, *The Prophets of Israel* (London, 1960) 75; L.J. Wood, *The Prophets of Israel* (Grand Rapids, 1979) 304.

43. Wilson, *Prophecy* 282. See also G. Hölscher, *Die Profeten* (Leipzig, 1914) 298. Kuhl (*Prophets* 124) expresses doubts about Ezekiel's priestly background.

44. Kuhl (*Prophets* 59) argues that 'From his acquaintance with geography, history, mythology, and legendary and proverbial wisdom, it is obvious that he was not an uneducated yokel'. Wood (*Prophets* 286) argues that his work with cattle, sheep, and sycamore trees adds credence to the claim of affluence. Cf. Wilson, *Prophecy* 268.

45. Kuhl, *Prophets* 61.

46. Wilson, *Prophecy* 275.

47. *Ibid.* 280. Cf. Wood, *Prophets* 321.

48. *Ibid.* 289.

49. *Ibid.* 229, 242; cf. Kuhl, *Prophets* 66.

50. J. Barton ('Ethics in Isaiah of Jerusalem', *JTS* 32 [1981] 3) remarks that prophets have increasingly appeared 'as primarily links in a chain of tradition, handing on standards of morality long accepted as authoritative within the circles in which they themselves moved, and seeking to recall the people at large, who had lost touch with the roots of their own traditional culture to a renewed allegiance to these uncompromising moral values.'

51. E.g. Isa 35.1-10; (2 Isa 45.14; 3 Isa 60.5); Ezek 36.8-10; Amos 9.14; Mic 4.13; Zeph 3.20; Zech 14.14; Jer 33.6-9; Hos 14.7.

52. Certainly in the prophets (plunder, n. 36 above), but probably even in the Psalms, reversal of fortune is forecast not within the nation but between the nations. See Birkeland, *Evil-doers* 60, 93.

53. E. Gerstenberger, 'The Woe-Oracles of the Prophets', *JBL* 81 (1962) 256-58; J.W. Whedbee, *Isaiah and Wisdom* (Nashville, 1971) 80-90; Barton, *Ethics* 4; *contra* E.W. Davies (*Prophecy and Ethics* [JSOTS, 16, Sheffield, 1981] 118), who argues that the origin is even more broad, and describes prophecy and wisdom as 'parallel forms of spiritual and literary activity'.

54. Proverbial form: Jer 17.11; Hos 12.7; wealth pride/self-reliance: Isa 2.7 (cf. v. 11); 10.3; 13.17; (cf. v. 11); Jer 22.21; 48.7; 51.13 (cf. Isa 13.17); Ezek 7.19; 28.4-5; Zeph 1.18. Cf. Job 31.24-25; Pss 10.3; 49.5-6; 52.7; 73.3; Prov 11.4; 11.28; 16.19.

55. I include these because twelve of seventeen passages with which we are concerned (those occuring in Pss 37, 49, 52, 73, 112, and 119) fall into the wisdom classification according to L. Sabourin, *The Psalms* (New York, 1974) 494; see also P.A. Munch, 'Das Problem Reichtums in den Psalmen 37, 49, 73', *ZAW* 14 (1937) 390-46, who argues that Ps 49 is typical international wisdom, 37 and 73 Jewish; and the ideals expressed are generosity, priestly righteousness, and detachment—not social change.

56. R. Gordis, 'The Social Background of Wisdom Literature', *HUCA* 18 (1943-44) 82; cf. Gerstenberger, *Woe-Oracles* 256; Malchow, *Justice* 121.

57. M.H. Pope, *Job* (Garden City, New York, 1973) xli, concerning Job; cf. Gordis, *Background* 91-92 for more general remarks.

58. Cf. note 34 above.

59. Gordis, *Background* 93-111.

60. *Ibid.* 81. I think Gordis goes too far when (105) he concludes that 'The Messianic hope on earth and the faith in an afterlife alike find no echo in their thought. Nowhere in the entire literature do we find the faith of the prophets in a dynamic world.' The parallels in the HW stratum suggest a common background between wisdom and prophecy writers, and there are notable exceptions to Gordis' points (cf. Prov 11.4).

61. According to the translation of Franz Delitzsch (*Biblical Commentary on the Proverbs of Solomon* [Edinburgh, 1884] 93): 'Whoever oppresses the lowly, it is gain to him; whoever giveth to the rich, it is only loss'.

62. According to the translation of E. Dhorme (*A Commentary on the Book of Job* [London, 1967] 60): 'Has not their excess of wealth been snatched from them?'.

63. I distinguish the second group, which is identical in form and argues that 'something bad with righteousness is better than something good with wickedness', thereby placing greater emphasis on the ethical aspect than the economic. In the first group poverty is not mentioned, leaving a greater contrast between righteousness and wealth. Cf. *The Instruction of Amenemope* 9.5 and Chapter 3 note 37 above.

64. An interesting variation on this theme is Eccl 6.2, where the author laments the case of a man who dies without enjoying his wealth. This might be construed as VW (see R.B. Salters, 'Notes on the Interpretation of Qoh 6.2', *ZAW* 91 [1979] 288-89) unless it is inferred that worry over wealth (i.e.

greed, hence unrighteousness) is that which precludes enjoyment (see R.B.Y. Scott, *Proverbs. Ecclesiastes* [Garden City, New York, 1965] 232).

Notes to Chapter 5

1. Inserted references to wealth (alternate translation possibilities in parentheses): (Deut 33.19); 1 Kgs 2.10; Esth 1.20; Job 27.18; Ps 9.29; 33.1; (36.3); 75.5; Prov 11.16; 13.23; 19.22; 23.4; 29.3; (31.3); 31.14; 31.28; 31.29; Isa 5.14; (16.14); 29.2; (29.5-8); (32.14); 32.18. Cf. note 11 below for divergences relevant to the justice imperative.

2. Prov 14.24 makes the crown of the wise their wisdom (σοφῶν; Heb עשרם); Prov 28.20 condemns ὁ κακὸς rather than ואץ להעשיר; Prov 18.23 is simply missing in the LXX text; and the following translate words other than עשר in a non-economic sense: הון: Ezek 27.12; 27.18; 27.27; המון: Ezek 29.19; 30.4; 30.10; חיל: Gen 34.29; Deut 8.17, 18; Ruth 2.1; 1 Sam 9.1; Job 5.5; Pss 10.5; 49.6; Isa 8.4; 10.13-14; Jer 15.13; Ezek 26.12; 28.4-5; Mic 4.13; Obad 1.11; Zech 9.4; 14.14. Only the translator(s) of Ezekiel could be said to have a tendency to omit economic references, but even these changes are not dramatic given the flexibility of חיל.

3. Without attempting a detailed examination of the arguments for dating each work, I have attempted to collate the conclusions of the following authorities: R.H. Charles (*APOT I-II* [Oxford, 1913]); J.H. Charlesworth (*The Pseudepigrapha and Modern Research with a Supplement* [Chico, California, 1981]; G.W.E. Nickelsburg (*Jewish Literature Between the Bible and the Mishna* [Philadelphia, 1981]); L. Rost (*Judaism Outside the Hebrew Canon* [Nashville, Tennessee, 1976], 199-201); C. Rowland (*The Open Heaven: A Study of Apocalyptic in Judaism and Early Christianity* [London, 1982] 266-67); P.W. van der Hoerst ('Pseudo-Phocylides and the New Testament', *ZNTW* 69 [1978] 188); *The Old Testament Pseudepigrapha*, 2 vols., ed. J.H. Charlesworth (Garden City, New York, 1983, 1085); *Jewish Writings of the Second Temple Period*, ed. M.E. Stone (Philadelphia, 1984). Abbreviations follow Charlesworth, *Research* 11-13.

4. Note: references are given in the order of Table 6. Passages in prophetic material: LXX Deut 33.19; 1 Kgs 2.10; Isa 5.14; 16.14; 29.2; 29.5-8; 32.14; 32.18; Sib Or III 41-42; 189; 234-36; 241-47; 345; 388; 436; 444-48; 531; 638-40; 657; 750; 783; Jub 23.19-21; T Jud 21.6; T Dan 5.7; 1 En 94.6-8; 96.4-5; 97.8-10; 98.2-3; 100.6; 102.9; 103.5-6; 104.2-7; 38.3-5; 46.7; 52.2-4; 52.7; 63.2; 63.10; Bar 3.16-19; Pss Sol 17.46; 2 En 10.5; 4 Ez 8.54; 2 Bar 24.1; 44.14; 70.4. Passages in historical or narrative material: LXX Esth 1.20; 1 Macc 6.2; 2 Macc 3.6; 7.24; 10.20; Ps-Philo 29.1; 58.2; Jos Asen 10-12; *BJ* II 119-123. Cf. notes 6 and 43 for a complete list of passages.

5. LXX Isa 5.14; Sib Or III 41-42; 189; 234-36; Jub 2.19-21; 1 En 94.6-8; 96.4-5; 97.8-10; 98.2-3; 100.6; 102.9; 103.5-6; 104.2-6; 46.7; 52.7; 63.2; 63.10;

Bar 3.16-19; Pss Sol 17.46; 2 En 10.5. Indeed, only Jub and Bar are unaffected by passages in the VW stratum: see note 6 below.

6. VW stratum: Ahik 2.51 [Syr A]; 2.64 [Syr A]; 2.66 [Arm]; 2.69 [Arm]; 2.70 [Arm]; 26.6 [Gk]; 26.10 [Gk]; LXX Deut 33.19; 1 Kgs 2.10; Ps 36 [Hb 37].3; Prov 11.16; 13.23; 31.3; 31.14; 31.29; Isa 16.14; 29.2; 29.5-8; 32.14; 32.18; Tob 14.2; Sir 3.4; 3.17-18; 8.19; 10.27 10.30-11.1; 11.4-6; 11.20-21; 12.8-9; 13.24-25; 14.3-10; 14.11-16; 18.25; 18.32-19.1; 20.14-15; 21.4; 21.30-31; 22.23; 24.17; 26.3-4; 27.28; 28.24; 29.22; 29.23; 30.19-20; 33.19-23; 40.28-30; 44.6, 11; 47.18b; Ep Arist 196; 205; 226; 242; 263; 282; 290; Sib Or III 241-247; 345; 388; 436; 444-78; 531; 638-40; 657; 750; 783; 1 Macc 6.2; 2 Macc 3.6; 7.24; T Jud 23.3; 25.4; T Zeb 6.4-6; T Jos 11.7; Ep Jer 35; 1 En 38.3-5; 52.2-4; Pss Sol 16.13-15; T Job 4.5-7; 8.1-2; 28.5; 44.7; Ps-Phoc 109-110; 2 En A 43.2-3; T Abr 1; 2 Bar 70.4. Critical equality: Ahik 2.35 [Arm]; 2.67 [Arab]; LXX Esth 1.20; Sir 10.22 [Gk only]; 11.14; 1 Es 3.18-19; Wis 6.7; cf., T Benj A 6.5. Figurative references to wealth: LXX Prov 31.28; Tob 4.21; Sir 6.14; 30.14-16; T Gad 7.5-6; 1 En 103.5-6; Bar 3.15; Pss Sol 1.3-8; 18.1; Wis 7.11-13; 8.5; 8.18; 10.11; T Job 26.2-3; Ps-Philo 50.5; 51.3; 4 Ez 6.5; 7.77; 8.36; 8.54; 2 Bar 24.1; 44.14; Odes Sol 9.5; 11.16; 18.1; cf. Sir 40.18-19. HW stratum: see n. 43 below. Justice imperative: (see n. 11 below.)

7. See discussion below, (nn. 32-36.)

8. See Mealand, *Poverty* 11, Gager, *Kingdom* 24, and Theissen, *Sociology* 32, 45.

9. Joint references that convey critical equality: Ahik 2.35 [Arm]; 2.67 [Arab]; LXX 1.20; Sir 10.22; 11.14; 25.2; 1 Es 3.18-19; Wis 6.7; VW: Sir 11.20-21; 13.24-25; 18.25; 18.33-19.1; 26.3-4; 29.22; T Jud 25.4 T Abr 1; 2 Bar 70.4; HW: Ahik 2.14 [Syr A]; LXX Prov 19.22; Sir 13.2-8; 13.5-20; 13.21; 13.22; 30.14; 31.1-4; Jub 23.19-21; T Jud 21.6; 2 En 10.5. Cf. Ps-Phoc 28-29 in the justice imperative stratum. LXX Prov 19.22 and Sir 30.14 fall into the pattern of Prov 37.16, making some higher value the consolation even of poverty and some misfortune the curse even of riches.

10. Pss Sol 5.2-3; 5.13; 10.7; 15.1-2; 5 Syr Pss 2.18; Wis 2.10. It may be significant that this phenomenon occurs only in psalmic material: perhaps these later psalmists recognized the poor-pious equation as a convention in this type of writing.

11. Note: * indicates passages containing the word ἐλεημοσύνη; ** indicates passages containing descriptions of almsgiving. LXX Ps 32.5;* Prov 3.3;* 15.27a [Hb 16.6];* 19.22;* 20.28;* 23.4; 31.28,* Isa 1.27;* 28.17;* Dan 4.27;* Tob 1.3;* 1.7-8; 1.16-17;* 2.14;* 4.5-11;* 4.16;* 4.17;** 4.21;* 7.7;* 12.8-10;* 13.6;* 14.2;* 14.7;* 14.9-11;* Sir 3.4;** 3.14 [Gk only];* 3.30 [Gk only];* 4.1-10; 7.10;* 7.32-35; 10.22 [Hb only]; 10.23-24; 10.30-11.1; 12.1-3;* 13.24-25; 16.14;* 17.22;* 17.29; 21.5; 22.23; 22.25-26; 25.2; 29.1-12;* 29.20;** 31.11;* 34.20-22; 35.2;* 35.9-11;** 35.12-14; 40.13-14; 40.17 [Gk only];* 40.18-26;* 1 En 10.20; Ep Arist 205;** 226;** 290;** Sib Or III 241-47;** Jub 13.25-26; 32.2; 1 Macc 14.14; 2 Macc 3.10; T Levi 13.5;** T Jud

21.7-8; T Iss 3.8;** 5.2;** 7.5;** T Zeb 6.4-6;** 7.1-8.3;** T Gad 7.5-6; T Ash 2.5-8;** T Jos 3.5;** T Benj 4.2;** 1 En 98.6-16; 99.12-15; Bar 4.22b; 5.9; Pss Sol 5.2-3; 5.13; 9.9;** 10.7; 15.1-2; 17.46; 18.2-3; 5 Syr Pss 2.18; Wis 2.10; T Job 9.2-15.5;* 25.3-4; 30.3; 32.2-8; 44.1-5; 45.3;** 53.1-6; Ps-Phoc 5-6; 22-23;** 28-29;** 2 En 9.1;** 10.5; A 44.4-5;** 50.5;** 51.1;** 52.7; A 61: intro;** 63.1-2;** Jos Asen 10-12; Ode Sol 20.5-6.

12. See M. Hengel, *Judaism and Hellenism*, 2 vols., ET (London, 1974) 35-57, esp. 56, where he states that 'An essential factor here is that in the economic sphere Hellenism brought about no radical break, but intensified developments which had already begun to take shape in Palestine in the Persian period through the mediation of the Phoenicians'. To this we might add the non-colonial injustice of the prophetic period.

13. צדקה: Ps 32.5; Isa 1.27; 28.17; Dan 4.27; חסד: Prov 3.3; 15.27a [Heb 16.6]; 19.22; 20.28; cf. Prov 31.28 (no Heb equivalent) and the following references best translated 'act of mercy' rather than 'alms': Gen 47.29; Deut 6.25; 24.13; Pss 24.5; 35.24; 103.6; Prov 14.22; 21.21; Isa 38.18; 59.16; Dan 9.16.

14. Tob 4.10; 12.9; 14.11; Sir 3.14 [Gk]; 3.30 [Gk].

15. Tob 4.7; 13.6; Sir 35.2; 35.11; 40.17 [Gk]; 40.24; T Zeb 7.1-8.3; 2 En 9.1; A 44.5; B 51.1; Jos Asen 10-12; 2 En 9.1; 44.5; 51.1-2; 63.1-2. See Klaus Berger, 'Almosen für Israel', *NTS* 23 (Ja, 1977) 180-207, who proposes that LXX Prov 15.27a, Dan 4.27, and Jos Asen 10 signify an atoning function of alms for the heathen in particular.

16. Ep Arist 205; 226; T Zeb 6.4-6; T Job 44.7; cf. 9.2-15.5.

17. Cf Prov 19.17; Tob 12.8; Sir 3.4; T Lev 13.5; Pss Sol 9.9; 2 En 50.5. For good works=treasure, see 4 Ezra 7.77; 2 Bar 14.12.

18. Tob 4.7; cf. Tob 8.1-2; 1 En 97.8; where ὑπάρχοντα is equated with πλοῦτος.

19. See Tob 4.7, 16; Sir 4.5; 14.3-10; 31.13; 35.9; T Iss 3.4; T Benj 4.2.

20. Cf. Chapter 4 note 36 and Table 3 above.

21. Hengel, *Riches* 18. It should be noted that Hengel makes this remark with reference to 1 En, but goes on to call it part of a 'tradition' stretching from David to Dante (19).

22. Grant, *Background* 107. See also Weber, *Sociology* 110.

23. Even where HW occurs, we find the passages notoriously silent about colonial domination. Only five passages clearly refer to Gentiles (1 En 46.7; 63.2; 63.10; Bar 3.16-19; Jos Asen 10-12; other passages in 1 En may be included because of similarity of context); the overwhelming majority are ethical equations and injunctions in the Semitic tradition.

24. See Scroggs, *Communities* 4 (Chapter 1 note 1 above).

26. Ahik 2.51 [Syr A]; 26.10 [Gk]; Sir 8.19; 10.27; 11.20; 14.11-16; 18.33-19.1; 20.14-15; 22.23; 28.24; 29.22; 29.23; 33.19-23; 40.28-30; cf. Sir 7.22; 8.12; 8.13 (lending).

27. Ahik 2.64 [Syr A]; 2.66 [Arm]; 2.69 [Arm]; 2.70 [Arm]; 26.6 [Gk]; LXX

Prov 31.3; 31.14; 31.29; Sir 3.4; 10.30; 11.4-6; 11.11; 12.8-9; 21.30-31; 26.3-4; 30.10-20; Ep Arist 242; 1 Macc 6.2; 2 Macc 3.6; 7.24; Ep Jer 35; 2 En 43.2-3.

28. Cf. Ahik 2.69 [Arm]; 2.70 [Arm]; Sir 10.27; 10.30-11.1; 12.8-9; 22.23; 29.23. Note also the distinction made in Sir 29.22 and implied in Ahik 2.51 [Syr A] that a poor man 'on the way up' is a step above a wealthy man reduced to begging. On independence see Sir 14.11-16; 18.33-19.1; 28.24; 29.22; 33.20-23; 44.6, 11.

29. In fact, when the reader is told to give according to his means (Tob 4.5-8, 16; Sir 29.20; 2 En 51.1), we may infer a command not to give beyond them rather than (or together with) a command to give proportionately.

30. Sir 14.3-10; Ep Arist 205; 226; 290; Sib Or III 241-47; T Ash 2.5-8; T Abr 1. Of course, any command to give alms that assumes a wealthy audience could be included here. Other qualifications of charity include humility (Sir 3.17-18; 11.4-6; 18.25; Ep Arist 196), fear of God (2 En A 43.2-3), endurance of affliction (Ahik 2.66 [Arm]), and a worthy soul (Ep Arist 282).

31. Only Sir 29.1-12, which makes no explicit negative statement about wealth; and Jos Asen 10-12, which makes no explicit mention of alms, can be included in the HW stratum.

32. Of the twenty-two refernces, five used the word 'treasure': Sir 6.14; Bar 3.15; 4 Ez 8.54; 2 Bar 24.1; 44.14 (cf Tob 4.9; Sir 29.11-12; 2 En 50.5). The other seventeen use 'wealth'; of these five use nouns alone: Tob 4.21 (ὑπάρχει); T Gad 7.6; Wis 7.11-13; T Job 26.2-3; Ps-Philo 51.3; five use nouns modified with a genitive or dative: Sir 30.16; 1 En 103.5; Pss Sol 1.3; Wis 8.18; Ode Sol 11.16; five use verb forms: LXX Prov 31.28a; Wis 10.11; Ps-Philo 50.5; Odes Sol 9.5; 18.1; two use adjectival forms: Pss Sol 18.1; Wis 8.5.

33. Cf. Prov 3.14, where the 'profit (תבואתה)' of wisdom is 'better than gold'; 20.15; where the 'lips of knowledge are a precious jewel'; and Isa 33.6, where 'the fear of the Lord is his treasure'.

34. LXX Prov 31.28a; Sir 6.14; Bar 3.15; Pss Sol 18.1; Wis 7.11-13; 10.11; 4 Ez 8.54; 2 Bar 44.14; Ode Sol 9.5; 18.1.

35. HW in the same context: Sir 30.14-16; 1 En 103.5-6; Pss Sol 1.3-8; Wis 8.5; figurative use as a foil: Tob 4.21; T Gad 7.5-6; Wis 8.18; T Job 26.2-3; Ps-Philo 51.3. Note that the latter group tends to use the noun 'wealth' modified with a genitive or dative.

36. See references in F. Hauck and W. Kasch, 'πλοῦτος', *TDNT* VI, 319; Liddell–Scott 1423.

37. D.S. Russell, *The Method and Message of Jewish Apocalyptic* (London, 1964) 28. Prophetic references to wealth are as numerous in the VW stratum as in the HW stratum (cf. nn. 4 and 6 above). Even in the earlier post-exilic struggle posited by Hanson (*The Dawn of Apocalyptic* [Philadelphia, 1975] 211-20) between oppressed groups in the prophetic tradition and hierocractic

groups, we encounter the same form and balance of ethical material (see ch. 4 nn. 37, 38, and esp. 51); cf. Hanson, *Dawn* 228, 240, 286, 400).

38.   In the VW stratum: [Ahik] 2.51 [Syr]; 2.66 [Arm]: 2.70 [Arm]: 26.10 [Gk]; LXX Ps 36.3; Prov 31.3; Sir 3.17-18; 8.19; 11.4-6; 11.20-21; 14.11-16; 18.33; 22.23; 28.24; 33.19-23; 40.28-30; Ep Arist 196; 205; 226; 242; 263; 282; 290; T Jud 23.3; T Job 4.5-7; Ps-Phoc 109-110; cf. 1st person references: Ahik 2.69 [Arm]; T Zeb 6.4-6; T Job 44.7; HW stratum: Ahik 2.14 [Syr A]; 2.71 [Syr A]; Tob 12.8-10; Sir 5.1-3; 5.8; 8.1-2; 8.12-13; 13.2-8; 13.9-13; 18.32; 25.21; 29.1-12; 31.12-13; Ep Arist 211; T Jud 17.1; 19.1-2; 21.6; T Ash 5.1; 1 En 96.4-5; 97.8-10; 98.2; 102.9; 103.5-6; 104.2-6; Ps-Phoc 53.34; 2 En 50.5; cf. 1st person references: Wis 5.8-9; 7.8-9; T Job 18.6-8; 33.3-5; Justice Imperative stratum: LXX Prov 3.3; 23.4; Dan 4.27; Tob 2.14; 4.5-11; 4.16; 4.17; 13.6; 14.9-11; Sir 4.1-10; 7.10; 7.32-35; 12.1-3; 22.25-26; 29.20; 35.9-11; 35.12-14; 13.5; T Iss 5.2; T Job 45.3; Ps-Phoc 22-23; 28.29; 2 En 51.1-2; Ode Sol 20.5-6; cf. 1st person references: Tob 1.3; 1.7-8; 1.16-17; T Iss 3.8; 7.5; T Zeb 7.1-8.3; T Jos 3.5; Wis 2.10; T Job 9.2.

39.   See (p. 93 n. 23) above.

40.   Nickelsburg, *Literature* 55-56.

41.   H. Stadelmann, *Ben Sira als Schriftgelehrter* (Tübingen, 1980) 26.

42.   Gordis, *Background* 93; cf. 77-118; cf. also Nickelsburg, *Literature* 56.

43.   Ahik 2.14 [Syr A]; 2.71 [Syr A]; LXX Job A 27.18; Ps 9.29; 33.1; 75.5; Prov 19.22; 23.4; Isa 5.14; Tob 12.8-10; Sir 1.22 [Syr]; 5.1-3; 5.8; 7.18; 8.1-2; 8.12-13; 10.23-24; 11.18-19; 13.2-8; 13.9-13; 13.15-20; 13.21; 13.22; 13.23; 25.21; 27.1-2; 28.10; 29.1-12; 30.14-16; 31.1-4; 31.5-11; 31.12-13; 40.18-26; Ep Arist 211; Sib Or III 41-42; 189; 234-236; Jub 23.19-21; 2 Macc 10.20; T Jud 17.1; 18.2; 19.1-2; 21.6-7; T Iss 4.2; T Dan 5.7; T Ash 2.5-8; 5.1; T Benj 6.2-3; 6.5 [Arm]; 1 En 94.6-8; 96.4-5; 97.8-10; 98.2-3; 100.6; 102.9; 103.5-6; 104.2-3, 6; 46.7; 52.7; 63.2; 63.10; 1 Bar 3.16-19; Pss Sol 1.3-8; 5.18-20; 17.46; Wis 5.8-9; 7.8-9; 8.5; T Job 15.7-9; 18.6-8; 33.3-5; 48.2; 50.1; Ps-Phoc 42-43; 53-54; 61-62; 2 En 10.5; 50.5; Ps-Philo 35.5; 39.1; 58.2; Jos Asen 10-12; 4 Macc 1.26; 2.8; *BJ* II 119-123.

44.   Cf. examples in Greek literature given by Liddell–Scott 1932; BAG 866. Cf. also Sir 31.5; T Jud 17.1; Ps-Phoc 42.

45.   Cf. Ahik 2.71 [Syr A]; LXX Job A 27.18; Ps 9.29; Isa 5.14; Sir 8.1-2; 8.12-13; 31.10; Jub 23.21; 1 En 96.5; 97.10; 102.9; 104.5-6; Pss Sol 17.46; Ps-Phoc 42-43; 61-62. The converse of the equation (i.e. 'the unjust are wealthy') is illustrated by the following passages: T Jud 21.6; T Ash 2.8; 2 En 10.5.

46.   Cf. Sir 13.3-4; 13.21; 13.22; 13.23; 31.3-4; 1 En 63.2. Cf. also the Armenian MS variant of T Benj 6.5, which condemns preference for the wealthy.

47.   The Hebrew replaces 'wakefulness' (ἀγρυπνία) with שְׁקַר ('disappoint-ment') and includes שְׁקַר ('care') in a marginal gloss.

48. Cf. 1 En 96.4-5; 103.5-6; 104.2-6; cf. also Jas 5.1-8, which exhibits many parallels to the Enoch passage.

49. G.W.E. Nickelsburg ('Riches, the Rich, and God's Judgment in 1 Enoch 92-105 and the Gospel According to Luke', *NTS* 25 [1979] 324-44) cites these and other similarities of content between Luke and the writer of 1 En 92-105 to posit 'some form of contact' (342)—a legitimately conservative conclusion. See also S. Aalen, 'St. Luke's Gospel and the Last Chapters of 1 Enoch', *NTS* 13 (1966) 1-13, who argues for literary dependence. Nickelsburg rightly notes (335) that 1 En is closer to Luke than Sir 11.18-19.

50. *BH* 1115. The context may favor the LXX reading, or at least justify the error: mention of the poor (עָנִי, v. 5) and material possessions (טוֹב, v. 13) set up a possible contrast, and no other reference is made to animals or other nature metaphors. On the other hand, Ps 10.9 (cf. 7.2) refers to the unjust wicked as lions; hence, the LXX translator may have been clarifying here.

51. Note the interesting parallels to Phil 3.7-8; the loss of 'all things (τὰ πάντα, cf. T Job 4.5; 8.2; 20.1)' and the 'consideration' of them (ἡγοῦμαι; cf. ἡγησάμην, T Job 18.7) as nothing.

52. This was 'ordained at Usha' (*b. Ketub.* 50a) where the Sanhedrin met after Jamnia, and where a rabbinical synod was held after the wars of Bar Cochba (I.W. Slotki, *Ketub.*, p. 283 n. 12).

53. Cf. the reading of the shorter Slavonic version: 'Lose gold or silver for a brother's sake, that you receive inexhaustible treasure on the judgment day'.

54. H.C. Kee ('The Socio-cultural Setting of Joseph and Asenath', *NTS* 29 [1983] 410) affirms that Asenath's gifts 'are not acts of charity but an easy way to rid herself of what she no longer values'. Kee contends that the book 'seems to have been addressed to an esoteric group of upper-middle class Jews and converts'.

55. Cf. Chapter 5.4 below. Josephus's account is considered here as a sympathetic report from an outsider evincing the dissemination of Essene ideas during the period.

56. This section appears in substantially its present form in *JSNT* (1983) under the title 'Hostility to Wealth in Philo of Alexandria'. Note: I follow F.C. Conybeare (*Philo and the Contemplative Life* [Oxford, 1895] 325-58) against P.E. Lucas (*Die Therapeuten und ihre Stellung in der Geschichte der Askese* [Strassburg, 1879] with respect to the authenticity of *Vita*: Conybeare argues persuasively for the authenticity of the work on linguistic grounds.

57. *ZNW* 69 (1978) 258-64. Mealand ('The Paradox of Philo's View of Wealth', *JSNT* 24 [1985] 111-15) and F.G. Downing ('Philo on Wealth and the Rights of the Poor', *JSNT* 24 [1985] 116-18) have responded to my article, Downing most helpfully by introducing a few texts that I had missed which show a greater degree of sympathy for the poor on Philo's part than I had originally supposed. I am grateful for their comments, which have led

me to modify my view in this respect. My conclusions, however, were not seriously challenged by either writer. Mealand, for example, appears to misunderstand the crucial distinction between involuntary and voluntary dispossession and the primary relevance of the latter to HW. Thus I can assent to all of the conclusions in Mealand's 'rejoinder'. His only defense of the charge that his earlier article relies unduly on SEC as determinative of Philo's attitude is a question-begging allusion to 'those who are allergic to sociological theory' (*Paradox* 113). Rather than to respond in kind by labelling others as *addicted* to sociological theory, I would prefer to extend the metaphor by appealing for a search for a medicinal use of this apparently potent substance.

58. Mealand, *Philo* 264, a claim in support of which he cites not ancient texts, but two sociologists and his own dissertation.

59. *Ibid.* 258. See also S. Sandmel, *Philo of Alexandria* (Oxford, 1979) 12; V. Burr, *Tiberius Iulius Alexander* (Bonn, 1965) *passim*.

60. See G. Mäyer, *Index Philoneus* (Berlin, 1974) 235 for a list of the 149 passages cited below.

61. Roughly half the references (see *ibid.* 42, 307) use ἄργυρος and χρυσός to denote wealth (abbreviations follow Sandmel, *Philo* xi-xii; parentheses indicate that the passage also contains πλοῦτος): L.A. II 107; Cher. 34; 48; 80; Sac. 21; 26; 55; Det. 20; 157; Post. 150; Deus 169; Ebr. 85-86; 95; Sob. 41; Conf. 93; Mig. 97; 103; Her. 44; 216-17; Congr. 112; 113-14; Fug. 15; (26); 35; Mut. 89-90; 93; Som. II 44; 57-62; Abr. (209); (220); Jos. 120; 125; 150; (258); Mos. I (152); (317); Decal. 4; (71); 133; Spec. I (21-25); Spec. II (20); Spec. IV (74); (158); 223; Prob. (9); 31; (65); (76); Vita 49; Flacc. (131); 142; Leg. (9, context includes χρήματα); (108); 343.

62. Op. 79; L.A. I 75; L.A. II 17; Det. 135; Post. 114; 117; Gig. (15); 36-37; Deus 163; Plant. 66; 171; Ebr. 22; Sobr. 67; Mig. 217; Her. (48); 92; Fug. (28); 39; Som. I 124; Som. II 128; Abr. 228; Jos. 76; 135; Mos. I 141; 267; 293; Decal. 151; (153); Spec. I 78; 104; 143; 151; Spec. II 93; Spec. III 70; 82; 139; 168; 181; Spec. IV 10; 33; 82; 87; (159); Virt. (82); 182; Praem. (104); 142; Prob. 55; 65; 145; Vita 14; 16; Flacc. 60; Leg. 9; 17; 156; 172; 232; 315.

63. Op. 23; L.A. I 34; 45; L.A. II 12; L.A. III 24; 39; 163; 211; Sac. 124; Det. 131; Post. 139; 144; 151; 174; Agr. 54; Plant. 66; Mig. 71; Her. 27; 48; 76; Congr. 76; Fug. 17; 102; Som. I 179; Abr. 25; Mos. I 153; 155; Mos. II 38; Decal. 178; Spec. II 23; 107; Spec. IV 75; 194; Virt. 5; 6; 7; 8; 10; 81; 85; 94; 148; Praem. 36; Prob. 8; 77; Vita 17; 35; Flacc. 63; Leg. 51; 141; 203.

64. See also Her. 148; Mos. I 153; 155; Spec. II 23; Virt. 85.

65. Post. 109; Her. 212; Congr. 5; Som. I 155; Som. II 35; Jos. 72; Spec. I 139; 277; Spec. IV 172. See also Post. 114; Deus 163; Plant. 66; Abr. 228; Jos. 135; Spec. I 104; 143; Spec. III 70; 82; 168; 181; Spec. IV 10; 33; 159; Leg. 156; 315; where χρήματα is used in a noncritical sense; and Op. 49; Post. 35; Plant. 126; Ebr. 141; Her. 246; Spec. I 342; Leg. 4; 215; 295; where χρῆμα is used for tribute money.

66. Jos. 144; Spec. II 71; 87; 107; Virt. 97; 169; Leg. 13; 199.

67. In answer to Mealand's challenge (*Paradox* 114), 'Is it vague?', my response is simply 'yes'. The passage in question (Praem 168) describes eschatological reversal, and the reference to 'wealth to each individually and all in common' requires no social program, much less a sacrifice on the part of the rich for the poor. Philo envisions an ideal of abundance without specifying its production or maintenance.

68. L.A. III 24; 86; 197; Sac. 19; 43; Sob. 21; 41; 61; Mig. 94; 103; 172; 217; Her. 216-17; Fug. 15; Mut. 88-89; 173; Som. II 44; Jos. 120; 150; 198; Mos. I 141; 293; 312-17; Spec. I 78; 151; Spec. II 87; 208; Spec. IV 223; Praem. 142; 168; Leg. 232. Another indication of the distinction is that the VW passages are almost all narrative whereas the HW passages are usually didactic.

69. See also Spec. IV 65; 87; 212; Virt. 82; Flacc. 130-31; 142.

70. See Cher. 34; Det. 157; Post. 150; Conf. 93; Her. 44; Mut. 226; Som. II 40; Jos. 125; 140; Prob. 31; 65.

71. Mut. 226; Abr. 221; Mos. I 141; Spec. I 23; 24; 281; Spec. II 78; Spec. IV 65; 212; 215; Prob. 21; Flacc. 60. See examples in Liddell-Scott 1670, 1679, which demonstrate the commonness of these words in Greek literature.

72. See Spec. III 139; Spec. IV 158; Virt. 85-86; 161-62; Prob. 72.

73. Cf. Cher. 48; 80; Det. 135; Gig. 15; Ebr. 95; Sob. 67; Her. 48; 92; Congr. 112; Fug. 39; Som. I 248; Abr. 220; Jos. 131-33; Decal. 133; Spec. IV 82; Praem. 24; Vita 14; Flacc. 148; 148; Leg. 17.

74. Post. 115; Mut. 214; Som. II 57-62; Decal. 4; Virt. 174.

75. Abr. 209; Decal. 71; 151; Prop. 9; Vita 49.

76. See also Det. 20-21; Ebr. 22; Fug. 28; Som. I 124; 126; Som. II 128; Mos. I 267; Spec. I 93; Vita 16; Leg. 172.

77. See also Sac. 26; Abr. 219-21; Jos. 76; Virt. 188; cf. Prob. 55.

78. Ebr. 85-86; Sob. 3; Congr. 113-14.

79. Sac. 55; Ebr. 52; Mig. 101; Virt. 182.

80. This caste is most noticeable in the use of words like φιλαργυρία and χρηματία, the substitution of virtue for justice and wisdom, and the comparatively large number of references to wealth as an entity rather than to the wealthy as a group.

81. Det. 33-34; Post. 112; Gig. 15; 35; Deus 169; Agr. 31-39; 54; Plant. 69; Ebr. 75; Mig. 97; Her. 48; Congr. 27; Fug. 17-19; 151; Som. I 179; Abr 262-65; Spec. I 311; Spec. III 1.

82. L.A. II 25; L.A. III 41; 238; Sob. 5; but see Mig. 92; Mos. I 38; Leg. 325, where physical action is implied.

83. The last sentence is my own translation. Loeb translates ἀγαθῶν as 'good': θέας γὰρ ἐμπιπλαμένη τῶν γνησίων καὶ ἀφθάρτων ἀγαθῶν εἰκότως τοῖς ἐφημέροις καὶ νόθοις ἀποτάττεται. See Mut. 32 for a similar use of ἀγαθῶν.

84. Ebr. 57; Fug. 26; 35; Mut. 32 (cf. 39); Jos. 258; Spec. II 18-23; Spec. IV

159; Praem. 54; 100; Prob. 86; Vita 13; Hyp. 11.4-5, 11.

85. Hauck/Kasch 319-23. The authors demonstrate a general VW tempered by attention to the *polis* and virtue (Plato and Aristotle) or by mental detachment (Stoics).

86. H. Bolkestein, *Wohltätigkeit und Armenpflege im vorchristlichen Altertum* (Utrecht, 1939); Hands, *Charities*; W. Den Boer, *Private Morality in Greece and Rome* (Leiden, 1979) 151-78. Den Boer challenges (weakly, I think) the traditional view that the Greeks and Romans neglected charity.

87. Mealand, *Philo* 259-63.

88. See e.g. Hor. *Sat* II. iii. 82-157, 225-80; Sen. *Epist* 20.9-13.

89. Hauck/Kasch, πλοῦτος 322 n. 30.

90. Diogenes: Dio 6.61-62; 9.12; Crates: Diog. L. 6.87; Demetrius: Sen. *Vita Beat.* 18.3; *Epist.* 62.3.

91. This is not the case, as Mealand suggests (*Philo* 259), in Philo's 'praise of poverty'. Philo values only voluntary renunciation, and does not praise poverty. Seneca values poverty however it comes, even voluntarily (see *Epist.* 4.9-11; 17.5 20.7; 62.3; 87.41; 98.13). Another important difference is Seneca's bent toward Stoic detachment (*Epist.* 20.9-13; 14.17-18).

92. Cf. note 10 above. Bolkestein (*Wohltätigkeit* 114) states that in Greece 'Mahnungen an die Reichen, den Armen Almosen zu geben, fehlen....'

93. Fug. 29 (needy *friends*); Spec. IV 74; 159.

94. Hands, *Charities* 26.

95. *Ibid.* 77-88. One notable instance in Philo is Spec. IV 176-81. Although 'widow', 'orphan', and 'incomer' are the words used, and there is no explicit mention of economic condition, Philo goes as far as to liken the Jewish race to an orphan, who gets help from God rather than from natural helpers. But any meritorious economic austerity implicitly referred to here is voluntary (179) and even then not necessarily contemporary (181). The passage cannot be adduced as evidence that Philo saw Jews as poor and therefore saw wealth as bad. Decal. 40-43 suggests that one become 'affable and easy of access to the poorest ... the lonely ... orphans [and] wives on whom widowhood has fallen' not out of sympathy or social consciousness, but 'because the lot ... may change to the reverse, ... but also because ... a man should not forget what he is'. *Fragments* II Mang. 678 states that 'Poverty by itself claims compassion, in order to correct its deficiencies, but when it comes to judgment ... the judgment of God is just'. Sympathy appears stronger here, but significantly, it does not extend beyond charity to identification of God —much less the writer—with the plight of the needy. Philo himself should be given the last word: 'If then I must give judgment, I will do so without favoring the rich man because of his great property, or the poor man from pity of his misfortune ...' (Jos. 72). See also E.R. Goodenough, *The Politics of Philo Judaeus* (New Haven, Connecticut, 1938) 94-95. Downing (*Rights* 116-17) has brought to light three stronger statements of Philo's sympathy for the plight of the needy: Spec. Leg. 1.308; 2.106-108; Virt. 91. Mealand

(*Paradox* 113) brings up the oppression under Flaccus (see Flacc. 56-58; 77). But neither of these rejoinders takes up the lack of connection between these passages and Philo's HW, which is the main point here. Philo's sympathy for the disprivileged and his HW remain independent concerns.

96. *Ibid.* 62, 115. Interestingly, when Philo mentions Caligula's grain doles, in which Jews were included as Roman citizens, he makes no mention of need. See Leg. 38; R.M. Grant, *Early Christianity and Society* (New York, 1977) 142.

97. *Ibid.* 26. See also Sir 12.1-7; Ps-Phoc 80.

98. Bolkestein, *Wohltätigkeit* 158.

99. S.C. Mott, 'The Power of Giving and Receiving: Reciprocity in Hellenistic Benevolence', *Current Issues in Biblical and Patristic Interpretation*, ed. G.F. Hawthorne (Grand Rapids, 1975) 72.

100. Hands, *Charities* 48-61.

101. A.J. Saldarini, 'Apocalyptic and Rabbinic Literature', *CBQ* 37 (1975) 348-58.

102. I follow J. Neusner, *The Rabbinic Traditions About the Pharisees Before 70*, 2 vols. (Leiden, 1971).

103. See SB I, 818-26; C.G. Montefiore and H. Loewe, *A Rabbinic Anthology* (New York, 1974) 412-50; J.M. Ford, 'Three Ancient Jewish Views on Poverty', in *The New Way of Jesus*, ed. W. Klassen (Newton, Kansas, 1980) 46-53; J.D.M. Derrett, *Jesus' Audience* (London, 1973) 73-81. For an excellent survey of rabbinic justic passages relevant to the Gospels, see G.F. Moore, *Judaism*, 3 vols. (Cambridge, Massachusetts, 1927) II, 163-79.

104. Following this story is an account of Eleazar's wealth; together, the two stories place the emphasis on Torah study and not on economic status. See the examples in note 106 below.

105. *m. Pe'a* 6.1-5; *m. Ma'aś. S.* 5.3; *y. Sheb.* 10.3; see also J. Goldin ('Hillel the Elder', *JR* 26 [1946] 275-77), who explains that Hillel's invention of the *prosbul* averted pre-sabbatical year economic freezes by allowing courts to collect debts and make restitution.

106. *y. Hor.* 3.7 (AD 80-120); *Lev. R. Behar.* 34.16 (AD 120-140); *m. 'Abot* 4.1; 6.9 (AD 120-140); 6.4 (c. AD 240).

107. *M. 'Abot* 4.1; 6.9 (AD 120-140); 6.4 (c. AD 120-140). An interesting late reference is *b. 'Abod. Zar.* 64a: '[some who would be proselytes] came before Rabbah b. Abbahu and he told them, "Go and sell all your possessions and then come be converted".' The context, interestingly, is a discussion of idolatry (cf. discussion of Luke 16.13-15 below). According to H. Strack/G. Stemberger (*Einleitung in Talmud und Midrasch* [München, 1982⁷] 94), Abbahu was 3rd generation Amoraim (died c. AD 300), a late pupil of Joḥanan and of Jose b. Ḥanina, principal of the school in Caesarea. He was a student of the Greek language and culture and engaged in disputations with Christians. Could this passage exemplify Jewish borrowing of Christian ideas? An anyonymous instance of alternative devaluation occurs in *Num. R.*

Maṭ xxii, 9: 'It is written, "The wise man's heart is at his right hand, but the fool's heart is at his left" (Eccles. x, 2). The wise are the righteous, who apply their heart to the Law, for the law is at the right hand, as it is said, "From His right hand came a fiery Law for them" (Deut. xxxiii, 2): the fools are the wicked who apply their heart to get rich, as it says, "At the left hand are riches" (Prove. iii, 16). Or, the wise man is Moses, while the fools are the children of Reuben and Gad (Num. xxxii, 1-32), who made the chief thing the secondary thing, and the secondary thing the chief thing, for they loved their money more than their souls'. Cf. *Sif. Num Kor.* §119 f. 39b: 'Gold and silver take a man out of this world and the world to come, but the Torah brings a man to the to the life of the world to come'. See also *y. Pe'a* i, I 15b; *b. B. Bat.* 11a; *t. Pe'a* iv. 18; *Pesiq. Rab.* xxv, for the dispossession of Monobazus, king of Abilene, when he converted to Judaism.

108. See note 106 above; but see *m. Pe'a* 8.9 (attributed to Joḥanan); *b. Nid.* 70b (AD 80-120); *b. Pesah.* 112a (AD 120-140); *m. 'Abot* 4.9 (AD 140-165); 6.8 (AD 200-220).

109. *Tan, d. b. El.* p. 181: 'God examined all the good qualities of the world, but found no quality so good for Israel as poverty, for through poverty they fear the Lord. For if they have no bread to eat, no raiment to wear, no oil for anointing, then they seek the Lord of mercy, and they find Him'.

110. If the pattern of aristocratic HW is consistent, we might posit an even greater measure of agreement from the Sadducees. But these may have reasoned beyond Jesus' valid challenge to the concept of wealth as a measure of happiness or value to the political threat inherent in an economic upheaval (the inevitable result of mass teleological devaluation).

111. Abbreviated *N, P, F, O, J,* respectively. *F* contains an accurate rendering of Gen 14.23 (MS Vatican Ebr. 440) and follows *N* in Lev 24.12; Deut 16.19; 32.15; 33.19. The Targum to Job (*The Targum to Job from Qumran Cave XI* [Jerusalem, 1974]) preserves only 29.11-16; 36.11; and 42.,10 of the passages cited in 2.2. In 21.7, the phrase 'they grow mighty in power(גברו חיל)' is translated 'they have increased their possessions (והסאין נכסין)'; a rendering justified by the context if not by the vocabulary. LXX deviations are not reproduced in the Targums.

112. J. Bowker (*The Targums and Rabbinic Literature* [Cambridge, 1969] 16-28) and A.D. York ('The Dating of Targumic Literature', *JSJ* 5 [1974] 49-62) discuss the dates of the Pentateuch Targums; S.H. Levey ('The Date of Targum Jonathan to the Prophets', *VT* 21 [1971] 186-96) gives 200-150 B.C. and some time after AD 640 as the limits of *J*. See also M. McNamara, 'Half a Century of Targum Study', *Irish Biblical Studies* 1 (1979) 157-68, and introductory chapters of the critical editions. In the last analysis, we must conclude with B. Chilton (*The Glory of Israel. The Theology and Provenience of the Isaiah Targum* [JSOTS, 23, Sheffield, 1983] 12) that Targums are 'specimens of extended exegesis', any of whose passages require for dating determination not only of historical and literary allusions, but also of the

relation betwen exegetical 'conventions' and historical circumstances. Chilton argues that the 'principal framework' of the Isaiah Targum can be dated to the period AD 70-135 (97, cf. 112-17). We must await the application and/or refinement of Chilton's work in order to determine with greater precision the provenience of the Targum traditions.

113. See F. Hauck, 'Μαμωνᾶς', *TDNT* IV, 388-90; H.P. Rüger, 'Μαμωνᾶς', *ZNW* 64 (1973) 127-31. Targum references: *O*, *P* Gen 13.13; *O* Exod 18.21; *N*, *O*, *P* Gen 37.26; Exod 21.30 *P* Lev 16.15; *N*, *P*, *F* Lev 24.12; *P* Num 5.7; *N*, *F* Num 9.8; *N* Num 27.5; *N*, *O* Num 35.31; *P* Deut 1.18; *P* Deut 17.8; *N*, *P* Deut 6.5 *N*, *F* Deut 16.19; *N* Deut 1.18; *P* Deut 17.8; *J* 1 Sam 2.5; *J* Isa 45.13; *J* Joel 2.8; *J* Mic 2.8; *J* Mic 3.2; *J* Mic 4.13. See also Sir 31.8; CD 14.20; 1QS 6.2; 1Q27 1, 2, 5; *m. 'Abot* 2.12; *m. Sanh.* 1.1; 4.1.

114. *J* Exod 18.21 (ממון־דשיקרא, erased by censor); *N* Exod 18.21 (שיקרא־ממון); *P* 1 Sam 8.3; 12.3; *J* 2 Sam 14.14; *J* Isa 5.23; 33.15; *J* Ezek 22.27; *J* Hos 5.11; *J* Amos 5.11 (ממון־דשקר); *J* Isa 5.24; *J* Jer 6.13; 8.10; 22.17; *J* Ezek 22.13; 33.31 (with אנס); *J* Hab 2.9 (ממון־דרשע). See also 1 En 63.10 (so Hauck, μαμωνᾶς 128).

115. *N*, *P*, *F* Lev 24.12; *N*, *F* Num 9.8; *N* Num 27,5; *P* Deut 1.18; *P P* Deut 17.8; cf *m. 'Abot* 2.12; *m. Sanh.* 1.1; 4.1.

116. *N*, *P* Exod 18.21; Elsewhere 'dishonest gain': *J* 1 Sam 8.3; *J* Jer 6.13; 8.10; 22.17; *J* Ezek 22.13; 22.17; 33.31; *J* Hab 2.9; probably *J* Amos 5.11, with no Hebrew equivalent. Cf. *J* 1 Sam 12.3 (for כפר); *J* Hos 5.11 (see note 126 below).

117. *N*, *O*, *P* Gen 37.26 (בצע); *O* Exod 18.21 (בצע); *J* Isa 45.13 (שחר); probably *J* Joel 2.8; *J* Mic 2.8; 3.2 with no Hebrew equivalent (see n. 127 below). Cf. *J* Mal 3.14.

118. *N*, *O*, *P* Exod 21.30 (כפר); *P* Lev 16.15 (כפר); *P* Num 5.7 (אשמו); *N*, *O* Num 35.31 (כפר).

119. Hauck, μαμωνᾶς 389; Rüger, μαμωνᾶς 129.

120. Further evidence for this view is afforded by the context. The pattern of promised economic prosperity (6.10-11) and a subsequent warning not to forget God (6.12) is repeated in expanded and more explicitly economic terms in 8.1-10, 11-18. חיל in 8.17-18 is translated by *N*, *O*, and *P* as נכסין.

121. *N*, *O*, *P*, *F* Deut 32.15; *N*, *F*, *O* Deut 33.19; *J* Isa 60.16; *J* Jer 12.2; 48.11-12; 50.26; 51.2; *J* Ezek 26.25; 31.16; *J* Zech 11.2.

122. *J* Isa 9.11; 9.19; *J* Jer 10.25; 19.9; 51.34; 51.44; *J* Ezek 34.3; 39.19; *J* Hos 7.9; *J* Zech 9.15; 11.9; 11.16; 12.6.

123. See also *J* Isa 10.2; 15.7; 33.23; 40.29; 53.12; 57.10; *J* Jer 2.16; *J* Ezek 16.13; 27.16; 28.13; *J* Hos 8.7; *J* Zeph 1.11; 1.12. Two additional passages are worthy of note: *J* Isa 5.22 translates חיל as נכסין, thereby strengthening the economic sense; *J* Ezek 29.19; 30.4, 10 translate המון as אתרגמותחתה ('multitude'), thereby diminishing the economic sense.

124. Translations of Targum Jonathan to Isaiah are from J.F. Stenning,

The Targum of Isaiah (Oxford, 1949). Other translations are my own.

125. See the interesting discussion of the East-West struggle in R. Eisler, ΙΗΣΟΥΣ ΒΑΣΙΛΕΥΣ ΟΥ ΒΑΣΙΛΕΥΣΑΣ (Heidelberg, 1929) ch. 19. Most of his discussion centers on soures that post-date the Synoptics and which may be adduced to support a late dating of this passage.

126. The Hebrew here is difficult. MT has צו, for which BH (997) proposes שוא, citing the LXX (τῶν ματαίων) and the Peshitta ﻫﻮﺑﻞ. See the bibliography of the discussion in H.W. Wolff, *Hosea* (Philadelphia, 1974) 104.

127. As in Mic 2.8; 3.2 (note 117 above), I take ממון here to signify 'bribe' and not 'wealth'. נסין נכסי is parallel to וממון יקרחון in Mic 3.2 (cf. *J* Isa 5.24; *J* Jer 6.13; 8.10; 22.17; *J* Ezek 22.13; 33.31; where אנס and ממון in combination translate בצע; and *J* Hab 2.9, where ראנים ממון דשקר translates בצע בצע). These linguistic considerations add to the contextual consideration that not taking wealth (i.e. plunder) would be inconsistent with a conquering army's purpose, whereas not taking bribes (i.e. avoiding violence) would be consistent with its purpose.

128. Karnaim is probably a place name. Its literal meaning, 'horns', is perhaps indicative of power and symbolic of pride. See H.W. Wolff, *Joel and Amos* (Philadelphia, 1977) 287.

129. *J* 1 Sam 2.5 curses Rome, but contrasts her to 'Jerusalem who is like a barren woman' and curses the king of Babylon in the same context (v. 3): the expansion of the Song of Hannah is almost certainly late. There may be some evidence for a late date to the *J* Isa passages. 27.10 employs the same seemingly formulaic expression ויבזון נכסהא (cf. *J* Hos 7.9; 8.7; *J* Zech 9.15; 11.16) which is employed in *J* Jer 51.34 as a probably reference to Babylonian persecution. 30.20 and 33.4 share with 27.10 proximity, content, and departure from an original nature image; thus, we may with some confidence attribute them to the same source. Of course, the late date of these traditions depends on the admittedly tenuous shift from clarification to historical commentary in *J* Jer 51.34. For other possible 1st cent. AD historical allusions, see P. Churgin, *Targum Jonathan to the Prophets* (Yale Oriental Series, Researches 14, New Haven, Connecticut, 1907) 22-26.

130. Four of the unsupported insertions (*J* Isa 14.8-9; *J* Amos 4.1; 6.6; 6.13) evince stage two equations of wealth and injustice; three others (*J* Isa 53.9; *J* Hos 5.11; *J* Mic 2.8) reflect the justice imperative.

131. D.L. Mealand, 'Community of Goods at Qumran', *TZ* 31 (1975) 138. He cites CD 19.9; 1QH 2.32, 24; 3.25; 5.13ff.; 1QpHab 12.2ff. See also B. Thiering, 'The Biblical Source of Qumran Asceticism', *JBL* 93 (1974) 431; H.J. Klauck, 'Gütergemeinschaft in der klassischen Antike, in Qumran und im Neuen Testament', *Rev Q* 41 (1982) 59.

132. See ch. 4 nn. 9-10, 33; ch. 5 n. 10.

133. Fourteen occurrences: CD 6.21; 1QH 2.32; 3.25; 5.16; 18; 5.22; 1QM 11.8-9, 13; 13.14; 1QpHab 12.2-3, 6, 10; 4QpPs 37 2.8-9; 3.9-10; perhaps 3.15

(see W.H. Brownlee, *The Midrash Pesher of Habakkuk* [Missoula, Montana, 1979] 198).

134. See L.E. Keck, 'The Poor Among the Saints in Jewish Christianity and Qumran', *ZNW* 57 (1966) 66-77, who argues that most of the so-called self-designation texts are not such and that the term 'poor' is not a regular, technical term for the group. Cf. K. Elliger, *Studien zum Habakuk-Kommentar vom Toten Meer* (Tübingen, 1953) 220-23; H.J. Kandler, 'Die Bedeutung der Armut in Schrifttum vom Chirbet Qumran', *Judaica* 13 (1957) 199.

135. עני is used in a figurative sense elsewhere: 1QH 2.34-35; 5.13-14; 14.7 (with רוח).

136. Zech 11.1-17, esp. 11.11. Zech 7.10 mentions the poor (עני) as objects of justice, but in the reiteration of the prophet's ethical demand closer to this context (8.16) the poor are not mentioned. In the shepherd oracle itself the sheep are rather ill-defined victims of wicked shepherds; i.e. Israel's corrupt leadership. They are not said to be poor, but are presumably righteous as (untainted) victims. This relative purity is more likely to be a focus of the Qumran community than economic status.

137. Keck, *Qumran* 68. 4QpPs37 3.10 is incomplete, but Keck (75; cf. H. Stegemann, 'Der Pešer Psalm 37 aus Höhle 4 von Qumran (4 QpPs37)', *Rev Q* 4 [1963] 265 n. 171) argues that the context requires a verb of receiving; thus, 'the congregation of the poor will take possession of all', not '. . . will [give] the inheritance of all' (Dupont-Sommer 272).

138. See also 1QS 4.5; 4.9; 5.4; 5.25.

139. 1QS 1.11-13; 3.2; 5.2-3; 5.14, 20; 6.2; 6.17-25; 7.25; 8.23; 9.7-8; CD 13.11; 13.15-16.

140. W.R. Farmer, 'The Economic Basis of the Qumran Community', *TZ* 11 (1955) 296-97. Farmer documents the abundant supplies of fresh water, grazing land, and opportunities for trade in the immediate vicinity of the Qumran community.

141. See the bibliography in Mealand, *Community* 129 nn. 1-2.

142. Cf. 6.24-25, where punishment is described for deceit in this area: and CD 13.11, where the Guardian 'examines' incoming members with regard to their property.

143. 1QS 3.2; 5.14, 20; 7.25; 8.23.

144. C. Rabin, *Qumran Studies* (London, 1957) 27-29; M. Black, *The Scrolls and Christian Origins* (Edinburgh, 1961) 34-35.

145. R. de Vaux, *Archaeology and the Dead Sea Scrolls* (London, 1973) 18-19, 22-23, 34, 37, 44: 166 coins were found in level Ib (c. 135-0 BC); 176 in level II (c. AD 0-66); 94 (most in groups) in the period of the First Revolt (AD 66-70); and 9 from later periods. No coins were found in level Ia, but this is not surprising since 'the modest nature of the buildings and the scarcity of archaeological evidence attest the fact that this first installation was of short duration' (5). To the coin total could be added the 65 coins found at 'Ain

Feshka, with similar chronological distribution.

146. *Ibid.* 57; see also 52-54.
147. *Ibid.* 56.
148. *Community* 137.
149. *Ibid.* 131.
150. BDB 1: destruction is at least as common as loss in the examples.
151. Mealand, *Community* 135.
152. אל יתערב is used again in CD 11.4 to prohibit 'mingling' (hardly 'merging') among the sectaries on the Sabbath: likewise, in 1 QH 16.14 the psalmist implores God to 'mingle (התערב) with the spirit of Thy servant . . .'. These are the only other instances in the Qumran corpus.
153. 7.24-25 may imply that a drop-out's possessions were not returned: indeed, without an honourable discharge and substantial liquid assets, the community might not have been able to return such property.
154. 1QS 5.14, 20; CD 6.15-16; 8.4-5, 7; 1QH 10.29-30.
155. Mealand, *Community* 130 n. 17; Klauck, *Gütergemeinschaft* 66.
156. Rabin, (*Qumran* 23) cites CD 9.9-14; 11.5; 13; 12.9-11; 13.15; 14.13; 16.14-15.
157. Cf. 9.21-23: although the translation is uncertain, Dupont-Sommer (96 n. 2) seems to catch the sense by interpreting the passage as a condemnation of hoarding, which is characteristic of the 'men of the Pit'.
158. This is a misquotation of Hab 2.5, which has היין in place of הון. The use of הון, however, seems to be justified by the context: see Hab 2.6, 9, 12, 15, 19. W.H. Brownlee ('The Placarded Revelation of Habakkuk', *JBL* 83 [1963] 323-24) argues that the original reading is 'probably that implied by the Septuagint and Syriac readings, namely, *hawwān* or *hayyān*, meaning "presumptuous"'. In any case, consideration of the verse in its context suggests that a specific historic reference (i.e. the Wicked Priest), and not a general indictment of wealth, is intended.
159. Kandler, *Bedeutung* 204. The coupling of אביון and הון also implies the non-economic nature of the Qumran אביונים: How can the poor have wealth?
160. See Dupon-Sommer 295-305.
161. See also CD 12.6-7, where the sectary is instructed not to kill or loot a Gentile 'for the sake of riches and gain'. Purity takes precedence over wealth.
162. Unfortunately, the sentence is incomplete. Dupont-Sommer supplies 'of wickedness' after וכה[ן], which would of course change the nuance from 'riches' to 'unjustly gained riches'.
163. BDB 1072: 'regard as an abomination'. In Isa 14.19, the word is parallel to the phrase 'cast out, like an untimely birth'.
164. See Chapter 5.1 above. I have not included here the descriptions of Essene practice by Philo and Josephus, removed as they were by space, time, and perhaps personal prejudice from accurate information. Moreover, they

may be describing a different group from that at Qumran: see Black, *Origins* 38; and Thiering, *Asceticism* 437, who contrasts the dualism of Greek ascetic religion with that of the Qumran sectaries. Philo and Josephus reflect more of the former in their descriptive vocabulary. Cf. also Pliny, *Nat. Hist.* 5.17.4 for a brief first-century description of the Essenes.

Notes to Chapter 6

1. R. Pesch, *Das Markusevangelium*, 2 vols. (Freiburg, 1976-77) 1.81; cf. Zech 13.4.

2. P. Gaechter, *Das Matthäus-Evangelium* (Innsbruck, 1963) 86. John's disciples do apparently imitate his fasting: see Matt 9.14.

3. A. Schlatter, *Der Evangelist Matthäus* (Stuttgart, 1959) 60-61. Schlatter goes too far when (62) he places John against not only the religious establishment but also riches and ruling Greek culture.

4. E. Best, *Following Jesus: Discipleship in the Gospel of Mark* (Sheffield, 1981) 169.

5. 1.36; 3.7; 6.1; 14.51; 14.54.

6. 2.15; 9.38; 10.52; 15.41.

7. V. Taylor, *The Gospel According to Mark*, 2nd edn (London, 1966) 170. Cf. D.E. Nineham, *The Gospel of St. Mark*, 2nd edn (London, 1968) 276; E. Lohmeyer, *Das Evangelium des Markus* (Göttingen, 1937) 216; J. Ernst, *Das Evangelium nach Markus* (Regensburg, 1981) 300.

8. 3.9; 4.1; 4.36; 6.45-52.

9. 1.29-31; 2.15; cf. 2.1; 9.33.

10. Taylor 170.

11. R. Bultmann, *The History of the Synoptic Tradition* (Oxford, 1963) 187; cf. Taylor 260-66.

12. Taylor 260.

13. For the equation of 'age' and 'word' see H. Sasse, 'αἰών, αἰώνιος', *TDNT* 1.203-204. For further discussion of the synonymity of 'world' and 'life' (either ψυχή or βίος), see the discussion below of 8.35, 12.41-44.

14. Luke 16.8; 20.34; Rom 12.2; 1 Cor 1.20; 2.6; 2.8; 3.18; 2 Cor 4.4; Eph 1.21; 2.2; 2 Tim 4.10; Tit 2.12; cf. 1 Tim 6.17; Heb 9.26; 11.3.

15. See e.g. Ps 52.7; Sir 8.2; Sib Or III 189; Jub 23.21; T Benj 6.2-3; 1 En 97.8-10; CD 4.15-19; 1QpHab 8.3. The two words are combined by Philo in Gig. 15, where he refers to 'glory, wealth, offices, and honours, and all other illusions which like images or pictures are created by the deceit (ἀπάτῃ) of false opinion by those who have never gazed upon true beauty'.

16. A. Oepke, 'ἀπατάω, ἐξαπατάω, ἀπάτη', *TDNT* 1.385; cf. *BAG* 81; Matt 13.22; Eph 4.22; Col 2.8; 2 Thess 2.10; Heb 3.13; 2 Pet 2.13.

17. Taylor (261) wrongly points to instances of πλοῦτος in Pauline writings, all but one of which refer to divine or figurative wealth: Rom 2.4;

9.23; 11.22, 33; 2 Cor 8.2; Eph 1.7, 18; 2.7; 3.8, 16; Phil 4.9; Col 1.27; 2.2.
1 Tim 6.17 is the exception. Cf. Heb 11.26, which employs the word in a
figurative sense.

18. Taylor 261.

19. See e.g. Rom 1.24; Jas 1.14; 1 Pet 1.14; 1 John 2.16.

20. F. Zimmerman, *The Aramaic Origin of the Four Gospels* (New York,
1979) 87.

21. *Ibid.* 88; see also Payne Smith 199-200; BDB 451-52.

22. J. Wellhausen, *Evangelium Marci* (Berlin, 1903) 46; *contra* J. Lagrange,
Évangile selon Saint Marc, 2nd edn (Paris, 1947) 151; Taylor 304, who makes
the valid point that 'the permission of the staff must be considered along
with the injunction to wear sandals in 9'.

23. H.B. Swete, *The Gospel According to St. Mark* (London, 1909) 116.

24. W. Lane, *The Gospel According to Mark* (Grand Rapids, 1974) 207,
referring to E. Power, 'The Staff of the Apostles, A Problem of Harmony',
Biblica 4 (1923) 241-66.

25. *Ibid.* 207-208, quoting U. Mauser, *Christ in the Wilderness* (Naperville,
Illinois, 1963) 133f. The reference to Exod 12.11 was made earlier by Swete
116. Lane adds that the injunction to avoid bread and bag can be equally well
understood in light of this allusion.

26. Pesch, *Markus*, 1.328; C.E.B. Cranfield, *The Gospel According to Saint
Mark* (Cambridge, 1959) 199; Nineham 168; H. Andersen, *The Gospel of
Mark* (London, 1976) 163.

27. Lagrange, *Marc* 152. This prohibition of a bag goes beyond the
familiar accouterments of wandering Stoic-Cynic philosophers: see M.
Hengel, *Nachfolge und Charisma* (Berlin, 1968) 28-29; *Diog. L.* 6.13:
'Antisthenes . . . was the first, Diocles tells us, to double his cloak and be
content with that one garment and to take up a staff and wallet'.

28. Swete 116.

29. J. Gnilka, *Das Evangelium nach Markus*, 2 vols. (Zürich, 1978-79)
1.239.

30. On the other hand, *JA* 17.5.7 refers to two tunics being worn at the
same time during a journey.

31. Swete 117.

32. Lagrange, *Marc* 153.

33. Pesch 1.328; cf. Luke 3.11.

34. W. Grundmann, *Das Evangelium nach Markus*, 3rd edn (Berlin, 1968)
124. See also *b. Ber.* 62b; *t. Ber.* 7.19(17); *y. Ber.* 9.8; cf. SB I, 565. The
parallel applies more closely to the Matthean and Lukan versions, which
prohibit staff and sandals.

35. Cranfield 200; Taylor 304.

36. Gnilka I, 239. The same word is used by Ernst, *Markus* 175. Cf. H.
Braun, *Spätjüdisch-häretischer und frühchristlicher Radikalismus*, 2 vols.
(Tübingen, 1957) 2.80: '. . . in der Jesusbewegung . . . meint der Verzicht . . .

ein Weggeben, welches den Verzichtenden auch für das materielle Leben total in die Unsicherheit und so in die Abhängigkeit von Gott stellt'. This, Braun argues, distinguished early Christianity from contemporary Judaism and Qumran piety.

37. Best, *Following* 28-29.

38. *Ibid.* 38-39.

39. E. Percy, *Die Botschaft Jesu* (Lund, 1953) 171-72. Cf. *Ber. R.* 56: 'Abraham took the wood of offering as one who bears his cross upon his shoulder'.

40. *Ibid.* 37.

41. Wellhausen (*Marci* 9) brings attention to the connection between leaving all in 10.28 and 8.34. K. Berger (*Die Gesetzauslegung Jesu* [Vluyn, 1972] 437) regards 8.34-38 as a discipleship-ethic agreeing in principle with 10.28f.

42. 1.16-20; 2.14; 10.21; 10.28-30.

43. B. Metzger (*A Textual Commentary on the New Testament* [Stuttgart, 1971] 99) regards the absence of ἐμοῦ καί as attributable only to scribal oversight, since the double expression is more in accordance with Mark's style, and since both Synoptic parallels (Matt 16.25; Luke 9.24) read ἔνεκεν ἐμοῦ. Taylor (382) adds that the saying in its present form is attested in Q (Luke 17.33; Matt 10.29) and is found in John 12.25.

44. D. Murchie, 'The New Testament View of Wealth Accumulation', *JETS* 21 (Dec. 1978) 337.

45. Note 13 above; see Matt 6.25; 1 Cor 7.33; Luke 21.34.

46. Note that both contain ὅλος as opposed to πάντα.

47. BAG 140; Liddell-Scott 283; cf. Zimmerman, *Aramaic* 107-108.

48. For 8.36, see Taylor 382. For 12.44, see *Lev. R.* 3.5: 'Once a woman brought a handful of fine flour, and the priest despised her, saying, "See what she offers! What is there in this to eat? What is there in this to offer up?" It was shown to him in a dream: "Do not despise her! It is regarded as if she had sacrificed her own life (נפשׁ)"'.

49. For 'gain' (κερδαίνω) see Matt 25.17-22; for 'loss' (ζημιοῦσθαι), see 1 Cor 3.15; Phil 3.7-8.

50. Cf. Luke 12.21; 16.9; Matt 13.45-46; which employ economic terminology to communicate the sacrifice involved in discipleship.

51. See LXX Ruth 4.7; Job 28.15; Jer 15.13; Sir 6.15; cf. Matt 13.44-46. The best parallel is Sir 26.14-15: 'A silent wife is a gift of the Lord, and there is nothing so precious as a disciplined soul (ἀντάλλαγμα πεπαιδευμένης ψυχῆς); a modest wife adds charm to charm, and no balance (σταθμὸς) can weigh the value of a chaste soul'.

52. Berger (*Jesu* 413-15 n. 1) describes some of the options for reconstruction of the passage; see also *ibid.* 402-404, 407, 412-13; E. Schweizer, *The Good News According to Mark* (London, 1971) 209; N. Walter, 'Zur Analyse von Mark 10.17-31', *ZNW* 53 (1962) 206-18. An example of the divergence of

views is that Braun (*Radikalismus* II, 74 n. 1) considers 10.25 one of the oldest traditions illustrating the incompatibility of possessions and the kingdom, while S. Légasse (*L'Appel du Riche* [Paris, 1965] 71) considers it a later community formulation that originally spoke of the general difficulty of being saved. For more recent reconstructions, see E. Haenchen, *Der Weg Jesu* (Berlin, 1968) 355-60; Pesch 2. 140-47; Gnilka 2. 84-85; Ernst, *Markus* 294-95; Best, *Following* 110-15.

53. R.W. Haskin, 'The Call to Sell All: A History of the Interpretation of Mark 10.17-23 and Parallels' (unpublished PhD dissertation, Columbia University, 1968) *passim*.

54. See (Ch. 5.1) above, esp. Tob 4.5-11; Sir 29.9-12; T Lev 13.4; Pss Sol 9.9; 2 En 50.5.

55. See (Ch. 5.3) above and J. Bowman, *The Gospel of Mark: The New Christian Jewish Passover Haggadah* (Leiden, 1965) 214.

56. See (Ch. 5.4) above and Bowman 214.

57. Percy, *Botschaft* 105; J. Leipoldt, *Der soziale Gedanke in der altchristlichen Kirche* (Leipzig, 1952) 105 n. 104.

58. H.C. Kee, *Community of the New Age* (London, 1977) 155.

59. C.E.B. Cranfield, 'Riches and the Kingdom of God: St. Mark 10.17-31', *SJT* (1951) 309.

60. See (5.3) above on *N, O, P* Deut 6.5. But cf. Mark 12.33, which appears to take the commandment in the traditional sense.

61. See e.g. Percy, *Botschaft* 91; M. Dibelius, 'The Motive for Social Action in the New Testament', in *Jesus*, ET (London, 1963) 55; Légasse, *L'Appel* 51; Braun, *Radikalismus* 2. 75 n. 1; Lane, 367.

62. Ernst, *Markus* 297; see also Dibelius, *Motive* 138.

63. W. Harnisch, 'Die Berufung des Reichen. Zur Analyse von Mk 10. 17-27', in *Festschrift für Ernst Fuchs*, ed. G. Ebeling, E. Jüngel, und G. Schunack (Tübingen, 1973) 172-73.

64. Mealand, *Disparagement* 295.

65. Nineham 272.

66. Walter, *Analyse* 213; Taylor 429; P. Davids, 'The Poor Man's Gospel', *Themelios* (1976) 37; Schweizer, *Mark* 127.

67. Lohmeyer 212; Percy, *Botschaft* 92-93; Harnisch, *Berufung* 175; Gnilka 1.88; cf. Mark 9.43-47 (kingdom=Life).

68. Berger, *Jesu* 421-28. He cites Acts 10.2, 30-32; Luke 19.1-10 as further NT evidence. We might also adduce as proximate some of Philo's equations between HW and pursuit of the true good. See e.g. Congr. 27; Deus 147-51; Plant. 66; Mos. I 152-55; Prop. 77. See also K. Berger, 'Almosen für Israel', *NTS* 23 (1977) 180-204, esp. 183-88, where he draws attention to the atoning function of alms in Tob 12.9; 2 Clem 14.4; LXX Dan 4.27, 33-37.

69. Although the usual division of the passage is between vv. 22 and 23, it is reasonable to include Jesus' initial lesson and the response of the disciples (vv. 23-24a) as part of the story. So Walter, *Analyse* 209: πάλιν is Mark's

indication of the transition. Cf. 206-18; Lane 364.

70. See note 52 above.

71. Swete 228. In the NT elsewhere only in the parallel Luke 18.24 and Acts 4.37; 8.18, 20; 24.26. LXX examples are numerous; see e.g. Job 27.17; Sir 34.8, 9; 2 Chron 1.11, 12. Zimmerman (*Aramaic* 60-61), similarly, maintains that 'the Aramaic did not have on this occasion the usual *atir* but מהיתר *meyattar*, "one who has abundance of things, who has more than he needs..."'.

72. Wellhausen, *Marci* 87; cf E. Hirsch, *Frühgeschichte des Evangeliums*, 2 vols. (Tübingen, 1951) 1.111.

73. Lagrange, *Marc* 268-69; Metzger, *Commentary* 104. Another dubious attempt to create harmony is the addition to v. 24b in later manuscripts of τοὺς πεποιθότας ἐπὶ χρήμασιν. A. Merx (*Die Evangelien des Markus und Lukas* [Berlin, 1905] 123-26) argues that this reading actually represents an older tradition (as in Ps 49.7; Prov 11.28) than the more ascetic Lukan version, and that it originally stood as a *Doppelung* with v. 23.

74. Cranfield 331-32. K.G. Reploh (*Markus—Lehrer der Gemeinde* [Stuttgart, 1969] 194) points out that this greater severity is the reason for the sharper reaction of the disciples in v. 26.

75. P. Minear, 'The Needle's Eye', *JBL* 61 (1942) 169.

76. Swete 229, who gives 4.31; Matt 23.24 as other examples. Taylor (431) adds Luke 6.41. Lagrange (*Marc* 269-70) documents the tradition of the rope in *Cyril contra Julian* 16 and the Jerusalem gate in Poloner (15th century). Lagrange also gives the parallel in *b. Ber.* 55b, where an elephant is said to pass through the eye of a needle.

77. Reploh, *Lehrer* 192; examples include 3.5: 3.34; 5.32; 9.8; 11.11.

78. See 1.27; 10.32 for θαμβεῖσθαι; 1.22; 6.2; 11.18 for ἐκπλήσσεσθαι.

79. For πάλιν in this context see 10.10; 10.32; 14.39; 14.61; 14.69, 70; 15.4; 15.12.

80. Lane 369. See also Bowman 214-15.

81. Reploh, *Lehrer* 196; cf. Minear, *Eye* 165-66.

82. Swete 229; Walter, *Analyse* 213; Haenchen, *Weg* 354; Reploh, *Lehrer* 194; Pesch 2.143.

83. Lohmeyer 215; Reploh, *Lehrer* 195; Anderson 251; cf. note 77 above.

84. Lagrange, *Marc* 271; Reploh, *Lehrer* 196.

85. Anderson 251; Schweizer 214.

86. The passage is usually divided at this point, but it is important to note that while ἤρξατο is a favourite narrative device of Mark's to indicate new activity (e.g. 1.45; 2.23; 4.1; 6.2), in conversation it indicates *response*. See 5.17, 20; 10.41; 13.5; 14.19; 14.69; 14.71; and especially 8.32, where 'Peter took him and began to rebuke him'. That the use of ἄρχω with the infinitive is probably an Aramaism is pointed out by J.W. Hunkin, 'Pleonastic ἄρχομαι in the New Testament', *JTS* 25 (1924) 390-402. This may suggest an early

provenance for the verse and even for the connection.

87. Cited first by Lohmeyer 215; see also Swete 230 and Lagrange 271, who also cite Gen 18.14 and Job 42.2—but these speak only of God's ability, and not of man's inability.

88. It occurs in different contexts in Mark 14.36; Luke 1.37; cf. also Mark 9.23. Reploh (*Lehrer* 196) regards these instances as evidence that the saying is secondary in 10.27.

89. It is an interesting coincidence, but almost certainly not intended, that these three 'possibility' sayings in Mark correspond to the three seed-destroyers in the explanation of the Parable of the Sower (4.11-20).

90. See note 86 above.

91. Lagrange, *Marc* 271.

92. E. Gould, *A Critical and Exegetical Commentary on the Gospel According to St. Mark* (Edinburgh, 1896) 195.

93. Reploh, *Lehrer* 203; Berger, *Jesu* 409; Pesch 2.145; Best, *Following* 113; Ernst 300.

94. Cranfield, *Mark* 333; see also Lane 371 n. 56.

95. Lagrange, *Marc* 272; Pesch 2.149.

96. Lagrange, *Marc* 272; Reploh, *Lehrer* 203. Gaechter (*Matthäus* 630) suggests that Jesus may have said 'house', not 'houses', and meant leaving family/clan (specified in the following phrases), not a building. In this view, 'fields' are added secondarily to make a set of seven.

97. BAG 13; cf. 15.21; 16.12. The Hebrew שדה has the same breadth of meaning (BDB 961).

98. Merx 126.

99. Nineham 276; cf. 1 Cor 9.5. Lagrange (*Marc* 273) points out that the corresponding omission in v. 30 is necessary because one cannot have a spiritual spouse. We might add that the connotation of a promise of one hundred wives would be compromising, if not horrifying.

100. Pesch 2.145; but see 1 Cor 4.15, where Paul calls himself the spiritual father of the church in Corinth.

101. Nineham 273; Haenchen, *Weg* 358; Reploh, *Lehrer* 207; Schweizer, *Mark* 214; Best, *Following* 114.

102. Lagrange, *Marc* 273; Taylor 435; Nineham 273; Mealand, *Poverty* 50; Gnilka 2.93 all make reference to Acts 2.44-45; 4.34-37. Swete (232) adds 1 Cor 3.22.

103. Swete (232) calls attention to John 19.26; Rom 16.13; Mark 3.34-35; Lagrange (273) adds Gal 4.19; Taylor (435) adds Phlm 10; 1 Tim 5.1. See also n. 101 above,

104. *Quis Dives* 13ff., quoted by Wellhausen (*Marci*, 88), who agrees with Clement's interpretation; translated by Taylor 435.

105. Taylor 435.

106. Zimmerman, *Aramaic* 90-91.

107. Best, *Following* 113; see also Wellhausen, *Marci* 88; Minear, *Eye* 169;

Berger, *Jesu* 407; Pesch 2.146.

108. BD 232.

109. Lagrange, *Marc* 273-74.

110. Cranfield, *Riches* 312; Reploh, *Lehrer* 209; Lane 372. Grundmann (214) and Gnilka (2.93) find room for both views.

111. Pesch (2.263) gives the most complete list: *Xenophon* I 3,3; *Hesiod* op. 336; Aristotle *Nic. Eth.* 4.2; Horace, *Carm.* III 23; J.B. Aufhauser, *Buddha und Jesus in ihren Paralleltexten* (Berlin, 1926) 13-16; Euripedes *Danae fragm.* 329; see also *Lev. R.* III, 5, quoted in note 48 above; Tob 4.5-8, 16; Sir 29.20; 2 En 51.1.

112. Grundmann, *Markus* 257.

113. Lohmeyer 266.

114. Taylor 496.

115. Gould 239.

116. *Ibid.*; this casts doubt on the judgment of K. Bornhäuser (*Der Christ und seine Habe nach dem Neuen Testament* [Gütersloh, 1936] 28), that she gave her wages and not her capital.

117. Swete 293.

118. Bowman 238; who draws attention to *t. B. Bat.* 10b, where the equivalent coin is called Perutah.

119. Schweizer, *Mark* 259.

120. Swete 294.

121. See note 111 above.

122. Ernst, *Markus* 366. The argument of A.G. Wright ('The Widow's Mites: Praise or Lament?—A Matter of Context', *CBQ* 44 [1982] 256-65), that the passage *laments* the widow's gift, rests on the mistaken premise that Jesus would not praise someone for contributing to 'religion' (256). Implicit in the parable is the notion that such a gift, by its nature and by its motive (not by its worldly recipients), is a gift to God.

123. Lane 493.

124. *Ibid.* 494. This is even more obvious in Matt 26.6-13, where the story is preceded by an explicit identification between Jesus and the poor (25.35-45).

125. Verse 23 may be in part an allusion to Lev 19.9-10; 23.22; etc.; and so an indication that the group was self-consciously poor.

126. Cf. the use of boats and homes (notes 8-9 above), none of which are said to be owned by members of the group.

127. *NovT* (1964) 195-209.

128. *Ibid.* 209.

129. *Ibid.* 201. For the first point, see numerous examples in 198-200; for the second point, see 201; Rom 1.11; 15.24, 27; 2 Cor 9.6-15.

130. *Ibid.* 202-203; cf. Liddell–Scott 1535; BAG 816.

131. See J. Finegan, *The Archeology of the New Testament* (Princeton, 1969) 44; Freyne, *Galilee* 129-30: Tiberius was founded between AD 15 and

20.

132. See *Student Map Manual*, ed. J. Monson (Grand Rapids, 1979) section 12-4; cf. G.A. Smith, *The Historical Geography of the Holy Land* (London, 1931) 429-36.

133. Buchanan, *Class* 204-205. Theissen (*Setting* 188) suggests that the parables 'must emphasize in their imagery the socially powerful. Only a relationship to something superior can serve to make transparent the relationship to God'. Theissen's view is less persuasive when seen in conjunction with other internal evidence of Jesus' audience (e.g. that addressees had the means to follow the teaching).

134. *Ibid.* 205-206.

135. *Ibid.* 206-207. Buchanan (208-209 n. 1) doubts the authenticity of the birth narratives in Matthew and Luke, which portray Jesus' parents in humble conditions (esp. Luke 2.24). But even granting the historicity of the stories, the legitimization of the marriage, the end of the family's wanderings, and the changes of opportunity during the course of twenty-five years could have changed their status.

Notes to Chapter 7

1. Mealand, *Poverty* 16; cf. 92; G.D. Kilpatrick, *The Origins of the Gospel According to Matthew* (Oxford, 1950) 124-25.

2. R.H. Gundry, *Matthew: A Commentary on His Literary and Theological Art* (Grand Rapids, 1982) 580: 'Modern doubts about the text-critical originality of "a rich man" in Isa 53.9 do not affect the probability that Matthew read the text that way. Furthermore, since wickedness and wealth often go together in the OT, the phrases "with the wicked" and "with a rich man" make a better parallel in Isa 53.9 than is sometimes recognized. That the rich man Joseph of Arimathea was not also a wicked man did not bother Matthew. His use of the OT easily surmounts such obstacles'.

3. *Ibid.* 109; P. Bonnard, *L'Evangile selon Saint Matthieu* (Paris, 2nd edn, 1970) 45.

4. E. Klostermann, *Das Matthäusevangelium* ((Tübingen, 1927) 29; Gaechter, *Matthäus* 114, who points out that Luke makes clear, by use of the divine passive, the ultimate control of God.

5. E. Lohmeyer und W. Schmauch, *Das Evangelium des Matthäus* (Göttingen, 1956) 59.

6. Gundry 62.

7. *Ibid.* 62-63; cf. W. Grundmann, *Das Evangelium nach Matthäus* (Berlin, 1968) 110 n. 4; A.H. McNeile, *The Gospel According to St. Matthew* (London, 1915) 46.

8. Gundry 62.

9. *Ibid.* 63.

10. So, similarly, but with greater accent on the involuntary nature of their poverty: Schlatter 133; Bonnard, *Matthieu* 56; Gaechter, *Matthäus* 146-47; D. Hill, *The Gospel of Matthew* (London, 1972) 111; R. Guelich, *The Sermon on the Mount* (Waco, Texas, 1982) 97; Gundry 67. The poor as those who hope in God's salvation are clearly in view in 11.5, where the allusion is even more clearly to Isa 61.1.

11. W.C. Allen, *A Critical and Exegetical Commentary on the Gospel According to S. Matthew* (Edinburgh, 3rd edn, 1912) 39; see Mealand, *Poverty* 101-102 for a brief recent discussion and bibliography.

12. Gundry 67. The same reasoning applies to v. 6, whether the addition of 'righteousness' refers to God's future vindication of the persecuted (Gundry 70) or to the present conduct of believers (B. Przybylski, *Righteousness in Matthew and his World of Thought* [Cambridge, 1980] 96-98).

13. Braun, *Radikalismus* 2.73; S. Schulz, *Q: Die Spruchquelle der Evangelisten* (Zürich, 1972) 81; Percy, *Botschaft* 45-81.

14. J. Wellhausen, *Das Evangelium Matthaei* (Berlin, 1904) 14; McNeile 50; M.J. Lagrange, *Évangile selon Saint Matthieu* (Paris, 1948) 82; Grundmann, *Matthäus* 120-21; J. Dupont, *Les Béatitudes*, 3 vols. (Paris, 1969-73) 3.385-471; Bammel, πτωχός 904; E. Schweizer, 'πνεῦμα, πνευματικός', *TDNT* 6.401. For relevant uses of 'spirit' see Josh 2.11; 5.1; Pss 34.19, 51.19; 77.3; 142.3; 143.4; Prov 16.19; 29.23; Isa 57.15; 61.1; 66.2; 1QM 7.5; 11.10; 14.7; 1QS 4.3; 1QH 18.14-15; Jas 2.5; Acts 18.25; 1 Cor 7.34; *m. 'Abot.* 4.4, 7, 10. Bammel (πτωχός 904) adds strength to this view from the immediate context by pointing to 5.5 as perhaps a parallel (independently circulating?) form of the first beatitude. M.D. Goulder (*Midrash and Lection in Matthew* [London, 1974] 263-64, 311), on the other hand, regards 6.19-34 as an exposition of 5.5, that the meek is he who trusts God and is liberal with his possessions.

15. E. Best, 'Matthew V. 3', *NTS* 7 (1961) 257.

16. G. Maier, *Matthäus-Evangelium*, 2. Teil (Stuttgart, 1979) 1.109.

17. For a recent discussion see C.M. Tuckett and M.D. Goulder, 'The Beatitudes: A Source-Critical Study. With a Reply by M.D. Goulder', *NovT* 25 (1983) 193-216.

18. G. Agrell, *Work, Toil and Sustenance* (Lund, 1976) 84.

19. Guelich, *Sermon* 222.

20. Bonnard, *Matthieu* 73-74. Interestingly, the poor here are implicitly contrasted not to the rich but to the violent, as in the OT.

21. Grundmann, *Mätthaus* 173.

22. Mealand, *Poverty* 21.

23. *Ibid.* 24-27.

24. M. Black, *An Aramaic Approach to the Gospels and Acts* (London, 3rd edn, 1967) 178; Hill, *Matthew* 141.

25. McNeile (84) and Guelich (*Sermon* 326-327) regard βρῶσις as a

reference to worms rather than rust. Goulder (*Midrash* 301), however, makes the valid point that 'the balancing of the material with the animal wasting agent would be more pointful, and more Matthean'.

26. See e.g. Lagrange, *Matthieu* 135; Gaechter 225; Légasse, *L'Appel* 154-56; Grundmann, *Matthäus* 211; Bonnard, *Matthieu* 90.

27. See e.g. Wellhausen, *Matthaei* 28; W. Pesch, 'Zur Exegese von Mt 6, 19-21 and Lk 12, 33-34', *Biblica* 41 (1960) 365; Goulder, *Midrash* 301.

28. See Chapter 5.1 above; Tob 4.5-11; Sir 29.9-12; T Lev 13.5; Pss Sol 9.9; 2 En 50.5.

29. Gaechter (225) rightly points out the change to singular and the different rhythm which set the verse apart from vv. 19-20, and the beauty and precision which mark it as a proverb.

30. So Guelich, *Sermon* 328.

31. Gundry 113; cf. Maier 1.220.

32. See e.g. Grundmann, *Mätthaus* 212-13; Hill 142; Guelich, *Sermon* 329-32.

33. See e.g. A. Jülicher, *Die Gleichnisreden Jesu* (Tübingen, 1910) 100-102; Allen 62; McNeile 85; Klostermann 61; H.J. Cadbury, 'The Single Eye', *HTR* 47 (1954) 69-74; Schlatter 222-23; Goulder, *Midrash* 302; H.D. Betz, 'Matthew VI. 22 and Ancient Greek Theories of Vision', in *Text and Interpretation: Studies in the New Testament Presented to Matthew Black*, ed. E. Best and R.McL. Wilson (Cambridge, 1979) 55-56; Gundry 113.

34. See e.g. 1 Chron 29.17; Prov 11.24-26; T Iss 3.4; Rom 12.8; 2 Cor 8.2; 9.11, 13; Jas 1.5; cf. Sir 35.9. See also Schlatter 222-23 for parallels in rabbis and Josephus.

35. See e.g. Deut 15.9; 28.54-56; Prov 23.6; 28.22; Tob 4.7, 16; Sir 14.10; 31.13; *m. 'Abot* 2.9; 5.13, 16; cf. Sir 4.5; 14.3-9; and especially T Benj 4.2: ὁ ἀγαθὸς ἄνθρωπος οὐκ ἔχει σκοτεινὸν ὀφθαλμόν. ἐλεᾷ γὰρ πάντας . . . .

36. See e.g. Luke 22.53; John 3.19; Acts 26.18; Rom 2.19; 13.12; 1 Pet 2.9.

37. See also 2 Pet 2.17 and its parallel, Jude 13.

38. See 8.12; 22.13; 25.30; the only other occurence is the description of the sky in 27.45; cf. σκοτία 10.27.

39. See insertions of πόσον in 10.25; 12.12; cf. Luke 11.35-36; Gundry 114. Cf. 7.27 for a similar addition to imply eternal punishment: '. . . it fell; and great was the fall of it'.

40. The semitic form μαμωνᾷ is probably retained because wealth is here personified as a potential master: McNeile 85; Gundry 115. See 5.3 above for targumic usage.

41. Murchie, *View* 337; Klostermann 61; Schulz, *Spruchquelle* 461; Percy, *Botschaft* 91: '. . . entweder dient man Gott oder dem Mammon, entweder hängt das Herz an Gott oder am Mammon—etwas Drittes gibt es nicht'. *Contra* Guelich (*Sermon* 334), who argues that the question is not 'of having possessions . . . but of loyalty'.

42. Gundry 115; Bonnard, *Matthieu* 93.

43. So Wellhausen, *Matthaei* 29; Klostermann 61; T.W. Manson, *The Sayings of Jesus* (London, 1937) 131; O. Michel, 'μισέω', *TDNT* 4.690; Gundry 113.

44. Gen 26.27; Exod 18.21; 20.5-6; Deut 5.9; 7.10; 23.13, 16; 24.3; Judg 11.7; Ps 26.5; 50.17; 97.10; 101.3-4; 119.104, 128, 163; Prov 5.12; 8.13, 36; 11.15; 13.5; 14.20; 15.10, 27; 19.7; 28.16; Eccl 2.18; Isa 33.15; 54.6; 60.15; Amos 5.14-15.

45. BAG 126.

46. E. Schweizer, *Das Evangelium nach Lukas* (Göttingen, 1982) 159.

47. McNeile 85; cf. Isa 57.13; 1 Thess 5.14; Tit 1.9.

48. Davids, *Gospel* 38; cf. Allen 63; Schlatter 225; Agrell, *Work* 70-71; Gundry 115; *Contra* Gaechter 230, who regards it as a loose connection and a change in emphasis.

49. M.F. Olsthoorn, *The Jewish Background and the Synoptic Setting of Mt 6, 25-33 and Lk 12, 22-31* (Jerusalem, 1975) 84; D.R. Catchpole, 'The ravens, the lilies and the Q Hypothesis. A form-critical perspective on the source-critical problem', *SNTU* 6/7 (1981-82) 82; J. Jeremias, *The Parables of Jesus* (London, 2nd edn, 1972) 215-16; Schulz, *Spruchquelle* 155.

50. Gundry 116, who adds that both 10.19 and Luke 12.11 are persecution texts, and therefore they can only be understood to employ the word in the sense of 'worry'.

51. 1 Cor 7.32-34; 12.25; Phil 2.20; 4.6; cf. LXX Isa 57.11; Jer 17.8; 42.16; Ezek 12.18; Sir 30.24-31.2; 42.9.

52. According to Gundry (117), Matt changes ζητεῖτε (Luke 12.29) to μεριμνήσητε to bring v. 31 into conformity with the prohibition of vv. 25, 34. Gundry's reasoning may be applied to the absence of the same alteration in v. 32, since that verse does not parallel the prohibitions.

53. LXX Exod 5.9; Prov 14.23; Bar 3.18; perhaps Luke 10.41. Cf. the possible parallel in John 6.27 and Légasse, *L'Appel* 174-75.

54. Jeremias, *Parables* 241; Schlatter 225; Agrell, *Work* 81; *contra* Olsthoorn (*Background* 21), who argues that the metaphors are not examples of human behaviour but of God's care, which should forestall worry. I do not regard as persuasive the argument of Jeremias (*Parables* 214; cf. Dupont, *Béatitudes* 3. 283) that labour is necessitated in 6.27, since worry and labour are equally futile in such a situation.

55. Jeremias, *Parables* 214, Schlatter 226.

56. E. Schweizer, *The Good News According to Matthew* (London, 1975) 164.

57. Olsthoorn, *Background* 24; cf. Gen 28.20; Deut 10.18; 24.6, 12; 29.4; Isa 4.1; Tob 4.16; Matt 25.34-46; Luke 12.19; 1 Cor 9.4; 1 Tim 6.8; Jas 2.15.

58. Gundry 107; cf. McNeile 79-80; LXX Exod 16.4; Prov 27.1.

59. Dupont, *Béatitudes* 3.286-87.

60.   So e.g. Wellhausen, *Matthaei* 30; Klostermann 64; Lagrange, *Matthieu* 141; W.D. Davies, *The Setting of the Sermon on the Mount* (Cambridge, 1964) 387-401; Grundmann, *Matthäus* 217; H. Wrege, *Die Überlieferungsgeschichte der Bergpredigt* (Tübingen, 1968) 122-27; Dupont, *Béatitudes* 3.275-77; Olsthoorn, *Background* 73; Agrell, *Work* 74, 82; Catchpole, '*Ravens*' 86.

61.   The same change is made in 5.44 from Luke 6.35 and in 26.24 from Luke 22.22; and in reverse in 18.7 from Luke 17.1.

62.   Gundry 118.

63.   Guelich, *Sermon* 342.

64.   Guelich, *Sermon* 342; cf. Gundry 118; W. Michaelis, 'πρῶτον', *TDNT* 6.868-70; H. Riesenfeld, 'Vom Schätzesammeln und Sorgen—ein Thema urchristlicher Paränese. Zu Mt VI, 19-34', in *Neotestamentica et Patristica* (NovTSup 6) ed. W.C. van Unnik (Leiden, 1962) 49. Cf. Syriac versions, which employ the word ܠܘܩܕܡ ('first of all') instead of the word ܩܕܡ ('before').

65.   The former reference makes unnecessary the distinction between 'his' righteousness and 'your' righteousness (5.20; 6.1; Gundry 118). If there is significance to the retention of 'his' in v. 33, it is probably that it 'stresses more expressly that it is God's will and pleasure which are decisive for the righteous life of the disciples' (Olsthoorn, *Background* 74).

66.   Dupont, *Béatitudes* 3.303; cf. Lagrange, *Matthieu* 141; Riesenfeld, *Schätzesammeln* 49; Légasse, *L'Appel* 176-78; Grundmann, *Matthäus* 217; Hill 145; Olsthoorn, *Background* 74; Przybylski, *Righteousness* 90. Against this view it is argued that the 'righteousness' here anticipates God's future vindication: McNeile 89; Schlatter 234-35; Schweizer, *Matthew* 166; Gundry 118-19.

67.   Olsthoorn, *Background* 77; cf. Lagrange, *Matthieu* 141.

68.   Riesenfeld, *Schätzesammeln* 49; Hill 145; Schweizer, *Matthew* 166; Gueluch, *Sermon* 345.

69.   So Agrell, *Work* 82.

70.   Schlatter 331; Bonnard, *Matthieu* 145; Gundry 186-87. McNeile (135) protests that this makes the bag, etc., forms of payment. But εἰς τὰς ζώνας ὑμῶν and εἰς ὁδόν sufficiently distinguish the two sets of prohibitions as pertinent to maintenance and preparation, respectively. For κτᾶσθαι in the sense of payment see Luke 18.12; 21.19; Acts 1.18; 8.20; 22.28; cf. 1 Thess 4.4.

71.   Kilpatrick, *Origins* 125.

72.   McNeile 135; Gundry 186: 'neither gold, nor silver, nor (even) copper'.

73.   Gundry 186, who notes correctly that Matthew 'leaves the bread to be supplied mentally as the contents of the knapsack'.

74.   See discussion of Mark 6.8-9 above, esp. ch. 6, n. 34 Bonnard, *Matthieu* 145; Manson, *Sayings* 181.

75. Hengel, *Nachfolge* 84.
76. Gundry 260.
77. *Ibid.*
78. J. Dupont, 'Les Paraboles du Trésor et de la Perle (Mt 13.44-46)', *NTS* 14 (1967-68) 417.
79. B. Gerhardsson, 'The Seven Parables in Matthew 13', *NTS* 19 (1972-73) 23; cf. Gundry 275, who gives reasons to regard the passage as a Matthean composition. These compositional elements, especially the use of ἄνθρωπος as a man who becomes a disciple (Gundry 276-78; cf. 8.27; 9.8; 13.25, 52), refute the claim of O. Glombitza ('Der Perlenkaufmann. Eine exegetische Studie zu Matth XIII, 45-46', *NTS* 7 [1960-61] 153-61) that the parables describe the saving activity of God in Christ. An interesting OT reference relevant to the parables is Prov 2.4: 'if you seek (Wisdom) like silver and search for it as for hidden treasures...'
80. E. Linnemann, *Parables of Jesus. Introduction and Exposition*, ET (London, 1966) 103; Goulder, *Midrash* 372.
81. Dupont, *Béatitudes* 3.417-18.
82. Jülicher, *Gleichnisse* 585, Klostermann 124; Manson, *Sayings* 196; Lagrange, *Matthieu* 276; Schlatter 446; Légasse, *L'Appel* 153.
83. C.H. Dodd (*The Parables of the Kingdom* [London, 1935] 112) points out that because 'the Kingdom of God was conceived by those whom Jesus addressed as the great object of hope and prayer, they did not need to be assured of its value'.
84. Jeremias, *Parables* 200; Gaechter 458.
85. Gerhardsson (*Parables* 23) is overly subtle when he argues that 'an oriental merchant who has made the discovery of his life is not so foolish as to reveal it by leaping for joy... until the transaction is over'. A wise peasant will surely be equally circumspect.
86. Linnemann, *Parables* 101; Dupont, *Paraboles* 3.409.
87. Wellhausen, *Matthaei* 72; Lohmeyer, *Matthäus* 226-27; Goulder, *Midrash* 372; Gundry 276.
88. Jeremias, *Parables* 199; J.D. Kingsbury, *The Parables of Jesus in Matthew 13* (London, 1969) 113; cf. Gundry 278-79.
89. For πρᾶξις with the connotation of moral conduct, see Luke 23.51; Acts 19.18; Rom 8.13; Col 3.4; elsewhere in the NT only in Rom 12.4. See also Prov 24.12; Sir 35.22.
90. Minear, *Eye* 164; Davies, *Setting* 395.
91. Davies, *Setting* 395; Berger, *Gesetzauslegung* 446-52.
92. Legasse, *L'Appel* 191; Grundmann, *Matthäus* 433; Schweizer, *Matthew* 388; Mealand, *Poverty* 14; Gundry 100; Guelich, *Sermon* 234-35.
93. Schweizer, *Matthew* 388.
94. Gaechter 624.
95. Mealand, *Poverty* 14.
96. Klostermann 158. Vaticanus reads πολλαπλασίονα.

97. According to Wellhausen (*Matthaei* 132), talents are 'Kräfte, Gaben und Güter' with which the community of the Lord is served.
98. Jeremias, *Parables* 61-62.
99. Wellhasusen, *Matthaei* 134-35; D.R. Catchpole, 'The Poor on Earth and the Son of Man in Heaven', *BJRL* 61 no. 2 (1968) 393; J. Mánek, 'Mit wem identifiziert sich Jesu? Eine exegetische Rekonstruktion ad Matt 25.31-46', in *Christ and the Spirit in the New Testament*, ed. B. Lindars and S.S. Smalley (Cambridge, 1973) 15-25. L. Cope ('Matthew XXV: 31-46—"The Sheep and the Goats" Reinterpreted', *NovT* 11 [1969] 39-44) concludes (44) that 'the ethic is a churchly sectarian one; it does not represent a significant advance in ethical thinking over the ethics of the Judaism of its day'. Cf. Tob 4.17; Sir 12.1-4; 2 En A 5.12 for examples of the limitation of alms to the pious.
100. J. Michaelis, 'Apostolic Hardships and Righteous Gentiles: A Study of Matthew 25.31-46', *JBL* 84 (1965) 29; Gundry 513; cf. 7.22; 25.26.
101. So Mealand, *Poverty* 21, quoting Michaelis, *Hardships* 27-37 and Cope, *Sheep* 32-44. I cannot find this view in either article.

Notes to Chapter 8

1. So L.T. Johnson, *The Literary Function of Possessions in Luke-Acts* (SBLDS 39, Missoula, Montana, 1977). Johnson limits his purpose 'to discover if these materials do make sense at the literary level as integral parts of the story', and he grants that 'the content of the material on possessions had a significance for the author and his readers not exhausted by their literary function' (129). It is that significance which comprises our focus here.
2. So D. Seccombe, 'Possessions and the Poor in Luke-Acts' (unpublished PhD dissertation, Cambridge University, 1978) 103, 286. This dissertation has been published in *Studien zum Neuen Testament und seiner Umwelt, Serie B* (Linz, 1983) but was not available to me at the time of writing. Seccombe also refers to 'the limitless character of discipleship' as the application of the HW passages in the Gospel (148, 175, 286), but this phrase would scarcely be comprehensible—or even recognizable—to a first-century believer. He also concludes, *non sequitur*, that since warnings against wealth such as Luke 18.18-30 are not repeated in Acts, they must not be generally applicable (286). Further consideration of Seccombe's view of the poor in Luke will occur in the context of the relevant passages.
3. So H. Degenhardt, *Lukas, Evangelist der Armen* (Stuttgart, 1965) *passim*.
4. So W. Schmithals, 'Lukas—Evangelist der Armen', *Theologia Viatorum* 12 (1975) 153-67.
5. P.S. Minear ('Jesus' Audiences, according to Luke', *NovT* 16 [1974]

88) argues persuasively that 'disciples' refers to all believers in both the Gospel and Acts. Cf. Luke 6.1, 13, 17; 7.18; 10.22-23; 11.1; 14.26-33; 19.37-39; 24.6; Acts 6.1, 2, 7; 9.1, 10, 19, 25, 26, 38; 11.26, 29; 13.52; 14.20, 22, 28; 15.10; 16.1; 18.23, 27; 19.1, 9, 30; 20.1, 30; 21.4, 16.

6. Seccombe (*Possessions* 9-10) points out that 'Luke never grounds the unreliability of possessions on the likelihood of losing them through persecution', and he rightly cites 8.13; 12.45-46; 17.26-37; 18.29 (no διωγμός); 21.34-36 as evidence that persecution was less of a problem than complacency. At the same time, one wonders what the difference is between Schmithals's attribution of the tradition to 'einer extremen Situation' (165) and Seccombe's application of the tradition only in 'a time of great crisis . . . in the extreme situation . . .'(148).

7. 1.52-53; 4.18; 7.22; 14.13, 21.

8. 5.11, 28; 8.14; 9.3; 10.4; 12.15; 14.33; 16.13-15; 18.24-30; 21.4.

9. 3.11; 11.41; 12.21, 33; 16.9-12; 18.22; 19.8.

10. In the midst of a 'world-wide' famine (Acts 11.27-30), Christians presumably ignore pagan victims and risk the danger of long-distance travel to supply believers in Judaea. Cf. B.E. McCormick, 'The Social and Economic Background of St. Luke' (unpublished BLitt dissertation, Oxford University, 1960) 186-91. See also the discussion of the poor as a revolving (as opposed to permanent) class in the first century, Chapter 1 above.

11. So Dupont, *Béatitudes* 3.193-200. Only in his summary (3.202-203, 206) does Dupont acknowledge what should be the main point, that possession of wealth involves the danger of dependence on earthly goods rather than God for security.

12. So Mealand, *Poverty* 28, 49.

13. Seccombe, *Possessions* 121.

14. D. Jones, 'The Background and Character of the Lukan Psalms', *JTS* 19 (1968) 44; cf. S.C. Farris, *The Hymns of Luke's Infancy Narratives* (Sheffield, 1985) 108-26.

15. Jones, *Background* 24-26; see esp. 1 Sam 2.5-8; Eccl 10.14; cf. Job 12.19 (καθεῖλεν δυνάστας); Ezek 21.26; Esth 1.1; Job 5.11; Ps 88.15; Isa 2.11; 10.33; Tob 13.2; 1QM 14.10.-11 (ὕψωσεν ταπεινούς). For other examples of OT reversal, see E. Hamel, 'Le Magnificat et le renversement des situations. Réflexion théologico-biblique', *Gregorianum* 60 (1979) 61.

16. Jones, *Background* 26. Cf. *J* 1 Sam 2.3-8; Chapter 5.3 above.

17. J. Ernst. *Das Evangelium nach Lukas* (Regensburg, 1976) 87.

18. For 'mercy', see 1.50, 54, 72, 78; for 'power', see 1.16, 33, 35, 49, 51; for 'salvation', see 1.47, 68-69, 77, 2.30; 3.6.

19. So H. Schürmann, *Das Lukasevangelium*, Erster Teil (Freiburg, 1969) 76.

20. So. I.H. Marshall, *The Gospel of Luke* (Exeter, 1978) 84.

21. Cf. the equation of wealth and pride in Prov 15.25; 16.19; Isa 2.7-11; 13.11, 17; Jer 51.13; Sir 13.20; 1 En 94.8; 97.8-9; 46.7; CD 8.7; 1QH 10.25;

1QpHab 8.3, 9-12; cf. also the connection between the mighty (Hb זרוע) and 'sent empty away' in Job 22.8-9.

22. M.-J. Lagrange, *Évangile selon Saint Luc* (Paris, 1948) 48; J. Schmid, *Das Evangelium nach Lukas* (Regensburg, 1960) 55; Dupont, *Béatitudes* 3.190-93.

23. Cf. 1.14-17, 32-33, 48, 76-78; 3.5-6.

24. One other recurring phrase is ἐξαπέστειλεν κενούς, which in Lukan composition appears in 20.10, 11; 24.49 (ℵ² B).

25. Dupont, *Béatitudes* 3.193.

26. J.A. Fitzmyer, *The Gospel According to Luke*, Volume One (Garden City, New York, 1981) 469.

27. H. Conzelmann, *The Theology of St. Luke*, ET (London, 1960) 102.

28. Manson, *Sayings* 253.

29. H. Sahlin, 'Die Früchte der Umkehr', *ST* 1 (1947) 54-57; cf. Schmid 99; see e.g. Job 31.17, 20; Isa 58.7; Ezek 18.7; Tob 1.17; 4.16.

30. So Degenhardt 60; Ernst, *Lukas* 144; Fitzmyer, *Luke* 465.

31. See J.C. Todd, 'The Logia of the Baptist', *ExpT* 21 (1909-10) 173-75; E. Bammel, 'The Baptist in Early Christian Tradition', *NTS* 18 (1971) 106.

32. Manson, *Sayings* 253; K.H. Rengstorf, *Das Evangelium nach Lukas* (Göttingen, 1958) 57.

33. W. Wilkens, 'Die Versuchungsgeschichte Luk 4, 1-13 und die Komposition des Evangeliums', *TZ* 30 (1974) 267-70, 72.

34. So Schürmann (*Lukasevangelium* 211 n. 174), who cites 2.1 and 21.26, only the former of which has a political connotation.

35. See 21.26; Acts 11.28; 17.6, 31; 19.27; 24.5; cf. Rev 16.14; Heb 1.6; *JA* 8.13.4; *BJ* 7.3.3. Luke clearly does not favor κόσμος: it occurs only in 9.25 (following Mark); 12.30; Acts 17.24.

36. For Satan as lord of the world, see 2 Cor 4.4; Eph 2.2.

37. Bammel, πτωχός 906.

38. See Chapter 4 above.

39. Seccombe, *Possessions* 67-81. Verse 19 does nor indicate a literal Jubilee year: see R. North, *Sociology of the Biblical Jubilee* (Rome, 1954) 43; Whedbee, *Isaiah* 94-96; Seccombe, *Possessions* 65-66; cf. 1QH 18.14. The allusion here to the Jubilee is a promise of social justice only by extension from the establishment of the Kingdom.

40. Thus the passage should not be regarded as disjointed because of the different responses in v. 22, 28. See Marshall 179-80; B.D. Chilton, 'Announcement in Nazara: An Analysis of Luke 4.16-21', in *Gospel Perspectives II*, ed. R.T. France and D. Wenham (Sheffield, 1981) 15-52; J.A. Sanders, 'From Isaiah 61 to Luke 4', in *Judaism, Christianity, and Other Greco-Roman Cults*, ed. J. Neusner, Part One: New Testament (Leiden, 1975) 92-104.

41. Schmid (122) notes the retention of the plural after the focus on Peter

in v. 10.

42. J. Wellhausen (*Das Evangelium Lucae*) [Berlin, 1904] 15) favors the D(e) reading as original: οἱ δὲ ἀκούσαντες πάντα κατέλειψαν ἐπὶ τῆς γῆς καὶ ἠκολούθησαν αὐτῷ. He argues that this reading is closer to Mark 1.18-20, where the disciples leave only their boats. But the D(e) reading awkwardly skips the landing of the boat, and 5.28 (D) has Levi leave all. It is likely, then that D here represents a later harmonization with Mark.

43. Both v. 20a and the wording in the second person make this clear. The originality of the second person form has been the subject of some debate: see Marshall 248-49.

44. Lukan beatitudes commonly have this conditional sense: 7.23, 11.28; 12.37, 38, 43; 14.14; Acts 20.35; cf. 1.45 (past tense); 10.23; 14.15 (future tense). With respect to woes, the conditional sense is clear in 17.1; 11.42-52 and 22.22 address opponents; and 21.23 is predictive.

45. Seccombe, *Possessions* 115-16. Seccombe later remarks that the essence of discipleship is attention to Jesus' teaching (132). Should this not apply to 6.20-26?

46. For 'poor', see 18.28-30; 21.1-4; for 'hungry', see 16.20-22; for 'weeping', see 10.13; for 'hatred of men', see 21.12-19; for 'rich', see 12.16-20; for 'full', see 12.19; 16.19, 22-24; 21.34; for 'laughing', see 12.19; for 'praise of men', see 11.43. Thus Seccombe is not specific enough when he reduces the beatitudes/woes to a requirement that one 'identify with Jesus and his cause' (118).

47. Luke's form is generally regarded as closer to the original than Matthew's, although there may have been two forms of the tradition: see Marshall 246-47. W. Grundmann (*Das Evangelium nach Lukas* [Berlin, 1956] 141) and Percy (*Botschaft* 40-45) contend that the Lukan form probably goes back to Jesus himself.

48. So R.J. Karris ('Poor and Rich: The Lukan *Sitz im Leben*', in *Perspectives on Luke-Acts*, ed. C.H. Talbert [Edinburgh, 1978] 118), who argues that 4.18 and 7.22 should be interpreted in light of 6.20-26 to indicate Christians of Luke's time who suffer want and persecution. Cf. note 2 above.

49. See 6.27-29; 10.10-12; 12.11-12; 21.12-19.

50. It would be awkward to have Jesus 'lift up his eyes on the great crowd of disciples'. The effect of v. 20 is to limit the attention to disciples as a category, not as a small group within the group indicated by v. 17.

51. Minear, *Audiences* 104; cf. Schweizer, *The Good News According to Luke* (Atlanta, 1984) 119; Dupont, *Beatitudes* 3.96. Dupont applies this passage to believers who have been persecuted and deprived of their goods.

52. Cf. Mark 10.30, νῦν ἐν τῷ καιρῷ τούτῳ. Luke (18.29) omits νῦν because it is redundant, not because he understands it only in the sense of a specific moment in time: cf. 19.42-44; Acts 15.10. In vv. 22-23, ὅταν is

parallel to ἐν ἐκείνῃ ἡμέρᾳ; together, the expressions support the connotation 'in this age' in vv. 21, 25. οἱ πτωχοί and τοῖς πλουσίοις probably lack νῦν because they are nouns and not participles.

53. Schmid 133.

54. A. Plummer, *A Critical and Exegetical Commentary on the Gospel According to S. Luke* (4th edn, Edinburgh, 1901) 180; cf. Percy, *Botschaft* 88-89; Braun, *Radikalismus* 2.73; Ernst, *Lukas* 217. See also Degenhardt (50-51) and Schulz (*Spruchquelle* 81-83), who argue (*contra* Schürmann, *Lukas-evangelium* 325-27; Seccombe, *Possessions* 121) that the literal poor are meant, and not merely the community (who may or may not be poor).

55. Rengstorf 87.

56. Degenhardt 51-52; Schürmann, *Lukasevangelium* 329, 341; *contra* P. Klein, 'Die lukanischen Weherufe. Lk 6.24-26', *ZNW* 71 (1980) 154-55. Klein's arguments on the basis of vocabulary can be explained as influence on Luke *from* this passage.

57. So H. Schürmann, 'Die Warnung des Lukas vor der Falschlehre in der "Predigt am Berge". Lk 6, 20-49', *BZ* 10 (1966) 74-76.

58. So Schweizer, *Luke* 119.

59. So J.M. Creed, *The Gospel According to St. Luke* (London, 1930) 92.

60. Minear, *Audiences* 104-108.

61. Cf. the Lukan addition of ἀλλά before οὐαὶ +ὑμῖν τοῖς φαρισαίοις in 11.42. See also 5.14; 11.33; 13.3, 5; 14.10, 13; 17.8; 18.13; 20.21; 22.26, 36, 42; 24.21, 22; Acts 1.4, 8; 2.16; 4.17, 32; 5.13; 7.39; 9.6; 10 20, 35; 15.11, 20; 16.37; 18.9, 21; 19.2, 27; 20.24; 21.13, 24; 26.16. 20, 25. Only Acts 5.4; 10.41; 13.25; 26.29 use ἀλλά of a change in audience.

62. Marshall (256) explains that 'the verb is used in the LXX of an evil kind of laughter, which looks down on the fate of enemies and is in danger of becoming boastful and self-satisfied'.

63. Minear, *Audiences* 108; Marshall 256; W.E. Pilgrim, *Good News to the Poor* (Minneapolis, Minnesota, 1981) 107.

64. See Schmid 134; Ernst, *Lukas* 221.

65. Degenhardt 54.

66. Lagrange, *Luc* 195-96; Marshall 264.

67. G. Schwarz, 'μηδὲν ἀπελπίζοντες', *ZNW* 71 (1980) 134; cf. Job 27.33; Ezek 6.11; 21.17. Schwarz makes the further point that the expression could be a pun on another meaning of ספק ('distribute'): ספקו ולא ספקון.

68. B. Witherington ('On the Road with Mary Magdalene, Joanna, Susanna, and Other Disciples—Luke 8.1-3', *ZNW* 70 [1979] 244) argues persuasively on linguistic grounds that the passage is a Lukan composition.

69. 4.39 par. Mark 1.31; 10.40; 12.37; 17.8; 22.26, 27 par. Mark 10.45; Acts 6.2; cf. Acts 19.22.

70. H.W. Beyer, 'διακονέω, διακονία, διάκονος', *TDNT* II, 86. Cf. διακονέω in Acts 19.22; 2 Cor 3.3; 1 Pet 1.12; διακονία in Acts 1.17; 2 Cor

11.8; 2 Tim 4.5; Heb 1.14.
71. Acts 11.29; 12.25; Rom 15.25, 31; 1 Cor 16.15; 2 Cor 8.4; 9.1, 12, 13.
72. Degenhardt 73-74.
73. G. Delling, 'τάσσω, κτλ.', *TDNT* 8.33 n. 3. Bornhäuser (*Christ*, *passim*, esp. 33-43) argues that τὰ ὑπάρχοντα refers only to movable goods, not one's substance. But Degenhardt (83) rightly charges that this is an arbitrary and unproven distinction. Moreover, it excuses unjustifiably the individual who is rich in nonmoveable goods.
74. E.g. πάντα: 5.11, 28; τὰ σά: 6.30; τὰ ἀγαθά: 12.18, 19; 16.25; τῆς οὐσίας: 15.12; ὅσα ἔχεις; 18.22; τὰ ἴδια: 18.28; βίον: 21.4; τὰ κτήματα καὶ τὰς ὑπάρχεις: Acts 2.45 (cf. 5.1)
75. 11.21; 12.15, 33, 44; 14.33: 16.1; 19.8; Acts 2.45 (ὑπάρχεις); 4.32. Elsewhere, significantly, the word occurs only in parallels (Matt 19.21; 24.47; 25.14) and in 1 Cor 13.3; Heb 10.34.
76. Even if Mary Magdalene and the 'many others' had little or no capital, their giving can still be understood in this context: cf. 21.4.
77. Witherington, *Road* 244 n. 9.
78. *Ibid.* 247-47.
79. That Mark (6.6b) and Matthew (9.35) have similar summaries of Jesus' activity during the period before the mission charge, but without the details of those who accompanied him, suggests a simple desire to provide details of historical interest: cf. e.g. 2.1-3; 3.1-2; 21.37.
80. Cf. Tit 3.3; Jas 4.1, 3; 2 Pet 2.13; see also Luke 7.25 (τρυφῇ).
81. The two instructions are not meant to be distinct, minute lists of rules; rather, they should ne taken in a general sense. This explains the conflation of the two in 22.35-36: see Lagrange, *Luc* 294; Johnson, *Function* 163.
82. Cf. 9.62; 12.16-20, 45; 14.18-20; 21.34.
83. Verse 31 is a rather awkward insertion from Mark 13.15-16. Luke makes explicit the reference to household goods (σκεύη, cf. τι in Mark, τὰ in Matt; see 8.16; Acts 9.15; 10.11, 16; 11.5; 27.17). The omission of reference to το ἱμάτιον (Mark and Matt) is probably influenced by 9.62.
84. Wellhausen, *Lucae* 61; G.B. Caird, *The Gospel of Luke* (London, 1963) 158; Black, *Aramaic* 2; F. Hauck, 'καθαρός, κτλ.', *TDNT* 3.425 n. 76. See also J. Neusner ('First Cleanse the Inside', *NTS* 22 [1976] 486-95), who argues that the saying was originally Jesus' contribution to a rabbinic controversy over ritual cleansing, subsequently changed to the position (of Jesus and) the Hillelites; the present form of the saying, however, came from 'writers who clearly did not know or care what their true position had become' (495). Perhaps the change was made precisely *because* this position was known.
85. C.F.D. Moule, *An Idiom Book of New Testament Greek* (Cambridge, 1963) 186.
86. C.C. Torrey, *Our Translated Gospels* (London, no date) 98-99, 101-103.

87. See N. Turner, *Grammatical Insights into the New Testament* (Edinburgh, 1965) 57; Degenhardt 58-59; Moule, *Book* 34; Marshall 495-96.

88. Rengstorf (154) argues on the basis of 18.12 that mere almsgiving is not sufficient for inner purification, but that the inner man must be given over to God. But 18.12 specifies tithes, not alms, and Luke employs ἐλεημοσύνη only in a literal sense elsewhere; 12.33; Acts 3.2, 3; 9,36; 10.2, 4, 31; 24.17.

89. A.R.C. Leaney (*A Commentary on the Gospel According to St. Luke* [London, 1958] 193) argues for this view. He is refuted by R.C. Lenski (*The Gospel According to Luke* [Columbus, 1943] 260), who observes that the contents of the cup are not mentioned in vv. 39-40 and that 'inside' and 'outside' are used figuratively from v. 39b on.

90. Ernst, *Lukas* 386; Turner, *Insights* 57; cf. 12.34.

91. Cf. Logia 72 of The Gospel of Thomas, which omits vv. 15, 21, and is secondary. See T. Baarda, 'Luke 12, 13-14, Tradition and Interpretation', in *Christianity, Judaism, and Other Greco-Roman Cults*, ed. J. Neusner, Part One: The New Testament (Leiden, 1975) 141, 155; Marshall 522.

92. Caird, *Luke* 163.

93. See H.J. Cadbury, *The Style and Literary Method of Luke* (London, 1920) 202-203; cf. vv. 16, 22.

94. CF. 2.8; 8.29; 11.21; Acts 12.4 21.25; 22.20; 23.35; 28.16. Plummer (323) draws attention to T Jud 18.2 as a possible parallel; J.D.M. Derrett ('The Rich Fool: a Parable of Jesus concerning Inheritance', *Heythrop Journal* 18 [1977] 102 n. 19) adds Philo, Spec. IV 149.

95. Derrett, *Fool* 136; cf. 9.17; 15.17; Acts 16.5; where περισσεύειν requires a noun to make its meaning clear.

96. *Ibid.*: cf. Degenhardt 73; Nickelsburg, *Riches* 336. Only in 21.4, following Mark, does Luke fail to qualify περισσεύειν.

97. C.F.D. Moule, 'H.W. Moule on Acts iv. 25', *ExpT* 65 (1954) 220; followed by Marshall 523. The awkward Greek of the saying is not satisfactorily explained as an allusion to Aristotle, *Nic. Eth.* 10, 8, 9-10 (Lagrange, *Luc* 358; Derrett, *Fool* 103 n. 25): there is not a single word of correspondence in the Greek.

98. Plummer 323; Degenhardt 74.

99. Schmid 218; J. Navone, *Themes of St. Luke* (Rome, 1970) 109.

100. Lagrange, *Luc* 358.

101. Derrett (*Fool* 135-36) documents the common occurrence in Luke of ἐν with the articular infinitive to indicate a temporal sense.

102. Lagrange, *Luc* 358; Jeremias, *Parables* 165.

103. Derrett, *Fool* 104.

104. So Jeremias, *Parables* 106, 165; Ernst, *Lukas* 397.

105. E.W. Seng ('Der reiche Tor: Eine Untersuchung von Lk xii 16-21 unter besonderer Berücksichtigung form- und motivgeschichtlicher Aspekte', *NovT* 20 [1978] *passim* cites extensive parallels to the parable to support the

view that this is a parenetic example story. Cf. Chapters 4–5.1 above; K.E. Bailey, *Through Peasant's Eyes* (Grand Rapids, 1980) 63.

106. See Nickelsburg, *Riches* 335; cf. 1 En 97.8-10; 100.6; 102.9.

107. *Ibid*.

108. Dupont, *Béatitudes* 3.185. I regard as overly subtle the suggestion of Pilgrim (*News* 111) that 'his act of hoarding may be perceived as a plan to drive up prices later'.

109. Wellhausen, *Lucae* 65; Jeremias, *Parables* 106; Degenhardt 79-80; Nickelsburg, *Riches* 335; Ernst, *Lukas* 404; Derrett, *Fool* 150; Marshall 521.

110. Dupont, *Béatitudes* 3.117 n. 1; see also 14.33; 15.10; 17.10.

111. *Ibid*. 115-17; *contra* H. Schürmann, 'Sprachliche Reminiszenzen an abgeänderte oder ausgelassene Bestandteile der Spruchsammlung—im Lukas- und Matthäusevangelium', *NTS* 6 (1960) 203; Degenhardt 78-79; who argue that at least v. 21a is pre-Lukan.

112. Schürmann (*Reminiszenzen* 203 n. 2) infers from this that v. 21b may be Lukan.

113. So Minear, *Audiences* 95.

114. H.L. Egelkraut, *Jesus' Mission to Jerusalem: A redaction-critical study of the Travel Narrative in the Gospel of Luke, Lk 9.51–19.48* (Frankfurt, 1976) 165 n. 3.

115. 19 of 31 NT references are in Luke–Acts; see esp. Luke 6.35; 22.22 (against Matt).

116. Marshall 530; Black, *Aramaic* 126.

117. Schulz (*Spruchquelle* 142) recounts the Lukan elements of v. 33, esp. πωλεῖν, τὰ ὑπάρχοντα, ἐλεημοσύνη, and βαλλάντιον.

118. See 5.11, 28; 11.41; 16.9; 18.22, 28, 29; 21.4.

119. See 8.3; Acts 2.45; 4.34-35.

120. See 6.30, 35; 12.21. I will argue below that 14.33 is an aoristic present and that 19.8 is a futuristic present or aoristic present.

121. E. Burton, *Syntax of the Moods and Tenses in New Testament Greek* (Edinburgh, 1898) 20; cf. discussion of Mark 1.16-20 above.

122. It must be acknowledged, in the case of v. 21, that the list would recall previously mentioned recipients of the gospel who fit the description in a literal sense: cf. 6.6-11; 7.1-10; 8.40-55; 13.10-17; 14.1-6.

123. O. Glombitza, 'Das Grosse Abendmahl', *NovT* (1962) 15; *contra* Degenhardt 105 n. 29, who cites the neat correspondence between the groups of four in vv. 13-14 as opposed to the expansive list of three preceding v. 21.

124. J.D.M. Derrett, *Law in the New Testament* (London, 1970) 129-32; P.H. Ballard, 'Reasons for Refusing the Great Supper', *JTS* 23 (1972) 341-50. For lists of those prohibited from participation in holy wars, see Lev 21.17-23; 1QSa 2.3-10; 1QM 7.4-6. H. Palmer ('Just Married, Cannot Come'. *NovT* 18 [1976] 248) maintains that such an allusion, 'for those who

catch it, adds extra spice', but it is too remote to be essential to the intent of the parable.

125. Marshall 585.

126. Dupont, *Béatitudes* 3.262-72; Karris, *Poor* 120-21; Marshall 588; Pilgrim, *News* 140-41. See also Bailey, *Eyes* 95-99 for a detailed description of the cultural background of the excuses.

127. J.A. Sanders ('The Ethic of Election in Luke's Great Banquet Parable', in *Essays in Old Testament Ethics*, ed. J.L. Crenshaw and J.T. Willis [New York, 1974] 264-65) suggests that the poor are included as an especially poignant critique of the self-designation of the Pharisees and Qumran communities as the Poor.

128. J.D.M. Derrett '*Nisi Dominus Aedificaverit Domum*: Towers and Wars (Lk XIV 28-32)', *NovT* 19 [1977] 246) contends that the parables are a midrash on Prov 24.3-6, and argues that the tower builder and king signify God, who will succeed in his endeavor. This view cannot be supported from the evidence before us. Prov 24.3-6 does not mention a tower, and it recommends wise counsellors rather than troops in wartime. Moreover, the parables appear to assume failure, not success. Finally, Derrett's understanding of Luke's application (258) stresses οὖν to the neglect of οὕτως.

129. Jeremias, *Parables* 196; cf. Plummer 364-65; Degenhardt 110; Schmid 248; Ernst, *Lukas* 449; Marshall 591.

130. Jülicher, *Gleichnisreden* 2.208; cf. Creed 193; Lagrange, *Luc* 412.

131. Wellhausen, *Lucae* 80.

132. Cf. vv. 8 and 12, where μήποτε introduces not a hypothetical, but an inevitable condition.

133. L.A. III 142-45; Deus 147-51; see Ch. 5.2 above.

134. L.A. II 25; L.A. III 41; 238; Sob. 5; Mig. 92; Leg. 325; cf. Mos. I 38 (active voice).

135. *JA* 8.354: 'he parted from (ἀποτάσασθαι) them and then went with the prophet'; *JA* 11.232: '(for three days) throwing herself on the ground and putting on a mourner's dress and refusing (ἀποταξαμένη) all food and drink and comforts . . .'; *JA* 11.344: 'he sent the Shechemites away (ἀπετάξατο)'.

136. Schweizer, *Luke* 241; cf. discussion of Matt 6.24 above.

137. Mark 6.46; Luke 9.61; Acts 18.18, 21; 2 Cor 2.13. See Delling, τάσσω 33.

138. Marshall 594; cf. Dupont, *Béatitudes* 3.575; Karris, *Poor* 121. This interpretation of the passage, without explicit appeal to the present tense, is followed by many commentators: e.g. Plummer 366; Schmid 248; Seccombe, *Possessions* 148.

139. BD 167; Burton, *Moods* 8.

140. A.T. Robertson, *A Grammar of the Greek New Testament in the Light of Historical Research* (Nashville, 1923) 880.

141. 8.3; 12.15, 33; 19.8; Acts 4.32.

142. So Plummer 366; W. Manson, *The Gospel of Luke* (New York, 1930)

156; N. Geldenhuys, *Commentary on the Gospel of Luke* (London, 1950) 399; Lenski 789.

143. Degenhardt 111; Ernst, *Lukas* 447.

144. ὁ κύριος in v. 8a could be either Jesus (Rengstorf 185; Schmid 258) or the master in the parable. I favor the latter not because Jesus would not make his point in this way (cf. 18.6), but because the parable is too open-ended without such a concluding statement (J.A. Fitzmyer, 'The Story of the Dishonest Manager (Lk 16.1-13)', in *Essays on the Semitic Background of the New Testament* [London, 1971] 166), and because 14.23 provides a precedent for re-introducing the master of the parable to make a comment. See K.E. Bailey, *Poet and Peasant* (Grand Rapids, 1976) 102-104.

145. Various suggestions as to the actual conduct of the steward have been put forward. Manson (*Sayings* 292) and Jeremias (*Parables* 181) contend that the steward falsifies his master's accounts in order to win favor from the debtors. P Gaechter ('The Parable of the Dishonest Steward after Oriental Conceptions', *CBQ* 12 [1950] 125) argues that the steward renounces his personal profit over and above his master's profit. J.D.M. Derrett ('Fresh Light on St. Luke XVI', *NTS* 7 [1961] 216-17) and Fitzmyer (*Story* 177) take a similar view, arguing that the steward was re-writing legal but originally usurious bills.

146. H. Kosmala, 'The Parable of the Unjust Steward in the Light of Qumran', *ASTI* 3 (1964) 114.

147. Derrett, *Light* 80; M. Krämer *Das Rätsel der Parabel vom ungerechten Verwalter* (Zürich, 1972) 173-83; Marshall 622. Only ἐκλείπειν (only here and in 22.32; 23.45; Heb 1.12) and φιλός (15 of 29 NT reference are in Luke, 3 in Acts) in v. 9 are distinctively Lukan words, but this may be due to his source here. Marshall (621-23) and Bailey (*Eyes* 110-18) argue persuasively for the Palestinian character and origin of vv. 8b-13.

148. So Plummer 385; R. Koch, 'Die Wertung des Besitzes im Lukas-evangelium', *Biblica* 38 (1957) 166-67; R.H. Hiers, 'Friends by Unrighteous Mammon: The Eschatological Proletariat (Luke 16.19)', *JAAR* 38 (1970) 30-36.

149. So Wellhausen, *Lucae* 87; Caird 188; F.E. Williams, 'Is Almsgiving the point of the "Unjust Steward"?' *JBL* 83 (1964) 295. Even less likely is the suggestion of D.R. Fletcher ('The Riddle of the Unjust Steward: Is Irony the Key?', *JBL* [1963] 29) that the verse is a sarcastic taunt: 'imitate the example of the steward, use the unrighteous mammon; surround yourselves with the type of insincere, self-interested friendship it can buy; how far will this carry you when the end comes and you are finally dismissed?' Another option, advocated by H.F.B. Compston ('Friendship Without Mammon', *ExpT* 31 [1919-20] 282) and P. Colella ('Zu Lk 16.9', *ZNW* 64 [1973] 124-26), is to posit an original ממון which was intended to mean 'and not mammon', as in some OT examples of the use of מן. But these examples are few, and the problem of Jesus recommending use of something evil disappears when

ἀδικία is properly understood.

150. Schmid 259-60.

151. So Derrett, *Light* 218; Nicklesburg, *Riches* 337. This view becomes nonsensical when one imagines almsgiving or dispossession of only the ill-gotten part of one's wealth.

152. Krämer, *Rätsel* 90; cf. 83-95. See also Kosmala, *Parable* 116; Marshall 621. The background of the phrase in Jewish writings (ממן דשקר, see 5.3 above; Sir 5.8; 1 En 63.10) does not determine its meaning in this context: Dupont, *Béatitudes* 3.169; Krämer, *Rätsel* 82; cf. 1QS 10.19 10.19; Braun, *Radikalismus* 2.78.

153. Degenhardt 123.

154. See 6.20-26; 12.15-21; 16.19-31; 17.28-33. Creed (205) and Kosmala (*Parable* 118-19) favor death; Krämer (*Rätsel* 99; cf. 95-98) prefers the Parousia. Cf. Marshall 621, who finds in 1 Macc 3.29 a precedent for the idea of mammon 'running out'.

155. Degenhardt 123; Marshall 621-23.

156. Ernst, *Lukas* 466.

157. Degenhardt 124; cf. Williams, *Almsgiving* 294.

158. The point would be strengthened if we were sure that the steward's conduct consisted in giving up all his own profit (see n. 145 above), but we need not press for so complete a correspondence between parable and application.

159. Against this common view, Bailey (*Poet* 110-18) makes a reasonable case for the original unity of the verses as a three-stanza poem on the topic of mammon and God.

160. So Schmid 259.

161. Rengstorf 191; Grundmann, *Lukas* 321; Marshall 623.

162. Lagrange, *Luc* 437; Schulz, *Spruchquelle* 459; cf. Acts 10.7. Degenhardt (168 n. 61) and Dupont (*Béatitudes* 3.172 n. 2) view this as a generalizing Matthean omission.

163. Grundmann, *Lukas* 322.

164. Degenhardt 135; Dupont, *Béatitudes* 3.167.

165. Minear, *Audiences* 99-100. Derrett (*Light* 368-70) does a commendable job of fitting vv. 16-18 into the context under the theme of obedience not only to the letter but to the spirit of the law. Thus, while at least in externals the Sadducees would fit better with v. 15 and the following parable, the Pharisees correspond best as antagonists in the overall scheme (see Manson, *Sayings* 295; Marhsall 625). It is at this point that we would desire more information about the Pharisees' attitude toward wealth. It appears from this passage that many equated wealth with God's blessing (cf. Ch. 5.4 above).

166. So e.g. Manson, *Sayings* 295-96; Caird 188; Schmid 262.

167. Cf. e.g. Deut 7.25-26; 1 Kgs 14.24; Ezra 9.11; Isa 44.19; see also Mark 13.14; Matt 24.15; Rom 2.22.

168. Dupont, *Béatitudes* 3.182; cf. Hirsch, *Frühgeschichte* 2.145.

169. So Theissen, *Sociology* 13; Mealand, *Poverty* 32, 46-47; Johnson, *Function* 142.

170. Schweizer, *Lukas* 173.

171. So C.H. Cave, 'Lazarus and the Lukan Deuteronomy', *NTS* 15 (1968-69) 319-25.

172. I do not regard the literal meaning of Lazarus's name, 'God helps', as more than a coincidence. The name was common enough in Palestine, and its meaning was lost on a Gentile audience. See Marshall 635; *contra* Grundmann, *Lukas* 327; Ernst, *Lukas* 473.

173. Dupont, *Béatitudes* 3.149; Mealand, *Poverty* 116 n. 31.

174. Plummer 390; Percy, *Botschaft* 104-105; Koch, *Wertung* 163; cf. Pilgrim, *News* 118.

175. O. Glombitza, 'Der reiche Mann und der arme Lazarus', *NovT* 12 (1970) 173.

176. Degenhardt (133 n. 10) cites twenty non-Lukan words and the unusual use of the historical present; cf. Jeremias, *Parables* 182-83; Mealand, *Poverty* 47.

177. See H. Gressmann, 'Vom reichen Mann und armen Lazarus', *Abhandlungen der königlich preussischen Akademie der Wissenschaften*, phil.-hist. Klasse 7 (Berlin, 1918), ET *AEL* 3.138-41. Gressmann contends that Jesus' story is closer to the Egyptian version than to several rabbinic tales which have certain affinities to it; cf. K. Grobel, 'Whose Name Was Neves', *NTS* 10 (1963-64) 376-78; SB 2.222-23. L.W. Grenstead ('The Use of Enoch in St. Luke xvi. 19-31', *ExpT* 26 [1915] 333) argues for dependence on 1 En 22; Jeremias (*Parables* 183) and Derrett (*Light* 376) posit Jewish re-telling before the Egyptian tale became known to Jesus; Cave (*Lazarus* 319-25) considers the whole a midrash on Gen 15 and Isa 1; R. Dunkerly ('Lazarus', *NTS* 5 [1958-59] 321-27) maintains that the raising of Lazarus was the occasion for the story.

178. Dupont, *Béatitudes* 3.58; Berger, *Gesetzauslegung* 454; see 14.1; 23.13, 35; 24.20; Acts 3.17; 4.5, 8, 26; 13.27; 14.5. The neutral instances cited by Seccombe (*Possessions* 155) do not refute this view; see 8.41 (Luke's source); 11.15 (Beelzebub); 12.58 (fictional judge); Acts 7.27, 35 (Moses); 16.19 (Gentile judges); 23.5 (the high priest).

179. Dupont, *Béatitudes* 3.57.

180. *Ibid.* 3.157; cf. Légasse, *L'Appel* 102.

181. Dupont, *Béatitudes* 3.157; Légasse, *L'Appel* 103.

182. See Luke 6.41, 44; 10.34; Acts 1.7, 19, 25; 3.12; 4.23, 32; 13.36; 20.28; 21.6; 24.23, 24; 25.19; 28.30.

183. Lagrange, *Luc* 482; cf. Swete, *Mark* 230.

184. Cf. discussion of Mark 10.29-39 above. Marshall (688) suggests that if οἰκίαν is understood as 'households', the list pertains entirely to personal relationships. But this requires understanding τὰ ἴδια as 'homes', a meaning unwarranted by Acts 4.32 and by the present context.

185. Dupont, *Béatitudes* 3.160-61; Ernst, *Lukas* 512; F.W. Hobbie, 'Luke 19.1-10', *Int* 31 (1977) 286; J. O'Hanlon, 'The Story of Zacchaeus and the Lukan Ethic', *JSNT* 12 (1981) 9.

186. W.P. Loewe, 'Towards an Interpretation of Lk 19.1-10', *CBQ* 36 (1974) 323-30.

187. So R.C. White, 'Vindication for Zacchaeus?', *ExpT* 91 (1979) 21. Self-vindication along the lines of 18.11-12 is hardly appropriate here: see Marshall 698.

188. N. Turner, *A Grammar of New Testament Greek*, Volume III: Syntax (Edinburgh, 1963) 63; Marshall 697; cf. BD 167-68.

189. Marshall 698; cf. Plummer 435.

190. For the amount given in alms, see *b. Ketub.* 50a (a reference to the 20% limitation imposed at Usha, A.D. 140) and SB 546-51; for the amount given in restitution, see Lev 6.1-5; Marshall 698; cf. Derrett, *Law* 284; 2 Sam 12.6; Exod. 22.1.

191. Seccombe, *Possessions* 172.

192. Plummer 435-36.

193. O'Hanlon, *Zacchaeus* 19.

194. *Ibid.* 1-9; *contra* Bultmann, *History* 20; J. Drury, *Tradition and Design in Luke's Gospel* (London, 1976) 72-75.

195. See L.T. Johnson, 'The Lukan Kingship Parable (Lk 19.11-27)', *NovT* 24 (1982) 139-59.

196. S. Brown, *Apostasy and Perseverance in the Theology of Luke* (Rome, 1969) 104 n. 430; cf. Seccombe, *Possessions* 247, 251.

197. 8.43 (some MSS); 15.12, 30; cf. 8.14. Elsewhere in the NT the word occurs only in Mark 12.44; 1 Tim 2.2; 2 Tim 2.4; 1 John 2.16; 3.17.

198. So Conzelmann, *Theology* 13, 199, 232-33; for this passage in relation to 9.3/10.4 see Schürmann, *Abschiedsrede* 135; Degenhardt 67-68; M. Hengel, *Was Jesus a Revolutionist?* ET (Philadelphia, 1971) 21; Ernst, *Lukas* 603; Theissen, *Sociology* 65; Schweizer, *Luke* 341.

199. Note that, in contrast to νῦν in 6.21-25 above, where the word is used in contrast to the kingdom, here it is employed in a contrast between commands in a punctiliar sense (ἀπέστειλα v. 35).

200. Marshall 825.

201. Plummer 505; cf. Marshall 825 for variations of this view.

202. P.S. Minear, 'A Note on Luke xxii 36', *NovT* 7 (1964) 131-33.

Notes to Conclusion

1. Meeks's work on the Pauline churches suggests that 'status inconsistency' in that context (e.g. wealthy women, upwardly mobile freedmen, well-to-do Jews in a pagan world) might explain the attractiveness of Christianity to such groups (*Urban* 191), but he does not suggest that the

group produced the attractive elements of the faith. Whether or not subsequent discoveries shed light on the social make-up of Palestinian believers, Meeks's work should serve as an example of careful research and careful conclusions.

2. We noted above that Luke 22.35-36 may hint in this direction.

3. See V. Mehta, *Mahatma Ghandi and His Apostles* (Harmondsworth, 1976) 56-65, 162-64, 250.

4. Weber, *Sociology* 116-17; cf. 105-16.

5. The reference of v. 3b to martyrdom is contested. C.K. Barrett (*A Commentary on the First Epistles to the Corinthians* [London, 1968] 302-303) and H. Conzelmann (*1 Corinthians*, ET [Philadelphia, 1975] 222-23) note the possibility of a reference to self-immolation, but this is much less likely to be on Paul's mind than occurrences of martyrdom by fire such as Dan 3, 2 Macc 7: see A. Schlatter, *Die Korintherbriefe* (Stuttgart, 1950) 159; H.D. Wendland, *Die Briefe an die Korinther* (Göttingen, 1965) 104; H. Lietzmann, *Korinther I-II* (Tübingen, 1969) 65. J. Héring (*The First Epistle of Saint Paul to the Corinthians* [London, 1962] 137-38) argues that v. 3b refers to the sale of one's freedom in order to give away the proceeds, in which case burning denotes branding as a slave. More recently, scholars have argued persuasively for the reading καυχήσωμαι rather than καυθήσομαι, in which case the reference is still to martyrdom, but the motive is 'glorying' as in 2 Cor 8.4; Phil 2.16, etc.: see Metzger, *Commentary* 563-64; W.F. Orr and J.A. Walther, *1 Corinthians* (Garden City, New York, 1976) 291.

6. See e.g. 1 Cor 14.39; 14.1; Rom 1.11-12; 2 Cor 11.23.

7. Cf. Judge (*Conformity* 23) on Paul's choice to forsake normal modes of status expression.

8. Hengel, *Property* 58; cf. 31-83 for an excellent treatment of the development from HW to 'effective compensation', in which the rich of the early Church gain the prayers of the poor in return for charity and inner detachment from their wealth.

9. Mealand, *Poverty* 92.

BIBLIOGRAPHY

Texts and Translations

Abraham, Testament of. *OTP.* ET E.P. Sanders. 1.871-902.
—*The Testament of Abraham.* Ed. M.R. James, ET M.E. Stone. *SBLTT* 2 (Missoula, Montana, 1973).
Ahiqar. *APOT.* ET F.C. Conybeare, J.R. Harris, and A.S. Lewis. 2.715-84.
—*Aramäische Papyrus und Ostraka aus einer jüdischen Militär-Kolonie zu Elephatine.* 2 vols. Ed. E. Sachau. (Leipzig, 1911). —*OTP.* ET J.M. Lindenberger. 2.479-508.
Ancient Near East. *Ancient Egyptian Literature.* 3 vols. Ed. and ET M. Lichtheim. (Los Angeles, 1973-80).
—*Ancient Near Eastern Texts.* Ed. and ET J.B. Pritchard (Princeton, 1950).
—*Babylonian Penitential Psalms.* Ed. and ET S. Langdon (Paris, 1927).
—*Babylonian Wisdom Literature.* Ed. and ET W.K. Simpson (New Haven, Connecticut, 1972).
—*The Literature of Ancient Egypt.* Ed. and ET W.K. Simpson. (New Haven, Connecticut, 1972).
—*The Literature of the Ancient Egyptians.* Ed. A. Erman. ET A.M. Blackman (London, 1978).
—*Near Eastern Religious Texts Relating to the Old Testament.* Ed. W. Beyerlin, ET J. Bowden (London, 1978).
—'Die Reformtexte Urukaginas', *Orientalia.* Ed. and German translation F. Diemal. 2 (1920) 3-31.
Apocrypha. *The Revised Standard Version, The Apocrypha/The Deuterocanonical Books* (New York, 1957).
—*Septuaginta.* 2 vols. Ed. A. Rahlfs. (Stuttgart, 1935).
Aristeas, Letter of. 'The Letter of Aristeus', ed. by H.St.J. Thackeray, in *Introduction to the Old Testament in Greek,* by H.B. Swete (Cambridge, 1902) 519-74.
—*OTP.* ET R.J.H. Shutt. 2.7-34.
Baruch, 2. 'Apocalypse of Baruch', *Peshitta.* Ed. S. Dedering. Part 4, fasc. 3 (Leiden, 1973) 1-50.
—*APOT.* ET R.H. Charles. 2.481-526.
—*OTP.* ET A.F.J. Klijn. 1.615-52.
Enoch, 1. *APOT* ET R.H. Charles. 2.163-281.
—*The Books of Enoch. Aramaic Fragments of Qumran Cave 4.* Ed. J.T. Milik (Oxford, 1976).
—*The Ethiopic Book of Enoch.* 2 vols. Ed. and ET M.A. Knibb. (Oxford, 1978).
—*OTP.* ET E. Isaac. 1.5-90.
Enoch, 2. *APOT.* ET N. Forbes. 2.431-69.
—*OTP.* ET F.I. Andersen. 1.91-222.
Ezra, 4. *APOT.* ET G.H. Box. 2.561-624.
—*Das 4. Buch Esra.* Ed. J. Schreiner (Gütersloh, 1981).
—'4 Esdras', *Peshitta.* Ed. R.J. Bidawid. Part 4, fasc. 3 (Leiden, 1973) 1-50.

—*OTP*. ET B.M. Metzger I, 517-60.
Greek Classics. *The Loeb Classical Library* (London, various dates).
Job, Testament of. *OTP*. ET R.P. Spittler. 1.829-68.
—*The Testament of Job*. Ed. and ET R.A. Kraft. *SBLTT* 5 (Missola, Montana, 1974).
—*Testamentum Jobi*. Ed. S.P. Brock (Leiden, 1967).
Joseph and Asenath. *Joseph and Asenath*. ET E.W. Brooks (London, 1918).
—*Joseph et Asénath: Introduction, texte, critique, traduction et notes*. Ed. and French translation M. Philonenko. (Leiden, 1968).
—*OTP*. ET C. Burchard. 2.177-248.
Josephus. *Josephus*. 10 vols. Ed. and ET H.St.J. Thackeray, R Marcus, A. Wikgren, and L.H. Feldman. (London, 1926-63).
Jubilees. *APOT*. ET R.H. Charles. 2.1-82.
—*OTP*. ET O.S. Wintermute. II, 35-142.
LXX. *Septuaginta*. 2 vols. Ed. A. Rahlfs (Stuttgart, 1935).
Maccabees, 4. *APOT*. ET R.E. Townshend. 2.653-85.
—'Machabaeorum IV', *Septuaginta I*. Ed. A. Rahlfs (Stuttgart, 1935) 1157-84.
—*OTP*. ET H. Anderson. 2.531-64.
Mishnah. *The Mishnah*. ET H. Danby (Oxford, 1933).
—*Mishnayoth*. 7 vols. Ed. and ET P. Blackman. 4th edn (New York, 1964).
New Testament. *Evangelion Da-Mepharreshe*. 2 vols. Ed. and ET F.C. Burkitt (Cambridge, 1904).
—*The New Testament in Syriac*. Ed. G.H. Gwilliam (British and Foreign Bible Society, 1920).
—*Novum Testamentum Graece*. Ed. E. Nestle, *et al.*, 26th edn (Stuttgart, 1979).
—*Synopsis Quattuor Evangeliorum*. Ed. K. Aland (Stuttgart, 1967).
Odes of Solomon. *The Odes of Solomon* Ed. and ET J.H. Charlesworth. SBLTT 13 (Missoula, Montana, 1977).
—*OTP*. ET J.H. Charlesworth. 2.725-71.
Old Testament. *Biblia Hebraica Stuttgartensia*. Ed. K. Elliger and W. Rudolph (Stuttgart, 1967-77).
Philo. *Fragments of Philo Judaeus*. Ed. J.R. Haris. (Cambridge, 1886).
—*Philo*. 10 vols. Ed. and ET F.H. Colson and G.H. Whitaker (London, 1929-43).
—*Philo Supplement*. 2 vols. ET R. Marcus (London, 1953).
Psalms of Solomon. *The Odes and Psalms of Solomon*. 2 vols. Ed. and ET J.R. Harris and A. Mingana (Manchester, 1916-20).
—*APOT*. ET G.E. Gray. 2.631-52.
—*OTP*. ET R.B. Wright. 2.639-70.
—'Psalms of Solomon', *Peshitta*. Ed. W. Baars. Part 4, fasc. 6 (Leiden, 1972).
Pseudo-Philo. *The Biblical Antiquities of Philo. Now First Translated from the Old Latin Version*. ET M.R. James (London, 1917).
—*OTP*. ET D.J. Harrington. 2.2977-378.
—*Pseudo-Philo: Antiquitates Biblicae*. Ed. C. Dietzfelbinger. JSHRZ II/2 (Gütersloh, 1975).
Pseudo-Phocylides. *OTP*. ET P.W. van der Hoerst. 2.565-82.
—'Pseudo-Phocylides'. ET B.S. Easton. *ATR* 14 (1932) 222-28.
—'Sententiae Phocylidis', in *Fragments Pseudepigraphorum Quae Supersunt Graeca*. Ed. A.-M. Denis (Leiden, 1970) 149-56.
Qumran. *The Dead Sea Scrolls in English*. ET G. Vermes (Harmondsworth, 1962).
—*Discoveries in the Judean Desert*. 6 vols. Ed. D. Barthélemy, J.T. Milik, *et al.* (Oxford, 1955-77).

—*The Essene Writings from Qumran.* Ed. A. Dupont-Sommer, ET G. Vermes (Oxford, 1961).
—*A Genesis Apocryphon.* Ed. and ET N. Aviyad and Y. Yadin.
—*Die Texte aus Qumran. Hebräisch und Deutsch.* Ed. and German translation E. Lohse (München, 1971).
Sibylline Oracles. *OTP.* ET J.J. Collins. 1.317-472.
—*Die Oracula Sibyllina.* Ed. J. Geffcken (Leipzig, 1902).
Sirach. *The Hebrew Text of the Book of Ecclesiasticus.* Ed. I. Levi (Leiden, 1951).
Syriac Psalms, 5. 'The Apocryphal Compositions', in *The Psalms Scroll of Qumran Cave 11.* Ed. and ET J.A. Sanders (Oxford, 1965).
—'Die fünf syrisch überlieferten apokryphen Psalmen'. Ed. M. Noth *ZAW* 48 (1930) 1-23.
—*OTP.* ET J.H. Charlesworth with J.A. Sanders. 2.609-24.
—'Some Apocryphal Psalms in Syriac'. ET W. Wright. *Proceedings of the Society of Biblical Archaeology* 9 (1887) 257-66.
Talmud, Babylonian. *The Babylonian Talmud.* 18 vols. ET (London, 1948, 1961).
Talmud, Jerusalem. *Le Talmud de Jerusalem.* 6 vols. Ed. and French translation M. Schwab (Paris, 1960).
Targums. *The Bible in Aramaic.* 4 vols. Ed. A. Sperber (Leiden, 1959-73).
—*The Fragment-Targums of the Pentateuch According to their Extant Sources.* 2 vols. Ed. and ET M.L. Klein (Rome, 1980).
—*Neophyti 1.* 6 vols. Ed. A.D. Macho. ET M. McNamara and M. Maher (Madrid-Barcelona, 1968-79).
—*Pseudo-Jonathan.* Ed. M. Ginsburger (Berlin, 1903).
—'A Study of Targum Jonathan to the Minor Prophets from Nahum to Malachi: Introduction, Translation and Notes', R. Gordon (Unpublished PhD dissertation, Cambridge University, 1973).
—*The Targum of Isaiah.* Ed. and ET J.F. Stenning (Oxford, 1949).
—*The Targum to Job from Qumran Cave XI.* Ed. and ET M. Sokoloff (Jerusalem, 1974).
Thomas, Gospel of. 'The Gospel of Thomas', in *The Nag Hammadi Library in English.* Ed. J.M. Robinson, ET H. Koestler and T.O. Lambdin (Leiden, 1977).
Twelve Patriarchs, Testaments of the. *APOT.* ET R.H. Charles. 2.282-367.
—*OTP.* ET H.C. Kee 1.775-828.
—*The Testaments of the Twelve Patriarchs.* Ed. M. de Jonge (Leiden, 1978).

Secondary Sources

Aalen, S., 'St. Luke's Gospel and the Last Chapters of 1 Enoch', *NTS* 13 (1967) 1-13.
Aberle, D.F., 'A Note on Relative Deprivation Theory as Applied to Millenarian and Other Cult Movements', in *Millenarian Dreams in Action,* ed. S.L. Thrupp (The Hague, 1962), 209-14.
Agrell, G., *Work, Toil and Sustenance* (Lund, 1976).
Allen, W.C., *A Critical and Exegetical Commentary on the Gospel according to S. Matthew* (3rd edn; Edinburgh, 1912).
Alon, G., *The Jews in their Land in the Talmudic Age* (Jerusalem, 1980).
Anderson, H., *The Gospel of Mark* (London, 1976).
Applebaum, S., 'Economic Life in Palestine', in *The Jewish People in the First Century,* 2 vols.; ed. E.S. Safrai and M. Stern (Assen, 1976), 2.631-727.

Baarda, T., 'Luke 12, 13-14, Tradition and Interpretation', in *Christianity, Judaism, and other Greco-Roman Cults*, ed. J. Neusner. Part One: New Testament (Leiden, 1975), 107-62.

Bailey, K.E., *Poet and Peasant* (Grand Rapids, 1976).

—*Through Peasant's Eyes* (Grand Rapids, 1980).

Ballard, P.H., 'Reasons for Refusing the Great Supper', *JTS* 23 (1972) 341-50.

Bammel, E., 'The Baptist in Early Christian Tradition', *NTS* 18 (1971) 95-128.

—'The Poor and the Zealots', in *Jesus and the Politics of His Day*, ed. E. Bammel and C.F.D. Moule (Cambridge, 1984), 109-29.

—'πτωχός', *TDNT* 6.885-915.

Baron, S.W., *A Social and Religious History of the Jews* (New York, 1958).

Barrett, C.K., *A Commentary on the First Epistle to the Corinthians* (London, 1968).

Barton, J. 'Ethics in Isaiah of Jerusalem', *JTS* 32 (1981) 1-18.

Bauer, W. *Orthodoxy and Heresy in Earliest Christianity* (ET: Philadelphia, 1972).

Beals, R.L. and H. Hoijer, *An Introduction to Anthropology* (3rd edn; New York, 1965).

Berger, K. 'Almosen für Israel', *NTS* 23 (1977) 180-204.

—*Die Gesetzesauslegung Jesu* (Assen, 1972).

Best, E., *Following Jesus: Discipleship in the Gospel of Mark* (JSNTS, Sheffield, 1981).

—'Matthew V. 3', *NTS* 7 (1961) 255-58.

Best, T.F., 'The Sociological Study of the New Testament: Promise and Peril of a New Discipline', *SJT* 36 (1983) 181-94.

Betz, H.D., 'Matthew vi. 22 and Ancient Greek Theories of Vision', in *Text and Interpretation: Studies in the New Testament Presented to Matthew Black*, ed. E. Best and R. McL. Wilson (Cambridge, 1979), 43-56.

Beyer, H.W., 'διακονέω, διακονία, διάκονος', *TDNT* 2.81-93.

Birkeland, H., 'The Evil-doers in the Book of the Psalms', *Auhandlinger Det Norske Videnskaps-Akademi* 2 (1955) 1-96.

Black, M., *An Aramaic Approach to the Gospels and Acts* (3rd edn; London, 1967).

—*The Scrolls and Christian Origins* (Edinburgh, 1961).

—'The Tradition of Hasidaean-Essene Asceticism: Its Origins and Influence', *Aspects du Judéo-Christianisme*, Colloque de Strasbourg, 23-25 avril 1964 (1965) 19-33.

Boer, W. Den, *Private Morality in Greece and Rome* (Leiden, 1979).

Bolkestein, H., *Wohltätigkeit und Armenpflege im vorchristlichen Altertum* (Utrecht, 1939).

Bonnard, P., *L'évangile selon Saint Matthieu* (2nd edn; Paris, 1970).

Bornhäuser, K., *Der Christ und seine Habe nach dem Neuen Testament* (Gütersloh, 1936).

Bowker, J., *The Targums and Rabbinic Literature* (Cambridge, 1969).

Bowman, J., *The Gospel of Mark: The New Christian Jewish Passover Haggadah* (Leiden, 1965).

Braun, H., *Qumran und das Neue Testament* (2 vols.; Tübingen, 1966).

—*Spätjüdisch-häretischer und frühchristlicher Radikalismus* (2 vols.; Tübingen, 1957).

Breasted, J.H., *The Dawn of Conscience* (London, 1934).

—*Development of Religion and Thought in Ancient Egypt* (London, 1912).

Brown, S., *Apostasy and Perseverance in the Theology of Luke* (Rome, 1969).

Brownlee, W.H., *The Midrash Pesher of Habakkuk* (Missoula, Montana, 1979).

—'The Placarded Revelation of Habakkuk', *JBL* 83 (1963) 319-25.
Bryce, G.E., *A Legacy of Wisdom: The Egyptian Contribution to the Wisdom of Israel* (London, 1979).
Buchanan, G.W., 'Jesus and the Upper Class', *NovT* 7 (1964-65) 195-209.
Burr, V., *Tiberius Iulius Alexander* (Bonn, 1955).
Burridge, K., *New Haven, New Earth* (Oxford, 1969).
Burrows, M., 'Prophecy and the Prophets at Qumran', in *Israel's Prophetic Heritage*, ed. B.W. Anderson and W. Harrelson (London, 1962), 223-32.
Burton, E., *Syntax of the Moods and Tenses in New Testament Greek* (Edinburgh, 1898).
Byatt, A., 'Josephus and Population Numbers in First Century Palestine', *PEQ* 105 (1973) 51-60.
Cadbury, H.J., 'The Single Eye', *HTR* 47 (1954) 69-74.
—*The Style and Literary Method of Luke* (London, 1920).
Caird, G.B., *The Gospel of Luke* (London, 1963).
Case, S.J., *The Social Origins of Christianity* (Chicago, 1923).
—*The Social Triumph of the Ancient Church* (Chicago, 1933).
Cassidy, R.J., *Jesus, Politics, and Society* (Maryknoll, New York, 1978).
Catchpole, D.R., 'The Poor on Earth and the Son of Man in Heaven', *BJRL* 61 (1968) 355-97.
—'The Ravens, the Lilies and the Q Hypothesis. A form-critical perspective on the source-critical problem', *SNTU* 6/7 (1981-82) 77-88.
Cave, C.H., 'Lazarus and the Lukan Deuteronomy', *NTS* 15 (1968-69) 319-25.
Charlesworth, J.H., *The Pseudepigrapha and Modern Research with a Supplement* (Chico, California, 1981).
Chilton, B., 'Announcement in Nazara: An Analysis of Luke 4: 16-21', in *Gospel Perspectives II*, ed. R.T. France and D. Wenham (Sheffield, 1981) 147-72.
—*The Glory of Israel, The Theology and Provenience of the Isaiah Targum* (JSOTS, 23; Sheffield, 1983).
Churgin, P., *Targum Jonathan to the Prophets* (Yale Oriental Series, Researches 14; New Haven, Connecticut, 1907).
Cohen, S.J.D., *Josephus in Galilee and Rome* (Leiden, 1979).
Cohn, N., 'Medieval Millenarism: Its Bearing on the The Comparative Study of Millenarian Movements', in *Millenarian Dreams in Action*, ed. S.L. Thrupp (The Hague, 1962) 31-43.
—*The Pursuit of the Millennium* (London, 1970).
Colella, P., 'Zu Lk 16.9', *ZNW* 64 (1973) 124-26.
Compston, H.F.B., 'Friendship without Mammon', *ExpT* 31 (1919-20) 282.
Conybeare, Fred C., *Philo about the Contemplative Life* (Oxford, 1895) 258-358.
Conzelmann, H., *I Corinthians* (ET: Philadelphia, 1975).
—*The Theology of St. Luke* (ET: London, 1960).
Cope, L., 'Matthew XXV.31-46—"The Sheep and the Goats" Reinterpreted', *NovT* (1969) 32-44.
Cranfield, C.E.B., *The Epistle to the Romans*, II (Edinburgh, 1979).
—*The Gospel According to Saint Mark* (Cambridge, 1959).
—'Riches and The Kingdom of God: St. Mark 10.17-31', *SJT* (1951) 302-13.
Creed, J.M., *The Gospel According to St. Luke* (London, 1930).
Cronbach, A., 'The Social Ideals of the Apocrypha and Pseudepigrapha', *HUCA* 18 (1943-44) 119-56.
Dalton, G., 'Primitive Money', *American Anthropologist* 67 (1965) 44-65.
Daube, D., 'Jewish Inheritance in Two Luke Pericopes', *Zeitschrift der Savigny-*

Stiftung für Rechtsgeschichte (Rome, 1955), 326-34.

Davids, P., 'The Poor Man's Gospel', Themelios (1976) 39-41.

Davies, E.W., Prophecy and Ethics: Isaiah and the Ethical Traditions of Israel (JSOTS, 16; Sheffield, 1981).

Davies, W.D., The Setting of the Sermon on the Mount (Cambridge, 1964).

Degenhardt. H., Lukas, Evangelist der Armen (Stuttgart, 1965).

Deissman, A., Light from the Ancient East (ET: London, 1927).

Delitzsch, F., Biblical Commentary on the Proverbs of Solomon (ET: Edinburgh, 1884).

Delling, G., 'τάσσω, κτλ.', TDNT 8.27-48.

Derrett, J.D.M., 'Fresh Light on St. Luke XVI', NTS 7 (1961) 198-219, 364-80.

—Jesus' Audience (London, 1973).

—Law in the New Testament (London, 1970).

—'Law in the New Testament: The Treasure in the Field (Mt. XIII, 44)', ZNW 54 (1963) 31-42.

—'Nisi Dominus Aedificaverit Domum: Towers and Wars (Lk XIV 28-32)', NovT 19 (1977) 241-61.

—'The Rich Fool: a Parable of Jesus concerning Inheritance', Heythrop Journal 18 (1977) 131-51.

—'"Take thy bond . . . and write fifty" (Luke XVI.6) The Nature of the Bond', JTS 23 (1972) 438-40.

Dhorme, E., A Commentary on the Book of Job (London, 1967).

Dibelius, M., 'The Motive for Social Action in the New Testament', in Jesus (ET from Kirche, Erkenntnis und Sozialethos (1934); London, 1963), 137-66.

Dodd, C.H., The Parables of the Kingdom (London, 1935).

Downing, F.G., 'Philo on Wealth and the Rights of the Poor', JSNT 24 (1985) 116-18.

Driver, S.R., A Critical and Exegetical Commentary on Deuteronomy (3rd edn; Edinburgh, 1902).

Drury, J., Tradition and Design in Luke's Gospel (London, 1976).

Dunkerly, R., 'Lazarus', NTS 5 (1958-59) 321-27.

Dupont, J., Les Béatitudes (3 vols.; Paris, 1969-73).

—'Les Paraboles du Trésor et de la Perle', NTS 14 (1968) 408-18.

Egelkraut, H.L., Jesus' Mission to Jerusalem: A redaction critical study of the Travel Narrative in the Gospel of Luke, Lk 9.51-19.48 (Frankfurt, 1976).

Einzig, P., Primitive Money (2nd edn; Oxford, 1966).

Eisler, R., ΊΗΣΟΥΣ ΒΑΣΙΛΕΥΣ ΟΥ ΒΑΣΙΛΕΥΣΑΣ (Heidelberg, 1929).

Elliger, K., Studien zum Habakuk-Kommentar vom Toten Meer (Tübingen, 1953).

Ernst, J., Das Evangelium nach Lukas (Regensburg, 1976).

—Das Evangelium nach Markus (Regensburg, 1981).

Farmer, W.R., 'The Economic Basis of the Qumran Community', TZ 11 (1955) 295-308.

Farris, S.C., The Hymns of Luke's Infancy Narratives (JSNTS, 9; Sheffield, 1985).

Fensham, F.C., 'Widow, Orphan, and the Poor in Ancient Near Eastern Legal and Wisdom Literature', JNES 21 (1962) 129-39.

Finegan, J., The Archeology of the New Testament (Princeton, New Jersey, 1969).

Finkelstein, L., The Pharisees. The Sociological Background of their Faith (Philadelphia, 1962).

Fitzmyer, J.A., Essays on the Semitic Background of the New Testament (London, 1971).

—The Gospel According to Luke (Garden City, New York, 1981).

—'The Story of the Dishonest Manager (Lk 16.1-13)', in *Essays on the Semitic Background of the New Testament* (London, 1971) 161-84.

Fletcher, D.R., 'The Riddle of the Unjust Steward: Is Irony the Key?,' *JBL* 82 (1963) 15-30.

Fletcher, V.H., 'The Shape of Old Testament Ethics', *SJT* 24 (1971) 47-73.

Ford, J.M., 'Three Ancient Jewish Views on Poverty', in *The New Way of Jesus*, ed. W. Klassen (Newton, Kansas, 1980), 46-53.

France, R.T., 'God and Mammon', *Evangelical Quarterly* 51 (1979) 3-21.

Freyne, S., *Galilee from Alexander the Great to Hadrian* (Notre Dame, Indiana, 1980).

Gaechter, R., *Das Matthäus Evangelium* (Innsbruck, 1963).

—'The Parable of the Dishonest Steward after Oriental Conceptions', *CBQ* 12 (1950) 121-31.

Gager, J.G., *Kingdom and Community* (Englewood Cliffs, New Jersey, 1975).

—'Robert M. Grant, *Early Christianity and Society: Seven Studies*; Abraham J. Malherbe, *Social Aspects of Early Christianity*; and Gerd Theissen, *Sociology of Early Palestinan Chrisitanity*', *RelSRev* 5 (1979) 174-80.

Gapp, K.S., 'The Universal Famine Under Claudius', *HTR* 28 (1935) 258-65.

Gardiner, A.H., *Egypt of the Pharaohs* (Oxford, 1961).

Geldenhuys, N., *Commentary on the Gospel of Luke* (London, 1950).

Gerhardsson, B., 'The Parable of the Sower and its Interpretation', *NT* 14 (1962) 165-93.

—'The Seven Parables in Matthew 13', *NTS* 19 (1972-73) 16-37.

Gerstenberger, E., 'The Woe-Oracles of the Prophets', *JBL* 81 (1962) 249-64.

Gibson, G.S., 'The Social Stratification of Jewish Palestine in the First Century of the Christian Era' (unpublished PhD dissertation, University of London, 1975).

Glock, C.Y., 'The Role of Deprivation in the Origin and Evolution of Religious Groups', in *Religion and Social Conflict*, ed. R. Lee and M.E. Marty (New York, 1964), 24-36.

Glombitza, O., 'Das Grosse Abendmahl', *NovT* 5 (1962) 10-16.

—'Der Perlenkaufmann', *NTS* 7 (1960-61) 153-61.

—'Der reiche Mann und der arme Lazarus', *NovT* 12 (1970) 166-80.

Gnilka, J., *Das Evangelium nach Markus* (2 vols.; Zürich, 1978-79).

Goodenough, E.R., *An Introduction to Philo Judaeus* (2nd edn; Oxford, 1962).

—*The Politics of Philo Judaeus* (New Haven, Connecticut, 1938).

Goodman, M., 'The First Jewish Revolt: Social Conflict and the Problem of Debt', *JJS* 33 (1982) 417-28.

Gordis, R., 'The Social Background of Wisdom Literature', *HUCA* 18 (1943-44) 77-118.

Gould, E., *A Critical and Exegetical Commentary on the Gospel According to St. Mark* (Edinburgh, 1896).

Gottwald, N., *The Tribes of Yahweh* (Maryknoll, New York, 1979).

Goulder, M.D., *Midrash and Lection in Matthew* (London, 1974).

Grant, F.C., *The Economic Background of the Gospels* (Oxford, 1926).

—'The Economic Background of the Gospels', in *The Background of the New Testament and its Eschatology*, ed. W.D. Davies and D. Daube (Cambridge, 1956). 96-114.

Greehy, J.G., 'Community of Goods—Qumran and Acts', *Irish Theological Quarterly* 32 (1965) 230-40.

Grenstead, L.W., 'The Use of Enoch in St. Luke xvi. 19-31', *ExpT* 26 (1915) 333-34.

Gressmann, H., 'Vom reichen Mann und armen Lazarus', *Abhandlungen der königlich preussischen Akademie der Wissenschaften* phil.-hist. Klasse 7 (Berlin, 1918).

Grobel, K., '... Whose Name was Neves', *NTS* 10 (1963-64) 373-82.

Grundmann, W., *Das Evangelium nach Lukas* (Berlin, 1956).

—*Das Evangelium nach Markus* (Berlin, 1968).

—*Das Evangelium nach Matthäus* (Berlin, 1968).

Guelich, R., *The Sermon on the Mount* (Waco, Texas, 1982).

Gundry, R.H., *Matthew: A Commentary on his Literary and Theological Art* (Grand Rapids, 1982).

Haenchen, E., *Der Weg Jesu* (Berlin, 1968).

Hahn, F., 'Das Gleichnis von der Einladung zum Festmahl', in *Verborum Veritas, Festschrift für Gustav Stählin zum 70. Geburtstag*, ed. O. Bocher and K. Haacker (Wuppertal, 1970), 51-82.

Hallo, W.W. and Simpson, W.K., *The Ancient Near East: A History* (New York, 1971).

Hamel, E., 'Le Magnificat et le renversement des situations. Réflexion théologico-biblique', *Gregorianum* 60 (1979) 55-84.

Hands, A.R., *Charities and Social Aid in Greece and Rome* (Ithica, New York, 1968).

Hanson, P.D., *The Dawn of Apocalyptic* (Philadelphia, 1975).

Harnisch, W., 'Die Berufung des Reichen. Zur Analyse von Markus 10.17-27', in *Festschrift für Ernst Fuchs*, ed. G. Ebeling, E. Jungel, and G. Schunack (Tübingen, 1973), 161-76.

Haskin, R.W., 'The Call to Sell All: A History of the Interpretation of Mark 10.17-23 and Parallels' (unpublished PhD dissertation, Columbia University, 1968).

Hauck, F., *Die Stellung des Urchristentums zu Arbeit und Geld* (Gütersloh, 1921).

—'καθαρός, κτλ.', *TDNT* 3.413-31.

Hauck, F. and Kasch, W., 'πλοῦτος, κτλ.', *TDNT* 6.318-32.

Heichelheim, F.M., 'Roman Syria', in *An Economic Survey of Ancient Rome*, ed. T. Frank, Volume IV (Baltimore, 1938).

Hengel, M., *Judaism and Hellenism* (2 vols.; ET: London, 1974).

—*Nachfolge und Charisma* (Berlin, 1968).

—*Property and Riches in the Early Church* (ET: Philadelphia, 1974).

—*Was Jesus a Revolutionist?* (ET: Phildelphia, 1971).

Héring, J., *The First Epistle of Saint Paul to the Corinthians* (ET: London, 1962).

Hiers, R.H., 'Friends by Unrighteous Mammon: The Eschatological Proletariat (Luke 16.9)', *JAAR* 38 (1970) 30-36.

Hill, D., *The Gospel of Matthew* (London, 1972).

Hirsch, E., *Frühgeschichte des Evangeliums* (2 vols.; Tübingen, 1951).

Hobbie, .W., 'Luke 19.1-10', *Int.* 31 (1977) 285-90.

Hoehner, H., *Herod Antipas* (Cambridge, 1972).

Hoerst, P.W. van der, 'Pseudo-Phocylides and the New Testament', *ZNW* 69 (1978) 187-202.

Holl, K., 'Der Kirchenbegriff des Paulus in seinem Verhältnis zu dem der Urgemeinde', in *Gesammelte Aufsätze zur Kirchengeschichte*, II: Der Osten (Tübingen, 1928), 44-67.

Hölscher, G., *Die Profeten* (Leipzig, 1914).

Hunkin, J.W., 'Pleonastic ἄρξομαι in the New Testament', *JTS* 25 (1924) 390-402.

Isenberg, S.R., 'Millenarianism in Greco-Roman Palestine', *Religion* 4 (1974) 26-46.

—'Some Uses and Limitations of Social Scientific Methodology in the Study of Early Christianity', *SBLASP* 19 (1980) 29-50.

Jeremias, J., *Jerusalem in the Time of Jesus* (ET: Philadelphia, 1969).
—*The Parables of Jesus* (ET: London, 1972).
Johnson, L.T., 'The Literary Function of Possessions in Luke-Acts', SBLDS 39 (Missoula, Montana, 1977).
—'The Lukan Kingship Parable (Lk 19.11-27)', *NovT* 24 (1982) 139-59.
—'On Finding the Lukan Community: A Cautious Cautionary Essay', *SBLASP* 16/1 (1979) 87-100.
Jones, D., 'The Background and Character of the Lukan Psalms', *JTS* 19 (1968) 19-50.
Judge, E.A., 'Cultural Conformity and Innovation in Paul: Some Clues from Contemporary Documents', *TynBul* 35 (1984) 3-24.
—*Rank and Status in the World of the Caesars and St. Paul* (Christchurch, New Zealand, 1982).
—*The Social Pattern of the Christian Groups in the First Century* (London, 1960).
Jülicher, A., *Die Gleichnisreden Jesu* (2 vols.: Tübingen, 1910).
Kandler, H.J., 'Die Bedeutung der Armut in Schrifttum von Chirbet Qumran', *Judaica* 13 (1957) 193-211.
Karris, R.J., 'Poor and Rich: The Lukan Sitz im Leben', in *Perspectives on Luke-Acts*, ed. C.H. Talbert (Edinburgh, 1978), 112-25.
—'Windows and Mirrors: Literary Criticism and Luke's Sitz im Leben', *SBLASP* 16/1 (1979) 47-58.
Käsemann, E., *Commentary on Romans* (ET: Grand Rapids, 1980).
Keck, L.E., 'On the Ethos of Early Christianity', *JAAR* 42 (1974) 435-52.
—'The Poor among the Saints in Jewish Christianity and Qumran', *ZNW* 57 (1966) 54-78.
—'The Poor among the Saints in the New Testament', *ZNW* 56 (1965) 100-29.
Kee, H.C., *Christian Origins in Sociological Perspective* (London, 1980).
—*Community of the New Age* (London, 1977).
—'The Socio-cultural setting of Joseph and Asenath', *NTS* 29 (1983) 394-413.
Kilpatrick, G.D., *The Origins of the Gospel According to Matthew* (Oxford, 1950).
Kingsbury, J.D., *The Parables of Jesus in Matthew 13* (London, 1969).
Kippenberg, H., *Religion und Klassenbildung im antiken Judäa* (Göttingen, 1978).
Klauck, H.J., 'Gütergemeinschaft in der klassischen Antike, in Qumran und im Neuen Testament', *RevQ* 41 (1982) 47-80.
Klausner, J., *Jesus of Nazareth* (ET: London, 1925).
Klein, P., 'Die lukanischen Weherufe Lk 6.24-26', *ZNW* 71 (1980) 150-59.
Klostermann, E., *Das Matthäusevangelium* (Tübingen, 1927).
Koch, R., 'Die Wertung des Besitzes im Lukasevangelium', *Biblica* 38 (1957).
Kosmala, H., 'The Parable of the Unjust Steward in the Light of Qumran', *ASTI* 3 (1964) 114-21.
Krämer, M., *Das Rätsel der Parabel vom ungerechten Verwalter* (Zürich, 1972).
Kramer, S.N., *History Begins at Sumer* (London, 1958).
Kraus, H.J., 'Die prophetische Botschaft gegen das soziale Unrecht Israels', *Evangelische Theologie* (1955) 295-307.
Kreissig, H., "Die landwirtschaftliche Situation in Palästina vor dem judäischen Krieg', *Acta Antiqua* 17 (1969) 223-54.
—*Die sozialen Zusammenhänge des jüdischen Krieges* (Berlin, 1970).
Kuhl, C., *The Prophets of Israel* (London, 1960).
Kümmel, W., *Introduction to the New Testament* (ET: London, 1966).
Kuschke, A., 'Arm und Reich im Alten Testament mit besonderer Berücksichtigung der nachexilischen Zeit', *ZAW* 57 (1939) 31-57.

238   Hostility to Wealth in the Synoptic Gospels

Lagrange, M.-J., *Evangile selon Saint Luc* (Paris, 1948).

—*Evangile selon Saint Marc* (2nd edn; Paris, 1947).

—*Evangile selon Saint Matthieu* (7th edn; Paris, 1948).

Lane, W., *The Gospel According to Mark* (Grand Rapids, 1974).

Lanternari, V., *The Religions of the Oppressed* (London, 1963).

Leaney, A.R.C., *A Commentary on the Gospel According to St. Luke* (London, 1958).

Leeuwen, C. van, 'Le développement du sens social en Israël avant l'ère chrétienne', *Studia Semitica Neerlandica* 1 (1955).

Légasse, S., *L'Appel du Riche* (Paris, 1965).

Leipoldt, J., *Der Soziale Gedanke in der altchristlichen Kirche* (Leipzig, 1952).

Lenski, R.C., *The Gospel According to Luke* (Columbus, Ohio, 1943).

Levey, S.H., 'The Date of Targum Jonathan to the Prophets', *VT* 21 (1971) 186-96.

Lietzmann, H., *KorintherI-II*. (Tübingen, 1969).

Linnemann, E., *Parables of Jesus, Introduction and Exposition* (ET: London, 1966).

Loewe, W.P., 'Towards an Interpretation of Lk 10.1-10', *CBQ* 36 (1974) 321-31.

Lohmeyer, E., *Das Evangelium des Markus* (Göttingen, 1937).

Lohmeyer, E. & Schmauch, W., *Das Evangelium des Matthäus* (Göttingen, 1956).

Lohse, E., 'Das Evangelium für die Armen', *ZNW* 72 (1981) 51-64.

Lorentzen, T., 'A Biblical Meditation on Luke 16.19-31', *ExpT* 87 (1975) 39-42.

Lucius, P.E., *Die Therapeuten und ihre Stellung in der Geschichte der Askese* (Strassburg, n.d.).

Maier, G., *Matthäus-Evangelium*, 2 Teil (Stuttgart, 1979).

Malchow, B.V., 'Social Justice in the Wisdom Literature', *BTB* 12 (1982) 120-24.

Malherbe, A.J., *Social Aspects of Early Christianity* (Baton Rouge, Louisiana, 1977).

Malina, B., 'Limited Good and the Social World of Early Christianity', *BTB* 8 (1978) 162-76.

—*The New Testament World: Insights from Cultural Anthroplogy* (London, 1983).

Maloney, R.P., 'The Old Testament Teaching on Usury', *Colloquium* 5 (1973) 42-51.

Mánek, J., 'Mit wem identifiziert sich Jesu? Eine exegetische Rekonstruktion ad Matt. 25.31-46', in *Christ and the Spirit in the New Testament*, ed. B. Lindars and S.S. Smalley (Cambridge, 1973) 15-25.

Manson, T.W., *The Sayings of Jesus* (London, 1937).

Manson, W., *The Gospel of Luke* (London, 1930).

Marshall, I.H., *The Gospel of Luke* (Exeter, 1978).

McCormick, B.E., 'The Social and Economic Background of St. Luke' (unpublished BLitt dissertation, Oxford University, 1960).

McNamara, M., 'Half a Century of Targum Study', *Irish Biblical Studies* 1 (1979) 157-68.

Mealand, D.L., 'Community of Goods at Qumran', *TZ* 31 (1975 129-39.

—'The Disparagement of Wealth in New Testament Times' (unpublished MLitt dissertation, Bristol University, 1971).

—'The Paradox of Philo's View of Wealth', *JSNT* 24 (1985) 111-15.

—'Philo of Alexandria's Attitude to Riches', *ZNW* 69 (1978) 258-64.

—*Poverty and Expectation in the Gospels* (London, 1977).

Merx, A., *Die Evangelien des Markus und Lukas* (Berlin, 1905).

Metzger, B., *A Textual Commentary on the Greek New Testament* (Stuttgart, 1971).

Michaelis, W., 'πρῶτος, κτλ.', *TDNT* 6.868-70.

Michaels, J.R., 'Apostolic Hardships and Righteous Gentiles', *JBL* 84 (1965) 27-37.

Michel, O., 'μισέω', *TDNT* 4.683-94.

Minear, P.S., 'Jesus' Audiences, according to Luke', *NovT* 16 (1974) 81-109.

—'The Needle's Eye', *JBL* 61 (1942) 157-69.

—'A Note on Luke xxii 36', *NovT* 7 (1964) 128-34.

Mondon, J. (ed.), *Student Map Manual* (Grand Rapids, 1979).

Moore, G.F., *Judaism* (3 vols.; Cambridge, 1927).

Mosley, A., 'Jesus' Audiences in the Gospels of St. Mark and St. Luke', *NTS* 10 (1964) 139-49.

Mott, J.C., 'The Power of Giving and Receiving: Reciprocity in Hellenistic Benevolence', in *Current Issues in Biblical and Patristic Interpretation*, ed. G.F. Hawthorne (Grand Rapids, 1975) 60-72.

Moule, C.F.D., 'H.W. Moule on Acts iv. 26', *ExpT* 65 (1954) 220-21.

—*An Idiom Book of New Testament Greek* (Cambridge, 1963).

Munch, P.A., 'Das Problem Reichtums in den Psalmen 37, 49, 73', *ZAW* 14 (1937) 36-46.

Murchie, D., 'The New Testament View of Wealth Accumulation', *JETS* 21 (1978) 335-44.

Navone, J., *Themes of St. Luke* (Rome, 1970).

Neusner, J., 'First Cleanse the Inside', *NTS* 22 (1976) 486-95.

—*The Rabbinic Traditions About the Pharisees Before 70* (3 vols.; Leiden, 1971).

Nickelsburg, G.E., *Jewish Literature Between the Bible and the Mishnah* (Philadelphia, 1981).

—'Riches, the Rich, and God's Judgement in 1 Enoch 92-105 and the Gospel according to Luke', *NTS* 25 (1979) 324-44.

Nickle, K.F., *The Collection* (London, 1966).

Nineham, D.E., *The Gospel of St. Mark* (2nd edn; London, 1968).

North, R., *Sociology of the Biblical Jubilee* (Rome, 1954).

Oepke, A., ἀπατάω, ἐξαπατάω, ἀπάτη', *TDNT* 1.384-85.

O'Hanlon, J., 'The Story of Zacchaeus and the Lukan Ethic', *JSNT* 12 (1981) 2-26.

Olsthoorn, M.F., *The Jewish Background and the Synoptic Setting of Mt 6.25-33 and Lk 12.22-31* (Jerusalem 1975).

Oppenheimer, A., *The 'Am Ha-aretz* (ET: Leiden, 1977).

Orr, W.F. and Walther, J.A., *1 Corinthians* (Garden City, New York, 1976).

Palmer, H., 'Just Married, Cannot Come', *NovT* 18 (1976) 241-57.

Patterson, R.D., 'The Widow, the Orphan, and the Poor in the Old Testament and the Extra-biblical Literature', *Bibliotheca Sacra* 130 (1973) 223-34.

Percy, E., *Die Botschaft Jesu* (Lund, 1953).

Pesch, R., *Das Markusevangelium* (2 vols.; Freiburg, 1976-77).

Pesch, W., 'Zur Exegese von Mt 6 19-21 und Lk 12.33-34', *Biblica* 41 (1960) 356-78.

Peterson, D.L., *The Roles of Israel's Prophets* (JSOTS, 17; Sheffield, 1981).

Pilgrim, W.E., *Good News to the Poor* (Minneapolis, Minnesota, 1981).

Plummer, A., *A Critical and Exegetical Commentary on the Gospel According to S. Luke* (4th edn; Edinburgh, 1901).

Pope, M.H., *Job* (3rd edn; Garden City, New York, 1973).

Porteous, N.W., 'The Care of the Poor in the Old Testament', in *Living the Mystery* (Oxford, 1967) 146-55.

Przybylski, B., *Righteousness in Matthew and his World of Thought* (Cambridge, 1980).

Rabin, C., *Qumran Studies* (London, 1957).

Rajak, T., *Josephus: The Historian and His Society* (Philadelphia, 1983).

Rengstorf, K. H., *Das Evangelium nach Lukas* (Göttingen, 1958).

Reploh, K.G., *Markus—Lehrer der Gemeinde* (Stuttgart, 1969).

Rhoads, D.M., *Israel in Revolution: 6-74 C.E.* (Philadelphia, 1976).

Riesenfeld, H., 'Vom Schatzesammeln und Sorgen—ein Thema urchristlicher Paränese. Zu Mt *vi* 19-34', in *Neotestamentica et Patristica* (NovTSup, 60 ed. W.C. van Unnik (Leiden, 1962), 47-58.

Robertson, A.T., *A Grammar of the Greek New Testament in the Light of Historical Research* (Nashville, Tennessee, 1923).

Rost, L., *Judaism Outside the Hebrew Canon* (ET: Nashville, Tennessee, 1976).

Rostovtzeff, M., *The Social and Economic History of the Hellenistic World* (3 vols.; Oxford, 1941).

—*The Social and Economic History of the Roman Empire* (2 vols.; Oxford, 1957).

Rowland, C., *The Open Heaven* (London, 1982).

Rüger, H.P., 'μαμωνᾶς', *ZNW* 64 (1973) 127-31.

Russell, D.S., *The Method and Message of Jewish Apocalyptic* (London, 1964).

Sabourin, L., *The Psalms* (ET: New York, 1974).

Sahlin, H., 'Die Früchte der Umkehr', *ST* 1 (1947) 54-68. Saldarini, A.J., 'Apocalyptic and Rabbinic Literature', *CBQ* 37 (1975) 348-58.

Salters, R.B., 'Notes on the Interpretation of Qoh 6.2', *ZAW* 91 (1979) 282-89.

Sanders, J.A., 'The Ethics of Election in Luke's Great Banquet Parable', In *Essays in Old Testament Ethics*, ed. J.L. Crenshaw and J.T. Willis (New York, 1974 245-71.

—'From Isaiah 61 to Luke 4', in *Christianity, Judaism, and Other Greco-Roman Cults*, ed. J. Neusner; Part One: New Testament (Leiden, 1975) 75-106.

Sandmel, S., *Philo of Alexandria: An Introduction* (Oxford, 1979).

Sasse, H., 'αἰών, αἰώνιος', *TDNT* 1.197-209.

Schlatter, A., *Der Evangelist Matthäus* (Stuttgart, 1959).

—*Die Korintherbriefe* (Stuttgart, 1950).

Schmid, J., *Das Evangelium nach Lukas* (Regensburg, 1960).

Schmithals, W., 'Lukas—Evangelist der Armen', *Theologia Viatorum* 12 (1975) 153-67.

Schniewind, J., *Das Evangelium nach Matthäus* (Göttingen, 1956).

Schulz, S., *Q: Die Spruchquelle der Evangelisten* (Zürich, 1972).

Schürer, E., *The Jewish People in he Time of Jesus Christ* (2 vols.; ed. G. Vermes and F. Millar; ET: Edinburgh, 1973).

Schürmann, H., *Jesu Abschiedsrede*, 3. Teil (Münster, 1957).

—*Das Lukasevangelim*, 1. Teil (Freiburg, 1969).

—'Sprachliche Reminiszenzen an abgeänderte oder ausgelassene Bestandteile der Spruchsammlung im Lukas- und Matthäusevangelium', *NTS* 6 (1960) 192-210.

—'Die Warnung des Lukas vor der Falschlehre in der "Predigt am Berge" Lk 6.20-49', *BZ* 10 (1966) 57-81.

Schwartz, M.J. and Jordan, D.K., *Anthropology: Perspective on Humanity* (New York, 1976).

Schwarz, G., 'μηδὲν ἀπελπίζοντες', *ZNW* 71 (1980) 133-35.

Schweizer, E., *The Good News According to Luke* (Atlanta, 1984).

—*The Good News According to Mark* (ET: London, 1971).

—*The Good News According to Matthew* (ET: London, 1975).

—'πνεῦμα, πνευματικός', *TDNT* 6.332-455.

Scott, R.B.Y., *Proverbs, Ecclesiastes* (Garden City, New York, 1965).

Scroggs, R., 'The Earliest Christian Communities as Sectarian Movement', in *Christianity, Judaism and Other Greco-Roman Cults*, ed. J. Neusner; Part Two: Early Christianity (Leiden, 1975) 1-23.

Seccombe, D., 'Possessions and the Poor in Luke-Acts' (unpublished PhD dissertation,

Cambridge University, 1978).

Seng, E.W., 'Der reiche Tor: Eine Untersuchung von Lk xii 16-21 unter besonderer Berücksichtigung form- und motiv-geschichtlicher Aspekte', *NovT* 20 (1978) 136-55.

Shepperson, G., 'The Comparative Study of Millenarian Movements', in *Millenarian Dreams in Action*, ed. S.L. Thrupp (The Hague, 1962) 44-54.

Smallwood, E.M., *The Jews under Roman Rule* (Leiden, 1976).

Smith, G.A., *The Historical Geography of the Holy Land* (25th edn; London, 1931).

Spangler, O., *The Decline of the West* (ET and abridged from *Der Untergang des Abendlandes*; 2 vols.; München, 1918) (London, 1961).

Sperber, D., "Costs of Living in Roman Palestine', *Journal of the Economic and Social History of the Orient* 8 (1965) 248-71.

—'Costs of Living in Roman Palestine II', *Journal of the Economic and Social History of the Orient* 9 (1966) 182-211.

Stadelmann, H., *Ben Sira als Schriftgelehrter* (Tübingen, 1980).

Stegemann, H., 'Der Pešer Psalm 37 aus Höhle 4 von Qumran (4QpPs37)', *RevQ* 4 (1963) 235-70.

Stern, M., 'The Province of Judaea', in *The Jewish People in the First Century* (2 vols.; ed. S. Safrai and M. Stern (Assen, 1974) 1.308-76.

Strack, H.L. and Stemberger, G., *Einleitung in Talmud und Midrasch* (7th edn; München, 1982).

Swete, H.B., *The Gospel According to St. Mark* (London, 1909).

Talmon, Y., 'The Pursuit of the Millennium: The Relation Between Religious and Social Change', *European Journal of Sociology* 3 (1962) 125-48.

Taylor, V., *The Gospel According to Mark* (2nd edn; London, 1966).

Thackeray, H.St.J., 'A Study in the Parable of the Two Kings', *JTS* 14 (1913) 389-99.

Theissen, G., 'Itinerant Radicals', *Radical Religion* 2 (1975) 84-93.

—*The Social Setting of Pauline Christianity: Essays on Corinth* (Philadelphia, 1982).

—*The Sociology of Early Palestinan Christianity* (London, 1977).

—'"Wir haben alles verlassen" (Mc. x 28). Nachfolge und soziale Entwurzelung in der jüdisch-palästinischen Gesellschaft des I. Jahrhunderts n.Chr.', *NovT* 19 (1977) 161-96.

Thiering, B., 'The Biblical Source of Qumran Asceticism', *JBL* 93 (1974) 429-44.

Todd, J.C., 'The Logia of the Baptist', *ExpT* 21 (1909-10) 173-75.

Topel, L.J., 'On the Injustice of the Unjust Steward: Lk 16.1-13', *CBQ* 37 (1975) 216-27.

Torrey, C.C., *Our Translated Gospels* (London, no date).

Tuckett, C.M. and M.D. Goulder, 'The Beatitudes: A Source-critical Study. With a Reply by M.D. Goulder', *NovT* 25 (1983) 193-216.

Turner, N. *A Grammar of New Testament Greek*, III: Syntax (Edinburgh, 1963).

—*Grammatical Insights into the New Testament* (Edinburgh, 1965).

Vaux, R. de, *Archaeology and the Dead Sea Scrolls* (London, 1973).

Walter, N., 'Zur Analyse von Mc 10.17-31', *ZNW* 53 (1962) 206-18.

Weber, M., *General Economic History* (ET: London, 1927).

—*Sociology of Religion* (ET: London, 1965).

Wellhausen, J., *Das Evangelium Lucae* (Berlin, 1904).

—*Das Evangelium Marci* (Berlin, 1903).

—*Das Evangelium Matthaei* (Berlin, 1904).

Wendland, H.D., *Die Briefe an die Korinther* (Göttingen, 1965).

Whedbee, J.W., *Isaiah and Wisdom* (Nashville, Tennessee, 1971).

White, R.C., 'Vindication for Zacchaeus?', *ExpT* 91 (1979) 21.

Wilde, J.A., 'The Social World of Mark's Gospel: A Word about Method', *SBLASP* 14/2 (1978) 47-70.

Wilkens, W., 'Die Versuchungsgeschichte Luk. 4.1-13 und die Komposition des Evangeliums', *TZZ* 30 (1974) 262-72.

Williams, F.E., 'Is Almsgiving the Point of the "Unjust Steward"?', *JBL* 83 (1964) 293-97.

Wilson, J.A., 'The Theban Tomb No. 4090 of Si-Mut, Called Kiki', *JNES* 29 (1970) 187-95.

Willis, J.T., 'The Foundations of Old Testament Justice', *Restoration Quarterly* 18 (1975) 65-87.

Wilson, B.R., *Magic and the Millennium* (London, 1973).

Wilson, R.R., *Prophecy and Society in Ancient Israel* (Philadelphia, 1980).

Witherington, B., 'On the Road with Mary Magdalene, Joanna, Susanna, and Other Disciples. Luke 8.1-3', *ZNW* 70 (1979) 243-48.

Wolff, H.W., *Hosea* (ET: Philadelphia, 1974).

—*Joel and Amos* (ET: Philadelphia, 1977).

Wood, L.J., *The Prophets of Israel* (Grand Rapids, 1960).

Worsley, P., *The Trumpet Shall Sound* (2nd edn; London, 1968).

Wrege, H.-T., *Die Überlieferungsgeschichte der Bergpredigt* (Tübingen, 1968).

Wright, A.G., 'The Widow's Mite: Praise or Lament?—A Matter of Context', *CBQ* 44 (1982) 256-65.

York, A.D., 'The Dating of Targumic Literature', *JSJ* 5 (1974) 49-62.

Zimmerman, F., *The Aramaic Origin of the Four Gospels* (New York, 1979).

INDEX

NEW TESTAMENT

APOCRYPHA

PSEUDEPIGRAPHA

Jubilees	
23.21	71

2 Baruch	
70.4	67

1 Enoch	
38.3-5	67
46.7	71
52.7	71
63.10	71
92–105	146
94.6	71
94.8	71
97.8-10	67, 72, 75
97.8-9	71
97.8	71
97.10	146
98.2-3	67, 71
99.10	67
100.6	71
103.5-6	64, 71
103.7-9	74
103.13-15	146
104.6	67, 73-74, 75

2 Enoch	
50.5	74
51.1	65, 74
51.2	65
61	74
63.1-3	65

4 Maccabees	
1.26	70
2.8	70

Testament of Job	
4.6-9	73

15.7-9	71
18.8	73
33.3-5	71
33.5-9	73
48.2	73
49.2	73
50.2	73

Pseudo-Philo	
35.5	73
39.1	70
58.2	70

Pseudo-Phocylides	
53-54	71

Sibylline Oracles III	
41-42	70
189	70
234-36	70
241-47	67
345	67
436	67
444-48	67
531	67
638-40	67
657	67
750	67
783	67

Psalms of Solomon	
1.3-8	64
1.4-6	71
5.16-17	72
18.2-3	65

Testament of Judah	
17.1	70
18-19	156

18.2	70, 156
18.6	156
19.1-2	70
23.3	67
25.4	67

Testament of Issachar	
4.2	70

Testament of Zebulun	
7.1–8.3	65

Testament of Dan	
5.7	70

Testament of Gad	
7.6	65

Testament of Asher	
2.5-7	65

Testament of Benjamin	
6.2-3	72

Joseph and Asenath	
10–12	74
10.11	74
10.13	74
12.12	74
21.41	74

Ahikar	
2.14	71
2.51	68
26.10	68

QUMRAN LITERATURE

CD	
4.15-19	99
6.16-19	91
6.16	90, 91
6.21	90

8.4-5	98
8.7	98
10.17-18	99
11.15	99
13.11	97

13.15-16	97
14.14	90
19.9	91

INDEX OF AUTHORS

JOURNAL FOR THE STUDY OF THE NEW TESTAMENT
Supplement Series

DATE DUE